# Faith
# and LEARNING

# Faith and LEARNING

## A Guide for Faculty

## PATRICK ALLEN &
## KENNETH BADLEY

Abilene Christian University Press

# FAITH AND LEARNING
*A Guide for Faculty*

ACU
PRESS

Copyright © 2014 by Patrick Allen and Kenneth Badley

ISBN 978–0-89112–411–5
LCCN 2014016095

Printed in the United States of America

LIBRARY OF CONGRESS CATALOGING-IN-PUBLICATION DATA
Badley, Kenneth Rea, 1951-
  Faith and learning : A Guide for Faculty / Kenneth Badley, Patrick Allen.
     pages cm
  ISBN 978-0-89112-411-5
  1. Learning and scholarship--Religious aspects--Christianity. 2. College teachers--Religious life. 3. Education (Christian theology) 4. Church and college. I. Title.
  BR115.L32B33 2014
  261.502'437812--dc23

                                                                    2014016095

Cover design and Interior text design by Sandy Armstrong, Strong Design

For information contact:
Abilene Christian University Press
1626 Campus Court
Abilene, Texas 79601

1-877-816-4455 toll free
www.acupressbooks.com

14 15 16 17 18 19 / 7 6 5 4 3 2 1

*We humbly dedicate this book to our wives, K. Jo–Ann Badley and Lori Allen. Their love and support have sustained us for many years, and certainly during this writing project. In the past months, they have listened to more ideas about faith and learning integration than any two persons should have to hear in a lifetime, and as they do in so many ways, they made our work and this book better.*

# Table of Contents

Preface.................................................................................................9

1   The Rich and High Calling of Faithful Teaching.............................13

2   What Is All the Faith and Learning Fuss About?............................25

3   Loving Jesus and Getting Promoted:
    What Faculty Need to Know and Do ................................................43

4   The Boyer Model...............................................................................69

5   The Scholarship of Teaching .............................................................89

6   The Scholarship of Discovery and Integration .............................. 117

7   The Scholarship of Engagement..................................................... 135

8   In Word and Deed:
    Assessing and Reporting your Work............................................... 155

9   The Productive Academic Writer..................................................... 171

10  Looking to the Future:
    Reconceiving the Faith-Based University ........................................205

Afterword ............................................................................................ 231

Notes ................................................................................................... 237

Acknowledgments................................................................................259

# Preface

We talked about faith and learning for more than three years over a series of Monday night dinners at a local sports pub in Newberg, Oregon. It finally came down to either writing a book together or buying stock in the tater tot distributor. We did not have much money to invest, so we went for the book idea instead! Well, that is not exactly how it happened. But we had been meeting regularly for dinner on Monday evenings for several years now, and at many points during our times together, we found ourselves discussing the integration of faith and learning. These conversations have given life to both of us.

One of us (KB) has been a scholar of faith integration for over thirty years, and one of us (PA) has been a chief academic officer for that same period of time. We realized that both of us have been participating in a sustained conversation over a number of years about faith and learning—parallel conversations to be more precise, one with the scholarly community and one with a professional community of deans and provosts. At times, these conversations have intersected, intertwined, and overlapped, but at other times our communities have been talking past each other like two ships passing in the night. We believed it was time to bring these two conversations together and we set out in this book to accomplish that.

We know that the concept of faith-learning integration can be confusing and daunting for new faculty members, particularly when first trying to figure out how to teach well, then how to establish a scholarly agenda.

And we know that new and veteran faculty alike find daily challenges in realizing faith-learning integration in our lives and practice. And, oh yes, there is that promotion and tenure process to navigate, too. Too often, the process becomes a mystery of sorts, one much more complicated than the faculty handbook describes. There are unwritten rules that must be followed. Sometimes the process can be downright hurtful. Added to all this, not only are faculty members expected to have a vibrant faith, they also must somehow show and share this faith in their teaching and integrate it into their research, documenting and assessing it along the way. Loving Jesus and getting promoted can be a very daunting task, indeed!

In Chapters One and Two, we try to make faith-learning integration more transparent and less confusing. We try to do the same in Chapter Three for the institutional conventions and conversations about faith and learning that arise during the promotion and tenure process. As you likely know from experience, on any campus one will hear various conceptions and conversations about faith and learning integration. Such conversations usually have a long and unique history. It is important to understand when and where these conversations occur, and how to navigate effectively the institutional terrain.

In Chapters Four to Seven, we introduce the life and work of Ernest Boyer, and the four dimensions of the Boyer model of scholarship (discovery, integration, teaching, and engagement), discussing ways to undertake these forms of scholarship effectively and faithfully. We believe that the Boyer model holds great promise for faculty serving in faith-based institutions. Truly it can be life giving. However, while every senior academic administrator we know is familiar with Boyer and *Scholarship Reconsidered*, exactly how most colleges consider and evaluate scholarship remains far from clear. In part, this is true because so many different voices and opinions enter into the faculty evaluation process—colleagues, peers, department chairs, deans, provosts, presidents, and trustees—and the voices keep changing. Too many times, this confusion rears its head during the promotion and tenure evaluation process, resulting in disappointment, frustration, and hurt. But what can faculty members do to make the promotion and tenure process go more smoothly for themselves and for others? In this volume, we share practical advice from provosts and presidents serving in faith–based institutions, and we offer our own specific strategies to assist anyone involved in the process. In the end, we will say that faithful scholarship is hard work, but it is good work—and it is sacramental work, too.

In Chapter Eight, we provide practical examples and guidance for assessing faith integration in the four scholarly dimensions. We share several helpful approaches we think will make this task more understandable and more approachable. Christian colleges have used faith-learning integration language for several decades already but we are collectively just now getting to the detailed work of assessing how successfully individuals and institutions have implemented this ideal. We will explore some of this fledgling work here.

In Chapter Nine, we offer some useful strategies for bringing scholarly habits to bear on faculty work. Certainly, writing and scholarship have a craft dimension; we believe that faculty can learn disciplines of the writing craft and thereby increase not just the substance of their CVs but the value of their teaching, the impact of their research, and their joy in academic work. We know far too many faculty who struggle to develop a scholarly agenda. It is not that they lack ideas or the intelligence or the desire to do so. Rather, they lack structure, support, and a disciplined approach to writing. For those dealing with such lacks, we trust that chapter nine will give life.

In the final chapter, we share our vision for the reorientation, realignment, and renewal of faith-based universities. With a few exceptions, we believe that faith-based institutions do not and should not conceive of themselves as research universities (R1 institutions). Instead, they should see themselves as transformational institutions (T1 institutions). That is, their central mission is the transmission of knowledge and the transformation of persons rather than the discovery and transmission of new knowledge. This is not a trivial distinction. We believe they can and do accomplish this transformative task in remarkable ways. Yet, the reward structures for promotion and tenure in these institutions borrow heavily from R1 institutions and their culture. In essence, T1 institutions reward one thing while hoping for another. We wonder what might happen if

Christian colleges and universities had the courage to be faithful to their heritage instead of trying to climb the ladder of academic status. We call for a rethinking of the academic institution as a wisdom community and for a corresponding realignment of reward and status structures. For those institutions willing to travel down that path—which may be a lonely path— we offer a few suggestions to guide the journey.

We end this preface with a confession. We claim different theological orientations. One of us is Wesleyan, the other Reformed. One of us is a practitioner, the other a teacher and scholar. We carry different passports, one Canadian, one American. We have worked in different types of institutions. We do not always see eye to eye on how to approach questions related to the integration of faith and learning, and we both see our conceptions and convictions moving and melding to some degree. And we know that we are jumping into an ongoing conversation. Should we replace the integration phrase or perhaps do away with integration language altogether? Are we beyond integration? Is this question no longer relevant? We do agree and believe deeply that bringing faith and learning together in a variety of meaningful ways is the rare air for Christian colleges and university faculties. We also believe that faith and learning integration is not a dead language. There is much about the integration discussion to commend it—no need to throw out the baby with the bathwater. One key, we argue, is to think about faith and learning as embodied in our scholarship, not just spliced to it with a scripture verse and a prayer. When it comes to faith-learning integration and, in fact, to the whole project of Christian higher education, the future holds both opportunities and pitfalls. In our view, the trick is to seize the opportunities and avoid the pitfalls. We trust that this book will guide faculty who are called and committed to this incredible journey.

## Chapter 1

# The Rich and High Calling of Faithful Teaching

All universities and colleges hire new faculty with the expectation that they will teach students and serve their institutions and, in some cases, their geographic communities. Many universities and colleges hire with the additional expectation that faculty will conduct research or engage in scholarship and participate in and serve the guild, the academy. Obviously, educational settings differ from each other, and the elements we have just named combine in different ways in different places. But some typical patterns hold, and universities and colleges expect their faculty both to accomplish great things and to demonstrate that they have accomplished those great things.

As one might expect, church-related colleges add another complex of expectations. They presume—rightly, we believe—that if a college names Christ and intends to offer education that is foundationally different from what is offered at institutions that do not name Christ, then faculty should be able to understand, embrace, and realize that difference. Furthermore, when faculty report to department chairs, deans, provosts, and the university committees that assess whether to grant promotion or tenure, they should be able to articulate that difference and their own success at realizing it.

Therein lies a problem. We believe that in Christian colleges two things may sometimes combine to make success appear out of reach for new faculty. First, figuring out teaching and academic life is not for the faint of heart; it is tough work. Even small colleges are very complex, open systems, and acculturation takes time and effort. It is a bit like solving a mystery—or joining one. Second, Christian colleges expect their faculty to add something beyond the usual trio of teaching, research, and service. Christian colleges do not all employ the same vocabulary to express this "added something," although many use the language of faith-learning integration. However they describe it, Christian colleges want their faculty to teach, think, and work as Christians, not just as faculty who happen to be able to spell the word *God* or who attend church. Professors are expected to profess something that is genuine and to do something that is truly distinctive: to teach, shape, and send. Hmm...

Christian colleges and universities produce reams of documents that advertise, mention, or attempt to explain what naming Christ means institutionally and educationally. Think of these typical documents: mission statements, statements of faith, strategic plans, recruitment brochures, syllabus templates, annual reports, websites, even the explanations and descriptions of how faculty are to structure and write their professional portfolios and assessments of their annual growth plans. This plethora of documents may leave faculty wondering exactly what characteristics or practices differentiate a Christian college from one that is not Christian. Faculty members, along with college administrators, parents, students, and board members, may ask themselves what differentiates a Christian education from an education which does not carry that honorific label. And faculty, left without translation software to interpret the many and possibly mixed messages about such differentiation, sometimes end up confused about what their colleges expect of them, uncertain about which understandings, characteristics, or practices trump others.

New faculty face an additional challenge. Whether they have come to college teaching from the academic world or from professional practice, they need to figure out teaching. Teaching is an interlocking set of jigsaw puzzles. Curriculum, for example, is a puzzle in itself. What are the core requirements and options within the different programs offered by the department? Why are they designed that way, and who decides? How do I structure a course so that I get through the material without rushing madly in the last few weeks of the term? How do I know which materials to focus on and which materials to leave in the background? These questions and many others cause new and veteran professors alike to lose sleep. Curriculum, by itself, is a jigsaw puzzle.

Instruction, too, can be intimidating. Do you mean that on the first day of the term, I have to stand up in front of all those people who do not know me, and some of whom wish they were elsewhere, and . . . what's that word? . . . start? Yes, and keep starting day after day for the whole term. And please vary your methods so students don't get bored. Oh, and please remember that their attention span is significantly shorter than the longer class blocks on Tuesdays and Thursdays, roughly the length of time between advertisements on TV or the time it takes to read a blog post. The list goes on. Instruction is a jigsaw puzzle, too. And so is assessment. And so is creating the classroom ethos in which we and our students do the good work of learning and teaching. All these puzzles are interlocking. None of them can be solved in isolation from the others. That is, teaching is a highly complex activity; it truly is not for the timid.

We do not want anyone to give up teaching right this minute because of what we have written here; we are simply trying to recognize the dual and very serious challenge of starting to teach in a Christian college. Beginning to teach is challenge enough. Beginning to teach while integrating faith and learning (whatever that means) can appear to be twice as difficult. We believe that those who read this book to the end will think differently about this perceived difficulty and will understand that both God and the colleges that name God expect them to teach out of their deepest, authentic selves. Faith and learning need not be confusing and intimidating; faculty can find ways forward. Teaching faithfully is a rich and high calling. It is a pilgrimage of faith, helping the now and not-yet Kingdom to come. It is expectant with deep relationships, personal growth, and intellectual development.

A large number of Christian colleges have adopted the language of *faith-learning integration* to express their vision for Christian education. In the next chapter, we will explore in more detail the history of both this bit of language and of some of the theological and cultural ideals its users intend to catch when they use it. But before we do that, we want to explore the three areas of expectations that we have mentioned: teaching, research, and service. What do colleges and universities expect when they tell faculty to teach, when they urge them to conduct research or engage in scholarship, and when they tell them to serve on committees?

## Teaching

We start with teaching. We do not apologize for colleges and universities that ask their faculty to teach. And we do not think those institutions should apologize either. Our refusals notwithstanding, someone must be sending out a different message to students. Both of us and, we expect, many of our readers have had students at our office door who began their query with these words: "Sorry for interrupting your work, but . . . ." Where did they learn that they were not part of our work? Who gave them that message? Presumably, someone did, but it was not us or our readers. Late in this book, we will argue that part of our mission in education, especially in Christian education, is to shape. We believe that shaping happens in the dormitory, in the gymnasium, in the commons, in the cafeteria and, to our point here, in the classroom. That is, we believe in teaching.

But many new faculty, even those who wholeheartedly support the teaching mission of their institution, legitimately wonder what they are supposed to do differently just because they and their employer name Christ. Does naming Christ in general imply making references to Christian faith in class? How about praying for one's students? What about mounting a cross over the classroom door or starting each class with a prayer or devotional? As faculty regularly ask us, "What difference does faith make in my teaching?" We consider that a great question, perhaps the key question that both faculty and their institutions need to be asking. What difference does faith make?

For many faculty, the difference does imply adopting practices such as praying in class or exploring whether Christian faith implies anything special or different about whatever subject matter happens to be at hand on a given day. Others attempt to realize their Christian commitment in quite different ways. In Chapter Two we discuss what we call *conceptions* of faith-learning integration. Each of us has a different understanding of what faith-learning integration means and of how we can or should try to realize it in our work as teaching faculty, as department and committee members, as researchers, as members of communities. It makes sense that we would understand the relationship between faith and learning differently given that we come to work having worshipped with different faith communities and having embraced different understandings of God, God's word, God's world, and our place in God's world. We have varying pictures of the ideal classroom, differing epistemologies, diverse approaches to the student-teacher relationship, and different understandings of the role of the teacher. With all these differences (and we know there are more differences and also many commonalities!), why would anyone expect all faculty to understand faith-learning integration in the same ways? We believe we will all be able to function more effectively at work and perhaps sleep better at home when faculty begin to appreciate the idea that we will inevitably arrive at different conclusions about—and conceptions of—faith and learning integration.

We will explore this question in much greater depth later in the book, but very briefly, *should* it make a difference? Not to be facile, but in one sense chemistry is chemistry in both a Christian college and a public college. The quadratic equation is the same everywhere. A debit can increase an asset or reduce a liability on any account ledger. The Democratic Republic of Congo is actually bigger than Greenland (yes!) regardless of whether the Mercator projection map that leads so many to the wrong conclusion hangs on the wall at a Christian college or at a public university. So, will there be curricular differences in the Christian college? Perhaps.

When it comes to information acquisition and skill development, Christians and Christian colleges have no exclusive territory to claim. At some level, R1 institutions (a Carnegie Foundation category that includes

institutions whose mission is to generate and disseminate new information) teach the same information and skills as community colleges. But
in addition to the lesson of the day, a chemistry professor in a Christian
college might also speak of the wonder of God's creation, of the nature of
truth, of different ways of truth seeking (of which the scientific method
is just one), of the centrality of vocation, of the call to use knowledge and
skills in ways intended not simply to earn money or increase happiness,
or of the sacramental nature of all learning. The list could go on and on.
Thanks be to God that many professors at R1 institutions find creative and
winsome ways to introduce ideas and questions such as these, even when
such queries are not expected or necessarily welcome. However, almost all
Christian colleges view such ideas and questions as central to teaching, as
essential aspects of their vocation. We will return to this matter late in the
book, in our call for colleges to clarify their mission, especially vis-à-vis
the tensions between teaching and research.

We believe that a realignment of the reward structure for promotion
and tenure at Christian colleges can do much to support and advance
this type of teaching beyond the lesson of the day. Faculty in many institutions perceive differences between their job descriptions and the institutional expectations they must meet for promotion and tenure. R. G.
Green, for example, writes of the "strikingly fundamental disconnect"
between workload and the role expectations that may "imped[e] morale,
well-being, productivity and recruitment."[1] It is a sad irony that some of the
best teachers at Christian colleges, recognized by colleagues and students
alike and showcased by admissions personnel to prospective students on
visit days, cannot earn a promotion or be granted tenure because they
do not possess a research doctorate or produce enough research. While
being recognized as teaching stars, they are relegated to the back of the
institutional bus and receive less pay, recognition, and job security than
do their peers who publish. Something is clearly misaligned. Later in this
book, we will discuss the folly of rewarding A while hoping for B, a classic
management mistake.

In Chapter Three, we will discuss some of the connections between
loving Jesus and getting promoted in a faith-based institution. As you may

already know, the connections can seem rather tenuous and the process can become quite complicated. After discussing several prevalent and pesky misconceptions that confuse the promotion process, we will examine and identify different institutional conversations—almost different languages—about faith and learning. As you will see, several of these conversations may take place on any given campus—and at the same time. It is important to know which jungle you are in if you wish to make it to your destination. What we will make clear is that different decision-makers in the promotion and tenure process may use the same words but in fact be speaking in entirely different languages. Some clarity at the inception of the promotion evaluation journey will go a long way in avoiding a train wreck at the other end or a derailment along the way.

In Chapter Four, we will introduce the framework that Ernest Boyer suggested as a way to help universities clarify their expectations of faculty. We think both faculty and their workplaces should take Boyer's framework seriously—and approximately a thousand have done so already—because his approach brings clarity to institutions seeking to understand their mission and mental health to faculty seeking to know what they should be doing. He reframes teaching, research, service, and the connections between the three in life-giving ways. After introducing Boyer in Chapter Four, we will suggest in Chapter Five an overtly Boyeristic framework for thinking about teaching.

We believe that Boyer offers a way to move teaching out of the silo that some keep it in, viewing it as a privatized, disconnected set of practices and responsibilities. Boyer also presents a challenge to those who view teaching as a scheduled irritant that gets in the way of "their work." No, teaching IS your work! It is our work. But along with his challenge, Boyer also offers help to those who are overwhelmed by the demands of teaching—and that includes many new faculty. Boyer presents a framework that brings a scholarly approach and scholarly habits of mind to the teaching task, allowing faculty to make creative and fruitful connections between their teaching and the research they wish they had more time to do.

# Research

Major universities consider research a central part of their mandate, per-haps the most important aspect (along with football). Many university and departmental rankings are determined by research production, leading to a situation where getting research grants and publishing research become critical. As we write, British universities continue to struggle as they try to adapt to government-imposed funding models whereby quantifiable research productivity, not student numbers, determines annual operating grants. We know of a prominent research university which, when preparing an accreditation report, seriously asked the accrediting agency if anything really needed to be mentioned about students or if a conversation about research was enough! After all, students were a means to an end, they were not of primary importance except to pay the bills (tuition) and serve as apprentices and lab assistants. What a sad commentary on that university's vision for higher education.

What about the Christian college? Where does research fit in an insti-tution whose primary mission is teaching? In Chapter Six, we will deal at length with this question and with Boyer's understanding of research. But as we did with teaching, we want to raise a couple of initial questions here to help locate our whole discussion and aid our readers in understanding the direction we take in the book.

Is there a place for research at a Christian college? Certainly, but we will argue later in this book that the most important research projects at a teaching institution are those that engage and shape students, paralleling the mission of the institution. What if those activities received the highest priority and funding? Teaching colleges do not exist primarily to support individual faculty research unrelated to their mission, but tenure and promotion processes might lead some to think that the most highly valued work is that of the autonomous researcher. And it seems strange to us that teaching institutions would release some faculty from a substantial part of their teaching assignment in order to provide them more time to do individual research, and then hold up that activity as a model for the rest of the faculty. Shouldn't the best and brightest faculty be in the classroom at a teaching institution, supporting the central aspect of the mission?

New faculty tend to hear a lot of conflicting advice about how much research and what kind of research they need to do if they want to keep their jobs and get promoted. Some, but not all, universities have a policy of "up or out," whereby faculty who do not move up the ranks from assistant to associate to full and being granted tenure are encouraged to "seek employment elsewhere," to use one of the many euphemisms available. And at many of those institutions, promotion depends heavily on the faculty member's success in an aggressive program of research and publication. In this environment, research and promotion become so tightly related that they actually become conflated in what some call social knowledge, the commonsense claims one hears in the hallway.[2]

We do want to note that there are a few Christian institutions (Notre Dame and Baylor among them) who want to be research institutions and compete in the R1 world. We see this as completely legitimate, but they are really few in number. So what about teaching institutions, a category that includes most of those using faith-learning language? Here we encounter a tension. Historically, Christian colleges have understood their mission to be teaching; they hire faculty to teach. But the larger academic ethos within which Christian colleges carry out their work is shaped by what we might call R1 culture. Somehow the air we breathe has in it the expectation that we are publishing research, even if the college where we teach states that its mission is to teach. Are we to be little R1s with Jesus as an added dimension?

Truly, faculty members at Christian colleges work in a particular college, but they also work in a discipline, in the academe, in the guild. We live in what we might call two kingdoms, to give Luther's concept only a partial twist. Living and working where we do, we get two kinds of messages. And those messages will not always be consistent with each other or the reward structures that support and perpetuate them. In Chapter Six, we will consider these tensions again, bringing to bear on them the liberating perspective of Ernest Boyer.

# Service

New faculty also wish for greater clarity about what their college expects by way of service. Does the word have a restricted and technical meaning inside the academy that differs from the ordinary sense of the word outside the academy? Some colleges define the word explicitly and clearly in the faculty handbook: service entails committee work as assigned and agreed within the department and school. Others, who define it equally clearly, include service within and to the larger community and church. Some offer no definition at all, leaving the faculty member to guess what counts as service and what does not, an approach that takes us back to social knowledge. "Well, I heard that the board wants this." "I know, but professor X on the tenure and promotion committee, apparently always asks about this." As one faculty member put it to one of us, "It's a moving target and the lights are off in the room. We won't tell you where it is, but we will tell you if you ever hit it."

With our readers, we recognize the moral wrong for a college to name an expectation but refuse to define how to successfully meet that expectation. We will not address the moral features of this situation other than to identify it. But we do want to suggest strategies for faculty to become effective in carrying out their service, in connecting their service to their research and teaching, and in appropriately describing their service so that their deans, provosts, departmental colleagues, and university colleagues serving on personnel committees will recognize that they have been effective in their service.

We noted our conviction that Ernest Boyer has offered colleges and faculty members a helpful framework to locate service within the overall work of the faculty. In Chapter Seven, we return to Boyer's understanding of service, which he calls *the scholarship of engagement* or *the scholarship of application*,[3] and offer some specific ways to bring scholarly habits of mind to faculty service—an often overlooked aspect of a professor's calling. We believe that this is a particularly helpful approach for faculty serving in professional disciplines.

## Faith and Learning Integration

Perhaps the most obvious commonality among many Christian colleges is their use of the language of faith-learning integration. In fact, member colleges of the Council of Christian Colleges and Universities use this phrase almost as a calling card. In Chapter Two, we will trace in detail both the history of this language and some of the reasons that faculty find it confusing. Here, we will simply note that people of faith have dealt throughout Christian history with questions of faith and reason. They have asked to what degree and in what ways naming Christ affects the work they do in the academy and in the world of ideas. Believers have engaged in the struggle to make the connections between faith and reason regardless of where they work in the world of ideas, whether in the monastic cell, in the study, in the classroom, in the laboratory, in the field, or in the library. Christians do not all agree on the many answers proffered to the question of how faith and reason connect, and, to further complicate matters, many of the answers appear to have solid scriptural warrants and certainly enjoy long historical support. We will find in this conversation a variety of traditions, all pointing to the Bible for endorsement.

Those who work in the academy and who claim Christ ask several related questions: How can we clarify and communicate that in our work as faculty we face the church and the world, not only the academy? How do we find language that suits our service orientation and recognizes that sheer volume of output is not likely to suit our institutions' stated missions and may not be what we, or God, or our students want? How does the typical lexicon of research filled with words such as "impact," "productivity," "output," "prolific," "effective", and "expert" fit within a Christian understanding of scholarship?

In the words of two professors, "Production speaks to an industrial model that seeks to meet demand and blacken bottom lines."[4] Can we nuance or differentiate "impact" as measured in the academy (acceptance rates of journals, prestige of journals, etc.) to words that incorporate widely held Christian values? And as for the right language, consider our "facing"; should we turn our face toward recognition from the academy or toward service to the world and the church? How do we combine and nuance these apparently competing values? How do live in this dissonance? How does our scholarship provide evidence that we love God and love others? We hope to provide ways to think carefully and faithfully about many of these questions, but you will have to arrive at your own answers. This is no "one size fits all" conversation.

Faith-learning integration language is rarely clear, which further complicates—and sometimes confounds—the efforts of faculty in Christian colleges to understand what their colleges expect of them. We believe it could be made clear. Colleges could stipulate a definition of this much -loved phrase, the same way that Humpty Dumpty stipulated his preferred meaning of the word *glory*. Note his interchange with Alice:

> "I don't know what you mean by 'glory'," Alice said.
>
> Humpty Dumpty smiled contemptuously. "Of course you don't—till I tell you. I meant 'there's a nice knock-down argument for you!'"
>
> "But 'glory' doesn't mean 'a nice knock-down argument'," Alice objected.
>
> "When I use a word," Humpty Dumpty said, in rather a scornful tone, "it means just what I choose it to mean—neither more nor less."[5]

A Christian college could specify that when they use the phrase "faith-learning integration," they mean a nice knock-down argument, or opening class in prayer, or selecting curriculum materials that will raise questions of justice or possibly indicate the presence of God's hand in the world.

We will not ask our readers to accept our understanding of faith-learning integration. We will outline a variety of conceptions of it, noting the traditions in which those conceptions locate themselves, how those conceptions work out in practice, and how faculty members might articulate their conceptions in the portfolios they prepare for purposes of promotion and tenure. Ultimately, faith-learning integration is a journey. We trust this book will serve to guide your professional journey, regardless of your present location or desired destination.

## Chapter 2

# What Is All the Faith and Learning Fuss About?

We noted in Chapter One the nearly ubiquitous belief among many Christian higher educators that the teaching, research, and service at their institutions should be different from the teaching, research, and service we would expect to find at a public institution. Different in what way, to what degree, and in what aspects? In short: Christian, high, and in all aspects of academic work.

We recognize that our answers are vague and circular. In fact, we intentionally answer that way to point again to the problem that new faculty, veteran faculty, deans, provosts, and personnel committee members all face: How do we answer the question of what difference Christian faith makes in education? Where does it show? How is the individual faculty member supposed to articulate it?

## History of a Popular Phrase

For good or ill, several decades ago, participants in this conversation latched onto the phrase *faith-learning integration*. The first use of this phrase appears in Frank Gaebelein's 1954 book, *The Pattern of God's Truth: The Integration of Faith and Learning*.[1] Gaebelein used the phrase to draw his readers' attention to the difference Christian faith should make to academic work. At the time and in the context in which Gaebelein wrote, many Christians had a limited and limiting understanding of the reach of Christian faith. In this truncated view, faith served as the foundation of a person's spiritual life, the basis of personal ethics, and the focus of one's worship and devotional practices.

After World War II, as the evangelical movement assessed its losses in the theological and church controversies of the early twentieth century, evangelical educators could not help but notice their educational losses, too.[2] Obviously, the evangelical movement lost many educational institutions. But it also lacked a vision for education that was sufficiently large or life-giving to energize the institutions it still controlled. Evangelical educators had retrenched. And in the mid-1950s, the time of Gaebelein's writing, it turned out that an understanding of Christian faith that extended to spiritual life, ethics, worship, and devotional practice but failed to account for education was not sufficient. In the view of Gaebelein and other contemporary educators, evangelicals came up short when articulating a posture toward the academic disciplines themselves or the work that academics did within those disciplines. In Gaebelein's view (and ours), Christian faith had been sold short. In this setting, Gaebelein called for Christians—especially the evangelicals in his own tradition—to see that faith had everything to do with teaching and academic research.

We must underline that Gaebelein and his evangelical colleagues were not the only Protestant educators calling for Christians to think as Christians about the world of learning and ideas. When Gaebelein's *The Pattern of God's Truth* appeared in 1954, many educators connected to Christian Reformed churches and colleges had already been working for decades in what some call a neo-Calvinist or Kuyperian framework (after Dutch philosopher, theologian and prime minister, Abraham Kuyper, 1837–1920). The Free University of Amsterdam (1880, Netherlands) and Calvin College (1876, Grand Rapids, Michigan) both worked in this tradition long before Gaebelein's book appeared. Today, many Reformed colleges throughout the United States, Canada, and the rest of the world explicitly work in this tradition. Many other colleges, while not explicitly Reformed, are heavily influenced by Reformed thought through evangelicals, such as Arthur Holmes of Wheaton College, who now present or formerly presented a Reformed vision for education and worldview. For philosophical and theological reasons we will not address here, many Reformed educators use worldview language rather than integration language when they discuss their visions for Christian education.[3] For the purposes of this book, we will restrict our focus to Gaebelein because, as far as we can determine, he coined the phrase *integration of faith and learning*.

We do not fault Gaebelein for deciding to use integration language. Having noted that, we do want to point out that he might just as easily have spoken of realizing a Christian worldview in the world of education. Admittedly, in 1954, the concept of worldview was still largely the province of philosophy, anthropology, and sociology; it had not yet entered the conversation about Christian views of culture or academic work. He could have written about Christian scholarship, and he could have spoken about teaching Christianly. Gaebelein could have cited Paul, who wrote in 2 Corinthians 10:5 about taking every thought captive to Christ, a phrase used in at least four book titles in the last several decades.[4] Gaebelein also might have lifted from Paul the idea that in Christ all things hold together (Col. 1:17). For that matter, he might have found the framework and language he needed in Richard Niebuhr's 1951 volume, *Christ and Culture*.[5] Might have. Could have. The language Gaebelein did choose was that of faith and learning integration, a phrase that—in the decades since *The Pattern of God's Truth* first appeared in 1954—has come to hold a powerful sway over the conversation about higher education in evangelical circles. Despite becoming immensely popular—or possibly because it has become immensely popular—the phrase also has problems, which we will discuss shortly.

We should note two things in Gaebelein's defense. First, if any of the *might-have, could-have* language we just suggested had achieved the popularity that faith-learning integration language has achieved in Christian higher education, it might have encountered many of the same difficulties that integration language has faced.[6] Second, Gaebelein chose his language to point to a gap and call people to bridge that gap. He was not alone in this effort, but for our purposes we must say that he succeeded; evangelical Christians in the academy heard the call to think, research, and teach like Christians. For all the problems with faith-learning integration language, the truth remains that it succeeded as part of Gaebelein's call inasmuch as it gave many Christian higher educators a way to address a pressing problem that confronted them.

In this chapter title, we ask what the faith-learning fuss is about. Simply put, we see *fuss* at two levels, both legitimate. First, if Christian higher education is going to be different from higher education that does not claim to be Christian, then we ought to be able to point to some differences. We ought to make some fuss about that. Second, faith-learning integration language, while dominant in this conversation, does not do all the work or precisely the work that some of its champions envision it doing. It works, to a degree, but a growing number of people, us among them, have pointed to its limits and weaknesses. Many find it vague and therefore confusing. For the purposes of this book, those limits and weaknesses present both you as our readers and we as the authors with a problem: we see the weaknesses inherent in integration language, but most Christian colleges still ask their faculty to use that language when they articulate their Christian vision for teaching, research, and service.

Because our purpose here is to help faculty articulate their own conception of Christian education, we will do our best to work in the language that so many colleges and individual educators use. Even so, we hope that you, our readers, will understand our serious reservations about that language, and so will detail those here.

## Problems with Integration Language: Introduction

We want to help our readers understand the wide range of Christian educational visions that energize Christian colleges. Because many such colleges use faith-learning integration language, we will examine that language, recognizing as we do that some may suspect that examining the language might distract us from the educational visions under discussion. In fact, we believe that the language of faith-learning integration actually offers us and our readers a window to see into the substance of those various educational visions, their common themes, and some of the features that differentiate them one from another. We believe the key phrase itself—faith-learning integration—is the source of some of the difficulties and so will explore some of the conceptual problems in ways that not only return our focus to Christian visions of higher education, but that also help faculty escape some of the conceptual thickets where they sometimes find themselves when they attempt to articulate their own understanding and vision.

Furthermore, faculty—especially new faculty—tell us the conceptual difficulties we treat in the following pages are the very ones that create frustration and apprehension as they attempt both to understand the work they have been hired to do in Christian colleges and to articulate that work in promotion portfolios and annual professional reports. So, the discussion that follows is not only linguistic analysis.[7] It is also very much an on-the-ground discussion of some important issues that new and veteran faculty face. A faculty member once lamented to one of us that it would be nice to be able to look up *faith-learning integration* in the dictionary. Would that it were that simple. It is a linguistic question. But it is so much more than that. It is also a biblical and theological question, a philosophical question, a historical question, and a question of curriculum and instruction. But let us begin.

## A Slogan: Faith-Learning Integration

First, and perhaps most obviously, faith-learning integration is a slogan. Slogans notoriously get slippery and ambiguous. People use slogans pro-grammatically, to call others to action, sometimes in the hope that they can bypass the critical capacities of those being called into action. So far, slogans sound rather dangerous. But slogans become slogans because they catch people's imagination and express important ideas.

We have no one to blame but ourselves for the fact that "faith-learning integration" has achieved slogan status. But *blame* may well be the wrong response if, in fact, a large number of Christian higher educators wish to express a particular vision for their work as educators. That is, *faith-learning integration* became and remains a slogan only because what it seems to resonate with so many people, although the term is a far-from-perfect expression of their vision. In 1994, one of us asked in a journal article whether the emphasis on faith and learning integration was merely a slogan or actually had some content.[8] Then, and now, the answer seems to be: *both*.

Linguistic philosophers noted decades ago that slogans are not incapable of conveying meaning. In fact, the opposite is true; slogans carry and convey rich meaning, and they usually do so very economically.[9] Educators interested in faith and learning have also explored how our phrase of interest functions, given its status as a slogan.[10] A quick check of either the advertising or the criteria for tenure and promotion at a few Christian colleges will confirm that *faith-learning integration* clearly retains the slogan status it had achieved as early as 1994. But simply because the phrase has slogan status does not prevent it from conveying meaning. For many faculty, the problem with the phrase becomes or remains the question, "What meaning?"

Should we get rid of faith-learning language because of this possibly dubious achievement of slogan status? We say both *no* and *yes*. We say *yes*, we should get rid of it, if the phrase serves only to generate confusion and frustration.[11] We say a pragmatic *no* if colleges insist on continuing to use it and requiring faculty to describe their work in such terms. And we offer a principial, albeit somewhat tentative, *no* if the phrase continues to catch—however inadequately—what so many Christian educators envision. Its status as a slogan is not, in our view, sufficient reason to jettison the term quite yet. Our readers may find other reasons more persuasive.

## Concepts and Conceptions of Faith-Learning Integration

Some faculty members may think their lives would be simplified if they could just look up *faith-learning integration* in a dictionary. We agree; life would be simplified, at least initially. But faculty might head in the wrong direction if they could do that since their direction would then depend on the combination of the character of the article and their critical skills.[12] We note that problems might arise out of this combination because much that is written about faith-learning integration presents one person's conception of integration as if it were the—pronounced *thee*—definition of the concept.

We will explore the concept-conception distinction because we think it helps explain how faith-learning integration language generates much of the frustration and confusion that educators experience. As it happens, this distinction relates to our discussion of slogans. In short, *faith–learning integration* has a dual function. It serves as both a concept and a conception.[13] The frequent appearance of such phrases as *faith–learning integration, Christian worldview,* and *Christian scholarship* indicate the deep and appropriate desire of many educators to make connections between our Christian faith and the teaching and research tasks that fill our days.

But—this is key to understanding how these popular phrases work in ordinary usage—Christian educators do not all envision the same kind or degree of connection. When answering the question of what kind of connection, some focus on the character of the professor, others on the tone of the classroom, others on the topics chosen for research, others on epistemology and curriculum or instruction. Even among those who focus on curriculum and instruction, one can distinguish six or seven models of integration. Some professors in Christian colleges would resonate deeply with the Pauline passages we cited earlier, that we are to take every thought captive to Christ (2 Cor. 10:5) or that in Christ all things hold together (Col. 1:17). Others might find the first of these passages insufficiently about engagement with the academy and too obviously about domination. Some might limit Paul's discussion of Christ's supremacy to a theological discussion that has no bearing on the academic disciplines. In short, we come at this question of the connections between Christian faith and our work as professors in many different ways.[14]

The distinction between a concept and a conception may help us frame these differences. At its simplest, this distinction starts with a dictionary definition. Obviously, the lexicographers will have an easier time defining words such as *book* and *car* than terms such as *democracy* or *justice*. Even simple terms can be deceptive. In response to a wonderfully written or beautifully printed book, we might be tempted to say, "Now that's a book!" or "That's what I call a book!" At the moment of our declaration, we are not negating what the dictionary has recorded, but we are demonstrating that we load our own values onto the basic concept of book (printed words bound between covers); our language inevitably becomes value-laden. If relatively nonnormative words such as *book* can become value-laden, normative language is even more likely to take on value connotations, to have built-in conceptions. *Democracy, justice*, and *faith-learning integration* are prime candidate terms to have their users load personal freight on top of whatever semantic load the dictionary has already assigned. In other words, they are particularly ripe for what some call "conception-building."[15]

Examples abound to illustrate how Christian educators build conceptions around normative concepts. Consider these typical—but quite different—expressions that arise out of Christian understandings of education, some of which their users would say are realizations of the ideal of faith-learning integration:

- I pray for my students privately, and I usually begin my classes with prayer.
- Within the departmentally specified objectives for this course, I try to develop curriculum materials that are most likely to allow students to raise questions related to faith.
- I want students to see God's hand in the subject matter they encounter in my class.
- I deliberately structure my courses so students will see that this whole discipline makes most sense when one approaches it with a Christian epistemology.
- Math is math, but I want students to see God's handiwork everywhere in this course.

For the sake of argument, let us say that all five of these comments came in response to a question about how professors try to integrate faith and learning. In such a case, we have a clear demonstration of the difference between a concept and a conception. The dictionary might say that faith-learning integration means something about the connection between Christian faith and academic work. The five faculty who made the claims above might all agree to the dictionary's definition. But if they talked long enough, and were honest enough, they might have to agree to disagree because their comments represent some very different conceptions of faith and learning integration.

We do not mean to solve a problem of disagreement here. We do not think all Christian professors *should* agree about faith and learning integration. We don't even agree with each other, one of us (Patrick Allen) being Wesleyan and one of us (Kenneth Badley) being Reformed. We would love to solve the problem that relates to conversation participants failing to notice the degree to which they disagree because they are using the same language. If our readers could grasp the concept-conception distinction, they might thereby be spared massive headaches and be prepared to show more respect for each other's understandings of—and attempts to realize—faith-learning integration in their respective programs of teaching and research.

One of us received a piece of advice before a tenure meeting with the academic sub-committee of a college board of governors. The advice was simple: tell the board that you love Jesus and, if you want to up the ante, tell them you led the taxi driver to Christ on your way to the meeting. The second bit was obviously a joke, but the first bit reveals something important about the institutions in which we work and the people who govern those institutions. Some board members may be concerned about the epistemic assumptions underlying the courses for which they, as governors, ultimately take responsibility. But others only want to know if the professors love Jesus. The kicker in this, of course, is that all the board members like the marketing brochure with its language of faith-learning integration; it's just that, like the professors they employ, the board members have different conceptions of faith-learning integration.

Understanding the concept-conception distinction can help Christian educators clear away some of the confusion that often arises when faith-learning integration language is used. A related concept, the essentially contested concept, may also help clarify the issue. The philosopher who originally suggested this category had in mind concepts that figure importantly in normative debates but whose users disagree as to their meaning. Democracy, justice, and faith-learning integration all serve as good examples of essentially contested concepts. Faith-learning integration figures centrally in a wide variety of statements of concern for Christian education. We used five bulleted statements a few paragraphs above to illustrate how conceptions get built onto concepts. The same statements illustrate essentially contested concepts. If one faculty member deeply believes that prayer is the key distinguishing feature of a truly Christian education, another deeply commits herself to professor-student relationships, and a third claims that curriculum and instruction are where students will see God's hand at work in the world, but all three use faith-learning language, then we would have a paradigm example of what Walter Bryce Gallie identified in 1956 as a contested concept.

An obvious, but practically difficult, way to resolve the contest regarding this particular contested concept is for each of us to accept that the other person, like us, is simply expressing what he or she understands to be the task of the Christian educator. That is, we will agree not to contest each other's understandings. Of course, to do so requires that we trust each other to be listening to God's voice as we individually and collectively discern what is God's best for us in our varied research, service, and work with students in our respective educational settings. Agreeing not to contest our different understandings also implies that we trust the Holy Spirit to lead people along different educational paths as we all seek to obey God in carrying out our scholarly vocations. In effect, we must trust God. And we must trust our colleagues to be listening to God, exactly what we are implicitly asking them to do with us.

When the Reign of Christ is fully realized, we will all know as we are known, and we then may all agree about how to define this key phrase (or we may agree to disagree, or we may stop worrying about it altogether). Until then, and for obvious reasons, we will more likely continue to prefer our own understandings of faith-learning integration, of Christian education, of the importance of helping students understand the concept of worldview. Preferring our own understandings—each doing what is right in our eyes—we may continue to wonder if others have got it right. In these circumstances, we may continue to need Gallie's idea of essentially-contested concepts to better enable us to function as colleagues with different understandings of the mission we collectively have set out to achieve. Grace can be a great healer.

## Some Models of Faith-Learning Integration

Having distinguished concepts from conceptions, we will survey briefly several models of faith-learning integration. As we noted in the section above, most people neglect to mention that they have in mind a particular model of or approach to the connections between faith and learning when putting integration language to work. Users of this language often assume a degree of univocality and clarity in issues they should actually assume to be problematic. We will distinguish seven distinct models or meanings here to show that the language is anything but univocal.

Some people, when speaking of faith-learning integration, seem to have in mind a kind of *fusion*, perhaps similar to the kind of fused curriculum created by combining biology, chemistry, geology, and physics into a junior high course called Science. Others imply some kind of *incorporation*, in which the professor or teacher incorporates faith elements or components into curriculum and instruction. Obviously, incorporation is a matter of degree. If Professor A mentions on the first day of the semester that Christian faith changes how we view and understand the subject matter but never mentions faith again, we would call this a low—nearly undetectable—degree of incorporation. Meanwhile, faith questions and connections saturate Professor B's course, illustrating a high degree of incorporation.

In *correlation integration*, the professor points to the connections and relationships between faith and the academic discipline, noting points of intersection or common interest. In correlation models, nothing is joined. Fusion and incorporation models (at least the more thorough versions of incorporation) tend to be structural and formal; correlation models involve pedagogical activity. *Dialogical integration* is either a first cousin of correlation integration or simply correlation integration performed at a high degree. In these models, Christian specialists in a discipline, and perhaps professors and students in classrooms, actually construct ongoing conversation between faith and the respective discipline.[16]

A fifth group of models we have called *perspectival integration* because all academic work in a discipline or subdiscipline is viewed from a particular worldview or perspective. A perspective or worldview yields coherence by making disparate and even conflicting elements fit into a larger framework of thought and practice.[17] We note the term "worldview" here because many Christian higher educators use the term. The two concepts, *worldview* and *faith-learning integration*, obviously connect at this point.

Other models might go by the name *incarnational* (used loosely), inasmuch as Christian academics show forth the life and redemptive work of Christ by their own lives. In the following section, we ask where integration is thought to happen and return to incarnational models, which some treat under the heading of character. Sadly, we must also include in our list what we call *appliqué* models of faith-learning integration. In these models, some cursory mention of faith is applied to the surface but has no transforming power within curriculum, instruction, assessment, or the classroom ethos. We know, for example, of a college where professors are to include a Bible verse for each day's plan. A former instructor there told us that "My brother Esau is a hairy man but I am a smooth man" (from Genesis 27:11) might even pass muster as long as it appears in the top corner of a lesson's printed material. In Chapter Four, we treat four more models or variations on these models. Now we turn to one more question that has vexed the discussion of faith-learning integration: what is the locus of faith-learning integration?

## Where Is Faith-Learning Integration Supposed to Happen?

By this point, some of our readers may be thinking that those calling for Christian higher education to get rid of this language must be right. *Faith-learning integration* can misfire in so many ways that it is a wonder anyone still uses it. Yet it persists. And its persistence probably points to two important facts. First, as we noted at the start of this chapter, it has achieved slogan status. Second, as we note throughout this book, it became a slogan for good reason: many Christian higher educators, motivated deeply by a concern to offer truly *Christian* education, remain on the lookout for shorthand ways to express their educational vision.

Still, we need to address at least one additional problem: where do people who use integration language think it happens? We already talked about the variety of conceptions of integration—some of them dramatically different from others—that give direction and energy to Christian educators' work. Asking where integration happens brings us back to those varying conceptions.[18]

Some say that integration happens in students' hearts and minds. In this account, integration is something students take away. Others point to the curriculum design process and instructional planning. Here, faculty plan curriculum and instruction that will point naturally to God's role in creation or in human history, to the ethical dimension of human activity, or to such biblical themes as justice and hospitality. Still others point to the Christian character of the staff and faculty that students encounter day to day on campus. For each different locus one might identify, the allocation of responsibility for realizing faith-learning integration shifts. We will explore several loci in turn, noting these shifts as we go.

## Curriculum

We start with the view that faith-learning integration depends on curriculum planning and structure. We assume that Christian colleges offer a curriculum meant to help students understand their studies in a fundamentally different way than do students who complete the same major or program in a college that does not name Christ. With that goal in view, the deans, the curriculum committee, faculty, and everyone else with curriculum oversight presumably asks how to design programs and curriculum that, in ways large and small, point students toward faith and God's reign. Anyone suggesting curriculum is where integration happens obviously assigns a good share of responsibility for the outcomes to those who plan curriculum.[19]

We believe that the curriculum answer is partly right. We would all voice our shock if Christian colleges ignored curriculum, shrugging it off as irrelevant to their Christian purposes. Yet we know that offering a perfectly Christian curriculum (whatever that might look like) will not guarantee that our graduates emerge from our programs with a coherent, Christian worldview deeply informed by Scripture. And on the other hand, we know of graduates from explicitly un-Christian, incoherent degree programs who nevertheless emerged with coherent, Christian worldviews deeply informed by Scripture. To use philosophical language for a moment, it appears that curriculum is neither necessary nor sufficient to produce the graduate that Christian colleges have in view.

### The Student

What if we identify the student as the locus of faith-learning integration? In the discussion of curriculum integration, which runs along lines somewhat parallel to the faith-learning discussion, several have suggested that students are, finally, the locus of integration. Integration must happen in their understanding.[20] A number of scholars have argued the same for what the Association of Theological Schools (ATS, the major accrediting association for seminaries) calls *integration*. For ATS, integration implies bringing the Christian Scripture and Christian tradition to bear on one's thinking about life in the world, a meaning quite compatible with what many Christian college educators mean when they speak of faith-learning integration.[21] Others have suggested the student as the locus with specific reference to the faith-learning integration discussion.[22]

Let us explore briefly where responsibility for faith-learning integration lands if one argues that the ultimate location is the student. Obviously, some responsibility must rest on students themselves; if they want to graduate or even finish a single course with a coherent and Christian understanding, they will have to do some of the work. So, do we as professors get off the hook? Not likely. If anything, this account leaves professors responsible to put forth real effort to understand our students both as individuals and as members of cohorts. We need to admit that the experiences we plan and the ways we structure our courses heavily shape how our students experience their education overall. If anything, identifying the student as the locus of faith-learning integration may leave us with more responsibility for integration than do curricular and epistemic models. If the student is the locus, we may need to study learning styles, we may need to expand our repertoire of teaching strategies, we may need to learn more about our students' interests and about current cultural attractions and distractions.

### Christian College Professors

The student-as-locus discussion brought into view our own work as faculty. We now turn to the argument that professors in the Christian college hold the key to faith-learning integration, that professorial character and classroom ethos are the keys. We noted that the discussion of curriculum integration runs along somewhat parallel lines to our own discussion of faith and learning integration. In the curriculum integration discussion, a persistent thread of scholarship has identified the professor as the locus of integration.[23] Some have proffered similar arguments for church-related education.[24] Research in this area confirms what common sense and perhaps Scripture both indicate: teachers carry heavy responsibilities here. We are on the hook every moment of every day, whether in our classrooms, our offices, or the hallway.

We believe that professors' classroom work can be summarized in a simple formula. We plan curriculum, we instruct, we engage in ongoing assessment, we revise our curriculum and instruction—for next time—in light of the assessment. Those three fundamental activities can be abbreviated with the letters *CIA* (easy to remember, but perhaps carrying unfortunate connotations). Think of curriculum, instruction, and assessment as the CIA rope. The sheath or mantel of that rope is the classroom ethos or atmosphere, which we build day by day and semester by semester as we carry out the core activities of teaching.[25] We recognize that this simplification misses some of the complexities of teaching in higher education. But it catches four key elements of the claim that the professor is key to the integration of faith and learning: in our course planning, in our instruction, in how we assess our students' work and our own work, and in the kind of ethos we construct and in which we and our students work together, we are showing that faith and learning connect in rich ways—or we are showing that they do not. This sounds like a heavy, almost intimidating, responsibility. Perhaps it should. In his epistle, James warned that not many should aspire to become teachers because teachers face a stiffer judgment than others (James 3:1). James might have addressed that warning to Christian college professors who want to determine who is responsible for realizing the ideal of integrating faith and learning.

We have explored at length three possible answers to the question of where faith-learning integration happens: curriculum, students, and professors and the classroom ethos they create. We will omit discussion of some other possible answers, although we recognize their validity. Arthur Holmes, one of the leaders of the faith-learning integration movement (if we may call it that) argued in a series of books for a campus-wide account of integration. He consistently gave a sort of all-of-the-above answer to this question.[26] His answer recognizes the importance of the student life department, chapel program, housing arrangements, and the campus chaplain. With Holmes and many others, we acknowledge the importance of these factors in shaping a student's experience and in assisting or hindering a student's attempt to gain a truly Christian education. Another obvious venue to consider is the students' local church and the campus fellowship group.[27] The faith character of students' families must figure into their success at integrating faith and learning, too. We recognize that there is much we do not discuss in depth here, but we note that what we have provided sufficiently demonstrates that there is no single adequate answer to the question of where faith-learning integration occurs, as it apparently happens at the nexus of a number of factors and conditions.[28]

## *Four Families of Models*

To summarize this discussion of the locus, we suggest thinking of four families of models. Those who focus on epistemology and curriculum tend to view faith-learning integration with reference to incorporation, fusion, correlation, dialogue, and perspective. Incarnational models tend to focus on the student's character or the professor's character. Pedagogical models have as their special interest the classroom ethos—the space in which students and educators do the work of learning and teaching, which is formed largely as the professor sets the tone, responding in either this way or that way in a thousand teaching moments. Finally, institutional models of faith and learning focus more on conceptual frameworks, mission statements, and the whole community of faith.

## Conclusion

In this chapter, we have described a variety of ways that Christian educators use and understand faith-learning integration language and have pointed to some of the reasons this language can cause confusion. Facing the reality of these circumstances, how should faculty respond when successful annual reviews or even chances for promotion or tenure depend on their ability to use language that has demonstrated such capacity for generating misunderstanding? Obviously, each faculty member will need to provide detailed descriptions of what he or she means when using such language, likely by providing details of their own specific practices and explaining the educational ideals or visions that underwrite those practices. Faculty may need to work within some of the categories we have offered here, reflecting, for example, on their own understanding of the locus of faith-learning integration. We will continue to address these questions in the remaining chapters of this book.

However, for most new faculty (and many veterans), getting a clear understanding of the semantics of faith-learning integration will remain only part of the challenge; they will also need to reconcile the apparently-competing expectations that they teach, serve, and conduct and publish their research. In Chapter Four, we will begin to engage with the work of Ernest Boyer, a higher educator who offered a framework some decades ago that many colleges have adopted and that we believe offers new faculty a way to understand and frame their work in ways that yield a significant measure of sanity and life. Before we do so, however, in the next chapter we want to discuss the challenge of loving Jesus and getting promoted. This is the territory where high ideals, deep faith, and local politics converge.

## Chapter 3

# Loving Jesus and Getting Promoted

## What Faculty Need to Know and Do

For new faculty at faith-based institutions, promotion and tenure conversations can be confusing and stressful. These discussions are particularly local in nature, and at times quite quirky and eccentric. Tip O'Neill, longtime U.S. Speaker of the House of Representatives, loved to say, "All politics is local."[1] So too are promotion and tenure decisions. As a professor joins the faculty, the conversation begins. New faculty members are advised to start thinking and preparing for promotion from their very first semester, and this is good advice. Unfortunately, while the goal of promotion may be identified early on, the promotion and tenure process can be extremely hard to understand, let alone navigate.

New faculty report that colleagues, department chairs, and deans are eager to offer their thoughts on the promotion process, so the good news is that there is plenty of advice to go around. The bad news is that new faculty hear so many perspectives—stories about how others succeeded or failed, varying interpretations of past events, evaluations of current decision-makers—and often receive conflicting advice about what elements are crucial to the process and what can be ignored. All this results in genuine cognitive dissonance, enough mixed messages to deliver a real headache. Because everyone seems to speak with such authority and certainty, new faculty can struggle to identify the most credible sources, a common academic malady.

Obviously, provosts are a voice of authority, but in most cases, they do not speak for the promotion and tenure committee or even serve as a member of that key faculty committee. And department chairs and departmental colleagues are usually quite willing to weigh in and tell it the way it really is, pointing out past difficulties faced by other faculty members—whether those faculty encountered their difficulties last year or in 1963. All this results in anxiety and uncertainty about how to proceed, and it can be accompanied by fear because failure has such professional and personal significance. We have heard provosts complain, "Why are the new faculty always so fearful about promotions? All they have to do is listen to me." Oh, that it were so simple!

## Four Realities that Affect the Promotion Process

Obviously, faith-based institutions do not want the promotion process to be mysterious and stressful, so why is it often that way? Behind the mixed messages and multiple sources of advice, four institutional realities are at work. Faculty should be aware of these, and colleges should acknowledge and address them so they can communicate clearly with new faculty.

### Turnover

The first of these four realities is turnover. Presidents, provosts, and deans come and go; average tenure is four to seven years, and sometimes much less. When such an important decision-maker arrives on campus, promotion criteria—even when they have the force of written policy and are committed to print in the faculty handbook—are open to reinterpretation. Each senior administrator brings his or her own understandings, priorities, and experiences to the table. And the composition of faculty committees changes, too; it is not unusual for a third of the members of a promotion and tenure committee to be new each year, with a new chair every two to three years. Such turnover makes it very difficult to maintain clear and consistent priorities, procedures, and decision criteria.

In addition, the makeup of the academic affairs committee of the board can change radically as well. Trustees are appointed to the board committee for a variety of reasons, not necessarily because they have deep interest in, expertise in, or understanding of higher education. This reality about board committees can be disconcerting to the academic leadership of the institution and debilitating to on-campus efforts to maintain an understandable and consistently fair approach to promotion and tenure decisions. Deans, provosts, and faculty committee chairs find themselves trying to interpret and explain the intent and actions of the trustee committee to new colleagues, and their explanations can be inconsistent, too. These difficulties are not lost on new faculty, who typically do not find their personal confidence bolstered by what they learn.

### Inadequate Documentation

A second institutional reality is the lack of adequate, up-to-date documentation of processes related to faculty affairs, including promotion and tenure, a perennial problem for many academic affairs offices. Simply put, processes and procedures change faster than some institutions' ability to update and document. Many faculty handbooks end up out of date, not reflective of current structures, persons, or procedures. Serious attention to such details usually waits until an accreditation team visit is just around the corner.

It is not that updating the handbook is not a high priority, but it is rarely the highest priority. Academic administrators must manage a dizzying array of problems, processes, personnel, and particulars at any one time, and often with limited help. Usually, handbook updates have to wait until the summer—or the next summer. This is understandable. In fact, we might worry if the chief academic officer's (CAO) highest priority was updating the faculty handbook. Still, new faculty find it disconcerting to learn that the handbook is not accurate.

## Mixed Messages

A third institutional reality that causes uncertainty and frustration for new faculty as they attempt to understand the promotion process is the disjunction between what is said to be important and what is actually rewarded. We will say much more about this in Chapter Ten, pointing to "the problem of rewarding A, while hoping for B."[2] Suffice it here to say that if the institution promotes itself as a teaching institution but faculty members are promoted largely on the basis of their research, new faculty will, at best, end up confused (and, at worst, sent into despair, especially if they are disinclined to research and write).

And if a dean stresses service to students and the department, but the promotion process typically gives such service little real consideration, colleagues of new faculty may advise them to avoid it whenever possible—because "it doesn't really count." At the end of the day, such mixed messages and misaligned rewards have great power to confuse.

## Institutional Culture

Finally, each institution has its own story, or more accurately, its own handful of stories. Stories take on a life of their own as powerful interpreters and promoters of the values and practices of an institution. A faculty member with experience at another institution often brings fresh ideas about how things could be done differently, but this experience may be unhelpful in trying to understand the local culture and traditions related to promotion or tenure. In fact, such ideas may get in the way. Comments like, "Well, at X university, we did it this way . . ." are honestly not welcome. New faculty who consistently recall graduate school or their service at another institution often have difficultly navigating the local terrain.

# What Faculty Need to Know

The four realities discussed above remain in the purview of deans and provosts, but they are beyond the job descriptions of new faculty members. In that sense, they are not the problem of individual faculty, although they can cause problems for individuals and the faculty as a whole. Having some insight into the nature of the local institution and the challenges faced by the academic administration can be instructive to faculty in these situations. Universities are never perfect; they always remain works in progress, a truth faculty should keep in mind.

So, what should new faculty at a faith-based institution know as they look ahead to the promotion and tenure process? We will examine in detail three important elements: (1) some misunderstood dimensions of academic work; (2) the institution's approach to the faith-integration conversation; and (3) the promotion process itself, including typical procedures, players, politics, and power dynamics.

## Misunderstood Dimensions of Academic Work

We want to discuss three generally misunderstood dimensions of academic work that make working at a faith-based institution confusing: the sheer complexity of higher education, the concept of shared governance, and the ongoing debate about promotion and tenure.

**The Complexity of Higher Education.** To use the language of those who study organizations, colleges and universities are complex, open systems. Their complexity defies easy description or explanation. They have multiple purposes, including teaching, scholarship, credentialing, job preparation, character development, counseling, and service to the church and community. They have multiple constituencies, including students, faculty, trustees, parents, alumni, donors, accrediting agencies, governments, vendors, neighbors, and denominational leaders, to name just a few. They have multiple academic cultures. William H. Bergquist and Kenneth Pawlak suggest there are six cultures at work in any college or university (up from the four they first suggested in 1992), a dominant culture and five others always in interaction and sometimes at odds with the dominant culture.[3] They suggest that the latest developing cultures are virtual, cultures that introduce further levels of complexity to academic settings.

As an open system, a physical campus has not only hundreds of points of entry and exit (making security a nightmare at times) but also thousands of daily digital points of contact and communication. What e-mail once made difficult for presidents and public relations officers, new social media have made impossible. It is simply unimaginable now to think that only authorized personnel using approved institution channels will communicate with the "outside" and speak for the university.

Even small colleges are amazingly complex, making it difficult for new faculty to find their way. It usually takes three years (and sometimes even longer) to establish solid relationships and feel settled at a new institution. We know of numerous new faculty members who worry because they do not feel at home after their first semester or two and do not have things all figured out (such as promotion expectations). We think they would feel less worried if they realized that settling into a complex, open organization takes time.

**Shared Governance.** Since medieval times, faculty have had a voice in academic matters. The concept of shared governance, the idea that faculty should have a dominant voice in academic matters and a prominent voice in institutional decisions that shape the nature and quality of academic programs, is widely recognized and supported in contemporary higher education. In fact, accrediting bodies all have standards directly addressing the faculty's role in institutional governance and recognizing it as a good thing. This recognition implies that faculty members have special standing in institutions of higher learning. They are not simply hired labor; they are that but, more so, they are knowledge specialists who carry in large part the ethos of the institution. They should have a say in how things go.

But shared governance is also messy. On what issues should the faculty be consulted? How and by whom? Faculties rarely have a singular point of view on an issue, so who speaks for the faculty? What happens if the faculty's sense of shared governance is violated? How is that grievance addressed? Simply put, there are no universal practices or correct answers to these questions. Such answers have to be conscientiously and consistently worked out at the institutional level. Internationally, including in North America, faculty in all kinds of educational institutions have lost voice in recent decades, with administrators increasingly assuming control. Whether in stable or changing circumstances, the way the administration and faculty work together to carry out their responsibilities is a serious matter, with real implications for the quality and integrity of educational institutions.

John Millett makes the helpful distinction between management, governance, and leadership and observes that all are at work at the same time in any college or university.[4] Management is the process of work planning, organization, performance, and evaluation. A university's organizational chart shows the management structure. Governance is the process of deciding institutional purposes, policies, programs, and allocation of resources. A faculty handbook that outlines the approvals process for new courses is outlining a governance process. Faculty governance usually involves lots of committees. Many faith-based institutions even have a Committee on Committees, simply to manage the committee process and ensure that committee work is shared somewhat fairly among faculty!

Leadership, both formal and informal, gives direction and energy to the management and governance processes. Faculty and administrators often confuse these processes, failing to differentiate their management roles from their governance roles. For example, faculty reorganization, a perennial change strategy for many presidents, provosts, and trustees who want "to get the faculty going," has serious implications for both management and shared governance. Reorganizing the management structure (who reports to whom, how to group departments, reorganizing schools and colleges, etc.) may or may not necessitate a change in how the faculty makes academic decisions. Sometimes, governance assumptions and structures change in the midst of management reorganization without notice or intent. The results can be damaging to shared governance. All faculty need to know how management, governance, and leadership processes are understood at their local institution. A good beginning point is to ask which faculty committees are governance committees and which are management committees. That question can start an intriguing conversation.

**Promotion and Tenure.** Promotion and tenure decision-making processes often look very much the same (and in some institutions, they actually are), but being promoted and gaining tenure remain two very different things. Promotion and tenure have different purposes and entail different obligations, and they often involve different decision-makers. Promotion—progress through the academic ranks—is the primary way for institutions of higher education to recognize faculty members as professionals. There are three standard ranks for faculty: assistant professor, associate professor, and professor (or full professor). Colleges publish in their respective faculty handbooks the criteria for each rank, which differ from institution to institution. Usually, initial appointments are determined by degree level earned (it is unusual to be named to the higher two ranks without a terminal degree), years of experience in higher education or related activities, and years in rank. After initial placement in rank, faculty are expected to serve for a specified number of years in that rank before being eligible for promotion to the next rank (usually five years, but in some institutions as few as three). In many institutions, salary is tied to years of service in a particular rank, meaning that promotion has its own financial rewards.

Expectations regarding quality teaching, research, and institutional service increase with each higher rank. Understandings of how professors are to connect faith and learning vary greatly from institution to institution but not usually from rank to rank.[5] We treat specific elements of documenting faith integration in teaching, scholarship, and service in Chapters Five to Eight. Faculty need to understand a key point here: in most institutions, promotions are considered to be management decisions, not governance decisions. Thus, department chairs, deans, and provosts are the prime deciders rather than faculty peers.

For example, at George Fox University (where we both teach), promotion recommendations originate with a school or college dean and proceed through the management structure, while tenure recommendations originate with a faculty personnel committee and proceed through the governance structure. It is interesting to note that the provost and president actually participate in both structures. In a survey of twenty CCCU institutions by the authors, fourteen reported differences in their promotion and tenure decision processes.[6]

Granting tenure is the highest honor an institution can bestow on an individual faculty member. It is literally a contract for life. While a few things can break this commitment (gross incompetence, moral turpitude, financial exigency, or sustained contempt for the mission and values of the institution), it rarely happens. Faculty members are usually considered for tenure in their sixth or seventh year of service at an institution. Sometimes, credit for service at other institutions is granted, reducing the time necessary for consideration. Tenure decisions can be "up or out," meaning that if tenure is not granted, the faculty member will not be offered a continuing contract and must seek employment elsewhere, or "up or not," meaning that the faculty member who is denied tenure may reapply after a specified period of time (in many instances, two years) or move to nontenure track status and serve with annual or multiyear contracts. Such faculty are not required to leave the institution, although some view tenure denial as encouragement to do so.

## The Role of Tenure

So, why would an institution give a faculty member a contract for life after six or seven years of service? For starters, it is a good way to keep faculty around. Tenure provides job security, to be sure, and recognizes and rewards those who best exemplify the highest standards of the institution. It is a way for an institution to say concretely, "You embody the best of who we are and want to be," and it is certainly a deterrent to turnover. A tenured faculty member will think twice before surrendering a tenured position for a nontenured appointment, regardless of the status of the new position. Indeed, it is a high honor to be tenured.

But tenure is also a solemn obligation. Actually, tenure is not an end in itself, but rather a means to an end. Faculty are given job security through lifelong contracts as part of an institutional insurance policy for the protection of academic freedom and a strong faculty voice. On faith-based campuses, tenure can plays a vital role in maintaining rich discourse. Simply put, history shows that presidents, provosts, trustees, donors, pastors, and church officials sometimes overstep their bounds. Conversations and meetings have been shut down, departments have been threatened, and faculty members have been warned, censured, silenced, and sometimes removed from their posts.[7] When such unilateral behavior happens, a chill runs through the faculty that can last a decade or even longer. The inappropriate use of power hurts individuals, and the resulting corporate fear weakens and sucks the life out of otherwise healthy institutions. Conversations go underground, and faculty members stay in their offices. Public discourse turns into whispers and private meetings.

Who can speak up in the face of such power? Faculty with tenure can, if they have the courage. In fact, the reason for tenure at a faith-based campus is to permit a group of senior faculty members to rise with impunity and say, "Stop! This action is unacceptable. You cannot do that here!" The concerns of a courageous and dedicated group of tenured faculty will be heard. History shows that they can cause the removal of a president or provost, admittedly with sacrifice and some pain. And it is the solemn obligation of tenured faculty members to do so in critical situations, for the sake of the mission and integrity of the institution.

Three other comments about tenure are in order. First, trustees and senior administrators sometimes express their concern that tenure protects deadwood and that it reduces the flexibility administrators need in uncertain financial times. Trustees should be vigilant to ensure that the institution maintains the highest expectations for tenure; there is no need to tenure a dead tree. It is our experience that deadwood is, in fact, rare among tenured faculty, and when it is present, most of the branches were losing their leaves long before the tenure decision was made. Sadly, no one had the courage to confront the decay and deny tenure. In other words, someone blinked. And we believe that a strong faculty voice can be maintained in a faculty that is twenty to twenty-five percent tenured, leaving plenty of room for flexibility. There is no need to tenure the entire faculty, or use it as a reason to abandon tenure altogether.

Second, some faith-based institutions do not grant tenure, stating that there is no need for tenure (we are *family*, or bad things will never happen on our campus) and there are other ways of guaranteeing a strong faculty voice (multiyear contracts, employment laws, etc.). We strongly disagree. We know of far too many instances where governors or administrators misused or abused their power; faith-based institutions have no immunity from such abuses. In fact, because of weak or absent checks and balances, such institutions are more vulnerable to bullying by a strong president or religious leader. New faculty members need to know that their work will be protected by the voice of tenured senior faculty.

Finally, tenure is the best protection yet devised for academic freedom in faith-based institutions. The idea of academic freedom, which finds it roots in German universities in the early part of the nineteenth century, is captured in two words: *Lernfreiheit* (freedom to learn) and *Lehrfreiheit* (freedom to teach). As a number of professors in the latter half of the nineteenth century returned from Germany with their doctorates in hand, the concept gained advocates on U.S. campuses. The idea of academic freedom was formalized in the United States in the classic 1915 Report of the Committee on Academic Freedom of the American Association of University Professors (AAUP).

A subsequent revision of the academic freedom statement in 1940 affirmed tenure as the way to protect academic freedom for faculty members in their teaching and scholarship. The statement also recognized the special nature of faith-based institutions and acknowledged that such institutions could limit academic freedom regarding matters of faith or other special aims, provided that such restrictions were clearly stated in writing at the time of appointment. Most faith-based institutions give assent to the 1940 statement but add their own particular caveat. Below is an excerpt from the George Fox University Academic Freedom Statement:

> The university recognizes that the AAUP statement provides an important pillar on which to rest its commitment to academic freedom, but it is not enough. The university and its faculty affirm the exemptions set forth in the AAUP statement (1940), sub-paragraph b. It is also important to fully integrate George Fox University's mission as a Christian liberal-arts institution with the concept of academic freedom. Whether in scholarship, teaching or service, the University recognizes the importance of integrating the role of faith and one's intellectual inquiry. Academic disciplines are intertwined with faith, which allows for the pursuit of truth that more fully reveals God and His creation. Consequently, the primary institutional objective is to teach all truth as God's truth, integrating all fields of learning around the person and work of Jesus Christ. This pursuit of truth affirms that all faculty have

freedom of academic inquiry, even if it leads to areas deemed controversial, within the limitations described herein.[8]

Notice that the George Fox statement affirms the 1940 AAUP statement, highlights the exemption granted faith-based institutions to limit academic freedom on religions grounds, and states that "the proper pursuit of truth reveals God and His creation, integrating all fields of learning around the person and work of Jesus Christ." However, the statement does not explain how this integration is to be done or how it translates into promotion and tenure expectations. All faculty members, particularly those entering the promotion and tenure process, need to know how their particular institution views and protects academic freedom and where the fault lines are buried. They also need to know how their place of work understands such key work expectations as *integrating all fields of learning around the person and work of Jesus Christ.*

In the remainder of this chapter, we will examine institutional conversations and expectations regarding faith integration as well some specifics of the promotion process. In Chapters Five to Eight, we will address specific ways that faith can be integrated and demonstrated in teaching, research, and service.

## Institutional Conversations about Faith-Learning Integration

As we noted in Chapters One and Two, the conversation about faith and reason began in the church's first centuries. Framed in the language of faith-learning integration, the conversation celebrates its sixtieth birthday in the year this book appears. Whether framed in the language of *faith-learning integration, teaching perspectivally, faithful learning, Christian education, faith integration,* or even *teaching from a Christian worldview,* this conversation takes place—usually openly and obviously—on every campus that operates in the name of Christ. Faculty, academic administrators, senior university officials, and trustees all desire to maintain a vital faith community. Observers of and even participants in this conversation sometimes miss one of its less obvious features: different constituent groups may employ the same phrases, such as those we italicized above, while honestly and earnestly talking past each other. We will highlight four such conversations.

## Slippery Slope

In what many call the slippery slope conversation, the fundamental fear is that the college will lose its Christian faith and become secular. This conversation concerns itself with keeping Christian colleges "Christian" or "Christ-centered," thereby avoiding the slippery slope of secularization.[9] Of course, some faith traditions are more concerned about secularization than others. For example, the sacramental view of all of life or a two-kingdoms view makes the idea of secularization a bit foreign for Catholics and Lutherans, and in many ways for Wesleyans, too, but very compelling in Reformed and Anabaptist traditions. When trustees and senior university officials speak of faith and learning or keeping the college Christian, they express their concern to avoid what they see as a slippery secular slope.

## Personal Faith

Participants in the personal faith conversation focus more on how faculty members (and administrators) maintain a vibrant personal faith while fulfilling the demands of the academy. Staying "spiritually alive" is the struggle, and the conversation often points to the practice of spiritual disciplines, the need for community, and time for personal renewal. Trustees are often concerned that faculty members are "all head and no heart." They want to hear a personal testimony and see tangible fruit that Christ is alive and at work. Of course, the flip side of this conversation is the concern that some colleagues love Jesus but do not do credible academic work. They are "all heart and no head." This conversation can quickly devolve into sniping at those who advocate a contrasting point of view, causing much pain and alienation.

## *Faith and Learning*

The faith-and-learning conversation focuses on bringing Christian faith to bear on the classroom and the curriculum.[10] How do professors make their teaching and the curriculum truly and distinctly Christian? One approach is to think about how to view and teach the academic disciplines from within a Christian perspective. The CCCU has supported the publication of a book series, *Through the Eyes of Faith* (history, biology, music, business, mathematics, psychology, literature), meant to help faculty who see that task as their own. Some insist that undergirding each course or the entire curriculum with Christian presuppositions or values is the essential course of action, while others urge faculty members to embody their faith before their students. Some stress both. Yet other Christian faculty members argue that personal faith is private; there is no need to confound the subject matter with one's beliefs. They would say that there is simply no such thing as Christian mathematics or Christian engineering, so there is no need to force Jesus into the mixture. All that is needed is a strong dose of rigor and integrity. As we noted in Chapter Two, this is a complex and at times confusing conversation.

## *Faith and Scholarship*

The faith-and-scholarship discussion actually came late to the larger integration conversation, but it is perhaps more robust. Is there such a thing as Christian scholarship? If so, what does Christian scholarship look like? What difference does it make for a scholar to be Christian? What are the obligations of a Christian scholar, particularly in a postmodern context? These and related questions provide the grist for numerous conferences, consultations, books, journal articles, and professional dialogues. Perhaps an identity crises lies behind this discussion of faith and scholarship. Such a crisis could find its roots in the insecurity of scholars in the evangelical community who want to be taken seriously by their colleagues in the academy and by those in their respective faith traditions. However, a consensus on how to do this is difficult to achieve. Late in this book, we will suggest that Christian scholars might benefit by rethinking the importance of being taken seriously by the academy. What might happen if Christian scholars were centered enough to stop pursuing the approval of the academy and simply accepted our minority role as persons of faith, speaking from that perspective? The King James Version of the Bible twice identifies Christ's followers as peculiar people (Titus 2:14; 1 Peter 2:9). Because our institutional missions and personal ambitions are to be different, perhaps scholars in faith-based institutions should wear that badge of peculiarity.

This editorial intrusion withstanding, we have made clear that integration language means many different things, and there are at least four distinct conversations about integration, each with a different focus. To complicate matters further, sometimes all four conversations are alive on a single campus. One management story has an explorer traveling through the jungle with a group of natives. The jungle was so thick that the party literally had to hack their way through with machetes. Every hour or so the leader would climb up a tree, look around, then climb back down and continue the difficult journey. The explorer finally asked the leader if he climbed the tree to be sure that the party was headed in the right direction. "No," he replied, "I want to see if we are still in the right jungle!" As faculty members begin to think about aspects of faith-integration in the promotion process, it is crucial to know which jungle they are traveling in. That is to say, what integration conversations are at work, and what are the expectations of that particular faith community? Integration conversations are, indeed, local.

### Institutional Expectations

Each faith-based institution will engage in integration conversations in distinctive ways, and over time, will develop a particular set of expectations regarding the demonstration of faith integration for faculty entering the promotion process. While it would be impossible to list and discuss every institution's expectations for faculty, we want to highlight five fundamental approaches operative in faith-based institutions: institutional embrace, personal testimony, theological assent, scholarly analysis, and embodied witness.

## *Institutional Embrace*

Senior leaders at most institutions want faculty members to embrace clearly and publicly the mission and values of the university. In effect, they want to hear that faculty love *this* place and want to pursue a calling *here*. We see this operative most often with trustees, but many senior administrators hold this sentiment as well. Randy Basinger, a seasoned provost at a faith-based institution, addresses the tension some faculty experience regarding whether to view themselves as members of the global academy or members of a single, local institution:

> There seems to be a built-in tension between some faculty members' self-understanding of being independent contractors who have been hired for their expertise and who are committed primarily to their own scholarship (and beliefs) and standing in their discipline and the administrators' understanding as faculty members who have been hired into a particular educational community because they want to be a part of that community and will willingly support that community.[11]

Note that Basinger recognizes that not all faculty experience this tension, but many do. And for those who do, reconciling the twin pulls of the global—the academy—and the particular—*this* academy—can become a source of job dissatisfaction.

## *Personal Testimony*

While not neglecting good teaching and scholarly activity, many institutions want their faculty members, first and foremost, to be transparent and public about their personal faith. In short, they want faculty members to be confessional, to testify that they love Jesus and have a personal relationship with him. This sentiment stems in part from churches and fellowships from the Holiness and Pentecostal traditions. It was standard practice in the late nineteenth and throughout most of the twentieth century for members in these traditions to testify regularly in a public meeting about the work of Jesus and the Holy Spirit in their lives—often at a midweek prayer and testimony meeting, and certainly at spring and fall revival services. While that practice is no longer as prevalent, the expectation remains in some circles that faculty members are able and willing to speak publicly about their faith. This sentiment sometimes crops up at promotion and tenure time, when senior leaders and board members who grew up in those traditions may express their desire to hear faculty testify of their personal faith journey. Three senior administrators speak to this sentiment.

> If a young professor focuses on loving Jesus, getting promoted will take care of itself. Tenure and rank should never be an end; if one does their work well rank and/or tenure are merely an affirmation, a sign, of work well done and a professional life well lived.[12]

> I operate on the assumption that you cannot integrate that which you do not possess. In other words, effective integration of faith and learning is only possible with faculty members who are faithful in their relationship to God. This faithfulness works itself out in every aspect of their lives—worship, stewardship, service, private life, public life, AND in their academic discipline.[13]

> I think it takes three or four years, saying it wrong, debating the fine points, hearing a fresh idea or two, to get what makes faith and learning come together. In the end I have always been convinced that this is spiritual work that must be lived out. Hiring those who come with a reservoir of faith and on a quest to know and love God is the most predictable way we get this done.[14]

In Chapter Two, we noted the range of models and meanings of faith-learning integration. We referred to incarnational models as those that focus more on the faculty member's or student's Christian life and character, that Christ indwells the Christian. Without identifying the model as such, these three administrators all work within incarnational models of faith-learning integration.

## Theological Assent

Many faith-based institutions describe themselves as broadly evangelical, denominationally affiliated, church-related, or simply Christian. If they have a statement of faith, it resembles the Apostles Creed or some other general statement of basic Christian beliefs. Prospective faculty members from a broad range of denominations and faith communities may sign and affirm such faith statements. However, other institutions are much more specific about the dominant theology and much more insistent that assent be given to certain theological positions. For example, here is an excerpt from the Calvin College Faculty Handbook:

> Calvin College faculty members are required to sign a synodically approved Form of Subscription in which they affirm the three forms of unity—the *Belgic Confession*, the *Heidelberg Catechism*, and the *Canons of Dort*—and pledge to teach, speak, and write in harmony with the confessions.[15]

This is a very small portion of an extended and detailed document. Faculty members must sign that they firmly believe all the articles and points of doctrine represented in the confessions, that they will teach and defend them, and that they will reject and refute all errors.

Here (in part) is the Lee University faith statement:

> As a part of his/her contract, each teacher is required to sign that he/she will not advocate in his/her teaching or publications anything contrary to the Declaration of Faith, which is as follows:

**We believe:**
1.  In the verbal inspiration of the Bible.
2.  In one God eternally existing in three persons: namely, the Father, Son, and Holy Ghost....
6.  In sanctification subsequent to the new birth, through faith in the blood of Jesus Christ, through the Word, and by the Holy Ghost....
8.  In the baptism with the Holy Ghost subsequent to a clean heart.
9.  In speaking with other tongues as the Spirit gives utterance and that it is the initial evidence of the baptism of the Holy Ghost.

10. In water baptism by immersion, and all who repent should be baptized in the name of the Father, and of the Son, and of the Holy Ghost.

11. Divine healing is provided for all in the atonement.

12. In the Lord's Supper and washing of the saints' feet.

13. In the premillennial second coming of Jesus. . . .[16]

These two faith-based institutions make clear that they have something very specific in mind for their faculty. Theological assent must be given in no uncertain terms *before* discussions of faith integration can even begin. Surely, these colleges' promotion and tenure processes deal with the faith-integration conversation in other ways and perhaps using other language, but that conversation is rendered inconsequential if the faculty member cannot assent to a very particular theological stance—and in some cases, without accompanying church membership. Put another way, the theological assent approach to faith-integration begins by identifying specifically the faith propositions or statements that are to be believed, defended, and taught. Teaching and scholarship must be informed by and integrated within those particular theological parameters.

## Scholarly Analysis

In the mid-1970s, Arthur Holmes's *The Idea of a Christian College* ignited a hopeful conversation in faith-based institutions about the integration of faith and learning, suggesting that professors could and should bring a Christian worldview and philosophical critique to their teaching. For the next twenty years, faith and learning conferences, symposiums, workshops, seminars, retreats, institutes, journals, and books about integration of faith and learning dominated the thinking of Christian college faculty and administrators. The scholarly approach became the gold standard for practice in Christian higher education. Educators in some traditions (for example, Wesleyan, Mennonite, and Quaker), were uncomfortable with this approach, fearing that it focused too much on belief as a starting point rather than on faithful living. These voices were largely ignored.

When Mark Noll complained in 1994 that the scandal of the evangelical mind was that there was no evangelical mind,[17] he touched a raw nerve in many faith-based institutions. They wondered if he meant to include them in his indictment. Perhaps he did. As we noted, many Christians in the academy have a deep-seated inferiority complex. Provosts share privately that they wish their institution had higher academic standards, better students, and more rigorous scholarship standards. Since the inception of the CCCU, a prime criterion for the informal but operative pecking order among institutions has been the scholarly nature of the college and university faculty, including their approach to the integration of faith and learning. As a result, many institutions have embraced the scholarly analysis approach, establishing or expanding faculty orientation programs that require a theological worldview statement, a philosophical disciplinary critique, and a scholarly, footnoted, academic paper or essay as the cornerstone of the faith-integration process.

## *Embodied Witness*

Over the past decade, the scholarly analysis approach has received some pushback.[18] Some scholars and administrators have suggested a different approach to faith integration—an embodied approach. Rather than a focus primarily on theological commitments, a Christian worldview, and the identification of underlying philosophical assumptions in an academic paper, this approach suggests that particular practices, values, and beliefs are to be lived out in community. For example, Quakers understand that their commitments to discernment, peace-making, social justice, and plain speaking are best expressed not in writing, but in living. And as they are lived out, integration (wholeness) is expressed. In this approach, the idea of faith and learning as two things that need somehow to be integrated does not make much sense. Rather the emphasis is on faithful learning, learning faithfully, or simply being a faithful presence in your work and community. Note this comment from a provost emeritus: "Providing that faithful presence of genuine discipleship and growth would be a wonderful life model for students to see."[19]

A current provost echoes those sentiments:

That (His Holy Spirit dwelling in us) is what empowers us to fulfill His calling on our lives. It seems to me that if we are living our lives in this way, and our work becomes our daily act of worship and obedience to Christ, then the notion that our faith and our learning as two separate things needing to be integrated tends to also take care of itself.[20]

We close this section with a cautionary note. We have heard presidents and trustees respond to the scholarly analysis approach during the tenure review process in this way, "I see that this faculty member is a capable scholar, but is she a Christian? Even a Buddhist could write this scholarly paper!" Obviously, these leaders wanted to hear the personal testimony or embodied witness approach while the faculty member was providing scholarly analysis. It is critical to identify carefully the operative institutional approach to faith integration and have agreement among the key decision-makers. If not, the result can be confusion and hurtful decision-making.

## Getting Promoted

Thus far in this chapter, we have highlighted several things that faculty members need to know: some misunderstood dimensions of academic work, the variety of different general faith-integration conversations, and some institutional expectations for faith-integration. We will now look specifically at typical promotion processes and procedures in faith-based institutions.

### *The Promotion Process and Players*

The faculty handbook at each institution outlines the promotion and/or tenure process. Colleges sometimes provide specific promotion documents or checklists to new faculty members, and new faculty orientations usually include this topic as well. At some institutions, faculty members initiate the process themselves (provided they have fulfilled the required probation); while at other institutions, academic administrators (chairs, deans, provosts) drive the process. We know of instances where faculty members received word of a promotion before they knew they were even being considered for one. The promotion was certainly appreciated, but the process left the recipient a bit mystified. Thankfully, such instances are not the norm.

The standard approach is to have a faculty member provide evidence of good teaching, research, and service. This evidence usually takes the form of essays and supporting documentation (such as syllabi, published works, student evaluations, action plans made in response to annual evaluations with department chairs, etc.). Some colleges require faculty members to provide a separate essay that articulates how faith informs those three aspects of their work. Other colleges ask the faculty member to address the faith dimension within each essay and component of their portfolio.

In the next five chapters, we address some of the specific ways that faculty can describe their work in teaching, research, and service and discuss ways to approach the questions of faith and learning. Here we will note simply that promotion and tenure procedures are usually clearly outlined in the faculty handbook, and the nature of the required documentation—application, essay(s), portfolio, and faith statement are listed, although faculty handbooks sometimes come up short in describing what faculty should include in these documents. Understandably, faculty find these gaps puzzling and stressful. Many institutions exhibit several portfolios or essays from some recently promoted or tenured faculty, and new faculty usually find such examples helpful.

Some colleges adopt the beneficial practice of assigning each candidate for promotion or tenure a mentor who has recently completed the process, knows the ropes, and can provide sound advice about critical aspects of the process. And some institutions have followed the lead of the assessment movement, developing and publishing rubrics that are used by committees and decision-makers in the promotion process. This practice is helpful because it forces institutions to be clear and public about their expectations and the range of acceptable evidence to be considered, and it gives candidates direct insight into the decision framework.[21]

The usual players in the process include a faculty review committee (by some name), department chairs, deans, provosts, presidents, and in many cases, trustee committees. The final decision often rests with the trustees, but as we shall discuss in the next section, they often serve more in a quality-control or pass-through function than in a hands-on function.

## *The Power and the Politics*

Most faculty handbooks outline the promotion and tenure process in detail and identify the different players in the process. However, given that colleges operate in the world below and not the heavens above, faculty often have difficulty identifying who really makes the decisions and on what criteria those decisions are made. In some institutions, the faculty committee serves as a strong gatekeeper, with the provost, president, and trustees accepting their recommendations as a matter of course. Other committees serve in advisory roles, with the provost and president making the decisions. Very rarely are trustees deeply involved in the decision process to the point of overturning a president's recommendation. For example, even though the trustee committee at George Fox University carefully reads and discusses each tenure portfolio and personally interviews each candidate, they have never to date overruled a president's recommendation. Thus, while they are engaged in the process, they are not key decision-makers. Rather, their role is to affirm the process and the participants. George Fox University's history on this question may not reflect the history of all Christian colleges, but it is the story at the majority.

Presidents are always interested in who is being promoted and tenured, but their engagement in the process varies significantly. Some presidents simply receive recommendations from the dean or provost and pass them on to the trustees, trusting the process while concentrating on other aspects of their work. Other presidents are deeply involved in the vetting of candidates, particularly, it seems, candidates from the religion department. Of course, presidents have good reasons to give attention to hiring in that department, but the main reason is that religion faculties are most likely to draw critique and criticism from trustees and church leaders from the sponsoring denomination and supporting churches. Whether directly stated or not, most faith-based institutions have an orthodoxy, and religion professors undergo a higher degree of scrutiny than most other faculty.

Trustees do not spend a great deal of time talking about the faculty, but when they do, it is often the religion department that is targeted. Given that the business professor, the chemistry professor, and the literature professor can all point students toward truth or away from truth, we suspect that this tendency to focus on one department may be a case of missing the Christian worldview boat.

At the center of the fray stands the provost or academic dean—the CAO. In most faith-based institutions, the provost is either the decision-maker regarding promotion and tenure or works most closely with the faculty committee and deans to make those decisions. This is as it should be. The CAO oversees faculty hiring, faculty orientation, and faculty evaluation and retains the best position to observe and comprehend the quality of faculty work across disciplines, departments, schools, and colleges. Appropriately, school deans and department chairs typically operate with their own interpretation of campus policies, and they advocate forcefully for their faculty colleagues. The provost must ensure that standards and expectations are applied evenly across the institution. In addition, the CAO usually meets with the academic committee of the trustees and is able to act as a *consigliere*—a trusted advisor to the board—explaining the work of the faculty to the trustees and the expectations and concerns of the trustees to the faculty.

To summarize, in most settings, the faculty handbook identifies clearly the procedures and the players in the promotion and tenure process. Usually, the process requires that the faculty member show evidence of faith-shaped, quality teaching, scholarship, and service. Typically, this demonstration requires a portfolio, possibly including a series of essays. Tenure decisions can include a personal interview with trustees or a peer committee. The politics vary from campus to campus, depending largely on how involved the president desires to be. At most institutions, the CAO is at the very center of the decision process.

## What Faculty Need to Do

In the next five chapters, we provide specific ways of thinking about and documenting one's work in instruction, research, and service using the model proposed by Ernest Boyer in 1990. Following our treatment of Boyer, we will return specifically to the matter of articulating and documenting how our work demonstrates that we research, teach, serve, and think as Christians. As we conclude this chapter, we offer four general words of advice to new faculty about getting promoted: study, listen, ask, lean in.

**Study.** Consider the faculty handbook to be the syllabus for the course on promotion and tenure. Read it, study it, and memorize it. As a professional, it is critical to know the institution's expectations and processes. Far too many times, we have seen faculty members enter the promotion process and ignore directions, fail to meet deadlines, or go off on a crusade. The success rate when doing so is understandably and needlessly very low.

**Listen.** Faculties have long memories, and every campus has its stories about those who were denied promotion or tenure or dismissed for one reason or another—and the administrators behind those decisions. These stories take on a life of their own and are told for decades. They are cloaked in mystery and generate clouds of suspicion; they become permanent fixtures in the collective memory of the faculty, even if important details have been lost to memory or omitted for greater effect. Newer faculty members hear these stories and become skittish about the promotion and tenure process, fearing that "things" (administrators) cannot be trusted. Undoubtedly, some faculty members have been mistreated and hurt during the promotion and tenure process at faith-based institutions, but these comprise a minority of cases. Institutions are proud of their faculties and work diligently to insure that faculty members are treated fairly in the promotion and tenure processes. Promotion and tenure are not intended to be punitive processes. Rather, they offer a way for faculty members to be recognized, affirmed, and rewarded. New faculty should listen to the stories that colleagues tell, but not get caught up in the drama or the implied politics. More often than not, there is more than one side to such stories.

**Ask.** Use your scholarly habits of mind. Know the faculty handbook and watch others go through the process. Ask questions for clarification from those who have the answers. When in doubt, ask the CAO. Ask to see examples and documentation from others who recently went through the process. Such examples are extremely helpful in highlighting approaches that have been judged successful. Ask to see the rubrics used in the process; if none exist, ask for some to be developed. And ask for a mentor, someone who recently navigated the process successfully. There is no reason to make this journey alone.

**Lean in.** Lean into this process. Do what is expected and do not be afraid. It is an essential aspect of faculty work, so approach the process as an opportunity. You can talk about what is important to you, demonstrate what you have already accomplished, and learn more about your craft to get better. Honestly, it can be fun!

David Alexander, president at Northwest Nazarene University, offers this wise advice: "Prepare well, keep learning, try new methods, be accessible, be genuine, pursue the incarnation of Jesus in all things."[22] Sadly, many faculty focus on what they call *building their CV*, a focus that can lead to many kinds of manipulation, inflation, and even downright academic fraud. In his comment, Alexander identifies some of the qualities of the opposite kind of faculty, those who succeed at promotion and tenure because they focused on their work and their enjoyment of it, rather than on adding new lines to their CV.

There is great promise in serving at a faith-based institution. Of course, the expectations are very high, but so too are the rewards. It is truly a wonderful calling, one in which faculty members trade money for time. Then, they turn right around and invest that time in the lives of their students, working at the very heart of Christian higher education to teach, shape, and send. A very high calling, indeed!

## Chapter 4

# The Boyer Model

Faculty, new and experienced, can frame their work in many different ways. Sadly, within some cognitive frameworks, conducting professorial work mainly brings a paycheck or a nice long holiday every summer. Happily, in other frameworks, professorial work helps make the world a better place: research advances human knowledge; teaching helps students advance toward their own learning goals.

Yet even professors who understand their academic vocation in these happier ways often face difficulty accomplishing all that their colleges expect of them and that they expect of themselves. We constantly must choose between competing goods: class preparation, grading, administration and departmental work, writing grants and proposals, research, writing. And that list includes only priorities at work; it excludes family, community. It even ignores errands.

In this chapter and the three that follow, we offer a framework that can help faculty make sense of and make connections between the competing—and often apparently irreconcilable—demands of academic work.

We do not claim this framework as our own. Rather we present it as a summary and application of the work of Ernest Boyer, an extraordinary and profoundly Christian higher educator, whose model has been adopted by over 1,000 colleges and universities as a way to frame and evaluate faculty work. In this chapter, we provide a background to his work, including some biography. In Chapter Five, we explore his understanding of teaching and what he called the scholarship of teaching. In Chapters Six and Seven, we offer treatments of research and service as parallels to the chapter on teaching. We do not offer such in-depth treatment of Boyer incidentally. Rather, we view his model as the most practical and life-giving approach to the competing vocational demands of academic work that we have encountered. Furthermore, because Boyer built on a deeply theological foundation, his model offers much to those who teach in Christian settings where faith-learning language is considered native.

The Boyer model expanded the way academics think and talk about scholarship, particularly in faith-based institutions. In a culture where research universities set the norms and status standards, Christian colleges have historically struggled for legitimacy, feeling like second cousins who must fight their own embedded insecurities to be accepted as part of the family. In some ways, the Boyer model was not all that new, but it was a profound combination of keen observation, scholarly synthesis, and personal convictions. And the timing could not have been better. In the 1980s, Parker Palmer and others advocated for a different approach to teaching and learning, one that was less objective, impersonal, and solitary. These calls for a new approach struck a chord in higher education; some, but not all, higher educators welcomed these voices. Boyer introduced his model in the wake of that conversation and, to some degree, rode the energy of its waves. "To him, it made no sense to force everyone through the sieve of discovery scholarship in order to get tenure."[1] The sieve was too restrictive, too specialized, too impersonal—and unrealistic. Boyer advocated a way forward that was more inclusive, positive, and helpful, offering a breath of fresh air to many professors who had grown disillusioned with their work.

In this chapter, we will look first at the life of Ernest Boyer, a remarkable man who lived out his Christian convictions in a genuine and hospitable manner, making his public work helpful and hopeful. We want to show how the Boyer model was shaped, in large part, by his personal convictions, allowing him to serve as a role model for Christians in higher education who desire to be faithfully engaged in the academy. We will then look closely at the "Boyer Model of Scholarship" proposed in a Carnegie Foundation Report in 1990. The report literally redirected the dialogue about faculty roles in higher education, bringing into focus concerns about the nature of faculty work, how professors should spend their time, and the institutional rewards for their work. This conversation was energizing for many faculty in Christian colleges who struggled with the established paradigm which privileged research as the most worthwhile activity for faculty effort. We will end this chapter by discussing the impact of the Boyer model on practices in faith-based institutions, moving on to specific strategies for using the model in teaching, research, and service in Chapters Five through Seven.

## Ernest Boyer's Early Life and Career

Ernest "Ernie" Boyer was a servant leader—and a very good one. A prominent higher educator, he served as chancellor of the State University of New York (SUNY), United States commissioner of education, and president of the Carnegie Foundation for the Advancement of Teaching. In some senses, he was a prophet, possessing the uncanny ability to see into the future, recognizing important currents and trends and their implications, and offering hopeful alternatives. He was influential, persistently and carefully arguing for what he saw while listening graciously to those who agreed and disagreed. He was a kind and gentle spirit, a thoughtful and gracious speaker, a meticulous writer, and a person of deep conviction. And he was a Christian, too.

Born in Dayton, Ohio, Boyer grew up in a Christian home and worked in his father's greeting card mail-order business where he learned valuable lessons about showing up early and putting in a full day's work, which helped establish his lifelong strong work ethic. His grandfather, a minister who ran an inner-city mission for the poor in Dayton, was a profound inspiration, teaching Boyer by example that service is the pathway to true humanity.[2] Ernie Boyer served his entire life.

As an undergraduate, Boyer attended Messiah College for two years, then transferred and graduated from Greenville College. While a senior at Greenville, he served as student body president, an early foray into politics, and not his last. Throughout his career in higher education, he maintained an interest in faith-based institutions, serving, for example, as a trustee for Messiah College, and speaking from time to time at faith-based institutions. After earning a doctorate in speech pathology at USC and teaching for a few years, Boyer turned his attention to academic administration, where he proved to be an innovator. While dean at Upland College, he started the first 4-1-4 semester program in the country; while chancellor at SUNY, he led the development of Evergreen State University, a nonresidential program for adults; a three-year baccalaureate degree; and undergraduate exchange programs with the Soviet Union and Israel.[3] Such innovations were certainly groundbreaking at the time. Boyer had the ability to see into the future and simultaneously get things done in the present, a rare combination. Boyer also serves as a good example of someone who worked out of a large vision but identified and completed the daily tasks necessary to fulfill that vision, a combination we address in Chapter Nine with reference to successful academic writers.

Boyer saw connections between secondary and higher education, and in response he expanded the purview of the Carnegie Foundation to include the high school experience. From our vantage point decades later, we see that Boyer had the gift of identifying and addressing the connections between things, a gift that stemmed in part from his own deep belief in the connectedness of all things. He was a person who thoughtfully lived out his convictions and gracefully embodied his Christian faith in the public arena. He was a person, to paraphrase James Baldwin, who stands as a witness that swimming in deep water and drowning are not the same thing.[4] With much good work finished, Ernest Boyer died on December 8, 1995. In some important senses, Boyer did not finish his work, and colleagues—both at the Carnegie Foundation and elsewhere—carried on the development of what so many now call the Boyer model.

## Boyer's Convictions

Boyer exemplified the Quaker notion of letting one's life speak. According to Douglas Jacobsen, distinguished professor of church history and theology at Messiah College, "Boyer was a pietist, not a creedalist, and accordingly his theology was driven by practice and not ideas."[5] He did not invest a lot of energy or quibble much about correct beliefs, but he cared deeply about convictions. For him, theology was more of a performing art than a cognitive science.[6]

You will grasp Boyer's approach to scholarship more easily if you understand these five central convictions, all of which he practiced faithfully.

### *Words Matter*

Even though Boyer avoided quibbling about correct beliefs, words did matter to him. For him, words had their own moral trajectory, so speaking them was always to be done carefully and truthfully. In Quaker circles, plain speaking is highly valued. Many Quakers will not give an oath in court "to tell the truth, the whole truth, and nothing but the truth" because it implies that at other times or in other circumstances they may not be telling the truth. Rather, they "affirm" that what they say will be the truth, a distinction rich in meaning and importance for Quakers. In his adult years, Boyer identified as a Quaker. For him, speaking plainly and writing carefully were spiritual acts, a sacred trust we take on whenever we use words.[7]

He pained over drafts of reports and speeches. Described by his colleagues as "a connoisseur of words," he "would rewrite a draft prepared by colleagues a hundred times, shaping it to reflect his own vision and turning the argument to speak his own voice. Reading aloud as he revised, Boyer would conjure up language that sounded as wonderful as it read."[8] Hearing him in person was always a personal and professional treat. Even now one has only to read one of his speeches to get a sense of the wonder and power of his words, doubtless one of the reasons his *Scholarship Reconsidered* has had continuing influence in the academy.

## *The Moral Context in Education and Life*

Boyer was not the kind of Christian who went around beating people over the head with a Bible or working to make everything Christian. Such an approach to faith would not fit with Boyer's Anabaptism, a tradition that stresses right living over right belief. But Boyer did understand that all learning has moral implications. After visiting the Holocaust Museum in Washington, D.C., he lamented that "even 'educated' men can listen to fine music and read great literature in their homes in the evening and the next morning go to the camp and slaughter their fellow human beings."

He continued, "Are we, in fact, educating for evil if we fail to place knowledge in a larger moral context?" At the end of the day, Boyer concludes, "our goal must be not only to prepare students for careers, but also enable them to live with dignity and purpose."[9] For Boyer, educational preparation for a life lived with dignity and purpose must include a moral dimension. And for him, that dimension did not entail attempting to convert others to proper belief. Rather it entailed a profound conviction that what we do and how we live matter deeply. As Boyer would say, we have neighbors.

## *The Connectedness of All Things*

Boyer believed that all things were connected, no matter how fragile and elusive the state of those connections. Affirming the longstanding Catholic tradition of viewing the unity of all truth, he joined Thomas Aquinas and Cardinal Newman, among many others, to argue for coherence over fragmentation, a malady Boyer saw in the modern academy. He loved to quote Barbara McClintock, a Nobel Prize-winning geneticist, who said, "There is no way to draw the line between things,"[10] and he also quoted Mark Van Doren, a Pulitzer Prize-winning professor at Columbia University, who wrote that the ". . . connectedness of things is what the educator contemplates to the limits of his capacity . . . the student who can begin early in his life to think of things as connected, even if he revised his views with every succeeding year, has begun the life of learning."[11] Regarding his convictions about the unity of truth, the connectedness of all things, and the sacramental principle that the natural world and humanity are intrinsically worthwhile, Boyer embraced a longstanding intellectual tradition that Christians from many communions embraced; his convictions were not parochial.

Boyer consistently argued that the great universities of our time should focus on the connectedness of all things. Note his concern in this quotation from a speech he gave to the American Association of Colleges in 1988: "In 1984, when we surveyed 5,000 undergraduates, 30% said that they had *nothing* in common with people in underdeveloped countries. Not one thing in common. What *are* we teaching in our colleges and schools?"[12] Such failure to see connections troubled Boyer deeply, and he noted that we quickly "affirm differences, but fail to capture commonalities. And in the absence of larger loyalties, we're settling for little loyalties. Students are hunkering down in their separate interests failing to find the relationships that bind."[13] He went on to identify eight universal experiences that connect all human beings: (1) the life cycle—the imperative of birth and growth and death; (2) language—our ability to use symbols; (3) the arts—our response to the aesthetic; (4) groups and institutions—group membership; (5) the natural world—the ecology of planet Earth; (6) time and space—our ability to recall the past and anticipate the future; (7) work—the ability to engage in producing and consuming; and (8) search for meaning—our search for a larger purpose.[14] Boyer suggested that a curriculum in higher education could be constructed with coherence if shaped around these eight human commonalities. Central to the concern of this book, he worried about the great divide between research and teaching and scholarship. His conviction about the connectedness of all things (including faculty work) compelled him to push for the reconsideration of scholarship in the academy.

## Community

Far too often, we live lonely, isolated lives. Commenting, at least in part, on the incessant individualism he saw in higher education, Boyer argued, "This leads me to another priority in higher education. I do not want to romanticize the notion of community in higher education. And yet, a college, regardless of its size, must be held together by something more than a common grievance over parking."[15] That something more, he suggested, included our shared practices, experiences, and traditions, as well as our ability to listen and speak carefully to each other. Simply put, Boyer believed in community.

Boyer always suggested walking alongside and finding things to agree upon, rather than contending with each other. He took the story of welcoming the stranger seriously. He was influenced by three Quaker practices: inclusion, discernment, and silence. We are quick to point out that these practices are not unique to Quakers, but Boyer was a practicing Quaker and therefore believed in and practiced inclusivity. All voices are welcomed in and understood as worship. Quakers teach that we must be open to the truth from whomever and wherever it comes, because everyone can know and express the mind of Christ. Other points of view are always invited, welcomed, and in fact, needed. In this framework, discernment becomes a communal act in which people get at truth by talking and listening together; again, we see that all voices are important. And silence is a communal act, too, with deep spiritual implications. Boyer explained his opposition to having a moment of silence to open the school day this way:

> I accept as a cardinal principle that no involuntary religious act or ceremonial engagement should be imposed on any student in the school. That includes prayer, whether spoken or in silence, since, as a Quaker, silence has a powerful religious significance to me. When the school prayer issue was being debated in the New Jersey legislature, I was appalled that silence was being pushed as an alternative, with the argument that it was just a moment to "do nothing." Silence that is intended to have a spiritual consequence is not a moment of doing nothing. It's a moment of doing something profoundly religious, and we cannot skirt the issue by suggesting that the process of prayer only include the utterances of words.[16]

Thus, for Quakers and for Boyer, community can be established and nurtured not only in the practices of talking together, but also in the practice of silence. However it is nurtured, Boyer saw it as a critical aspect in the positive formative education for both students and faculty.

## Service

Boyer believed that a Christian college with coherence could be a place where "students come to know that to be truly human one must serve."[17] As we noted, he learned the importance of service by watching his grandfather run an inner-city mission in Dayton. Readers of Boyer's speeches will notice that almost all of them include a comment or two about service. For him, service was faith in action.

Ernest Boyer was a person of deep faith and of lived convictions. He loved to recite parts of *The Leaden Eyed,* a poem written by Vachel Lindsay, when he concluded a speech:

> It is the world's one crime
> its babes grow dull
>
> . . . . . . . . . . . . .
>
> Not that they sow,
> but that they seldom reap,
>
> Not that they serve,
> but have no gods to serve,
>
> Not that they die
> but that they die like sheep.[18]

Boyer would often add, "The tragedy is not death. The tragedy is to die with commitments undefined, convictions undeclared, and service unfulfilled."[19] There was no tragedy in Boyer's death. He left this world with commitments defined, convictions declared, and service fulfilled. It was his declared conviction that all can serve and all have something worthwhile to offer humanity. That conviction, along with his strong belief in the connectedness of all things and the necessity of community, compelled him to argue for an understanding of scholarship very different from the model in place when he began his life's work. Compared to the traditional model that viewed research, teaching, and service in silos and that privileged research above the other two, Boyer's model—what so many now call *the Boyer model*—was more inclusive, affirming, positive, and connected.

It embraced all the skills and contributions of those who teach and work together in the academy.

## The Boyer Model

Since the release of *Scholarship Reconsidered: Priorities of the Professoriate* in 1990, faculty and administrators in colleges and universities have reconsidered the relationships between various kinds of academic scholarship. The traditional roles for a professor in higher education are instruction, research, and service (which we refer to as the IRS model). At different times in history, first teaching and then service were considered to be preeminent, but throughout most of the twentieth century and certainly by the time of Boyer's report, research had emerged as the primary and most legitimate academic task. In reality, the academy had adopted an iRs model. The framework offered by Ernest Boyer and the Carnegie Foundation for the Advancement of Teaching recognized that *scholarship* and *research* are not synonymous. In the report, Boyer upends the troika of *"scholarship, teaching, service"* by arguing that scholarship takes many forms, including research, which Boyer calls the *scholarship of discovery*. Faculty also engage in the *scholarship of teaching*, and in service, *the scholarship of application*.[20] Since the appearance of Boyer's *Scholarship Reconsidered*, some have called service the *scholarship of engagement*.[21]

Boyer further upends the traditional three-part formula and possibly presents his greatest challenge to the academy by identifying a category he calls *the scholarship of integration*, that kind of scholarship that finds, draws, synthesizes and helps students see connections between academic disciplines and the communities that form among those who pursue discipline-based academic work. In the two decades of conversation that have followed Boyer's *Scholarship Reconsidered*, the *scholarship of teaching* has garnered the most attention. In the next chapter, we will draw your attention specifically to that dimension of scholarship.

The academy has given significantly less attention to *the scholarship of integration* than to Boyer's other categories. We believe with the apostle Paul that every thought ultimately belongs to Christ (2 Cor. 10:5) and that both the natural world and the world of scholarship cohere only because in Christ "all things hold together" (Col. 1:17). With such a solid theological and epistemological foundation, we believe that Christian academics can model interdisciplinary and integrative conversation for the whole academy, and particularly so regarding elements of the academic life that bring faith and spirituality to bear on one's work. Moreover, faculties at faith-based institutions have been attending to the *scholarship of integration* regarding issues of faith for a very long time. It is second nature to us. In a time when the academy is asking questions about what gives purpose and meaning to the curriculum, how does it cohere or if it even should cohere, Christians have an excellent opportunity to demonstrate the integrative power of a common, shared narrative: in our case, the Christian story. We can do this every day.

Considering the *scholarship of discovery*, on Boyer's account, research adds to the stock of human knowledge but also enriches the instructional environment of the university. Boyer himself traces the introduction and subsequent narrowing of the term *research* between its introduction in the 1870s and 1990, the date of his landmark publication. Boyer and those who have followed in his tradition have concerned themselves with the tendency of the academy to define scholarship solely in terms of the *scholarship of discovery* (research) as if the two were co-extensive. Boyer sees this equation producing a more restricted view of scholarship, one that limits it to a hierarchy of functions. Basic research has come to be viewed as a first and most essential form of scholarly activity, with other functions flowing from it. Scholars are academics who conduct research, publish, and then perhaps convey their knowledge to students or apply what they have learned. The latter functions grow *out of* scholarship; they are not to be considered a part of it. But knowledge is not necessarily developed in such a linear manner.[22]

The institutional arrangements Boyer describes in this passage, and the cognitive framework they underwrite, have both been in place for so many decades that some might wonder why anyone would think we should organize our thinking and our institutional reward systems in any other manner. That the citation may appear, on first blush, to make this kind of sense underlines the need for Boyer's argument. Along with the *scholarship of integration*, he wants the terms *research, teaching,* and *service* to connote three separate but connected aspects of *scholarship.* Boyer is not against research; he praises the scholarship of discovery at many points. But he wants to include more than research in the definition of the key term.

We accept and applaud Boyer's redefinition, and we suggest that his categories actually can help two groups of faculty. First, Boyer's categories give all of us as faculty a more helpful way to frame, fulfill, and assess our professorial vocations in the context of our respective colleges and universities. Second, Boyer's categories may help members of any particular academic community understand more clearly the character of the scholarship conducted by its various faculty members.

Turning to teaching and service, Boyer recounts that teaching for the purpose of building moral character marked the first chapter in the history of American education, a view few dispute. The later 1800s saw a shift in the college's purpose toward national and community service. Research and teaching were to serve useful ends—to apply to actual problems—the shift that supplied Boyer with the name he assigned to service: *the scholarship of application.* Adoption of German models of the university in the latter decades of the 1800s meant the eclipse of both teaching and service. The discovery of new knowledge became the highest calling for the university. In Boyer's own words, "in just a few decades . . . the focus had moved from the student to the professoriate, from general to specialized education, and from loyalty to the campus to loyalty to the profession."[23]

In many institutions, the state of affairs Boyer described in 1990 remains, and it remains the source of tension for institutions and individual faculty. Large research universities struggle to find ways to meet the obligations they have taken on to teach their own undergraduates. On the other hand, smaller universities and colleges—including most Christian colleges and universities—that want to provide teaching excellence to a primarily undergraduate population struggle against the cognitive stranglehold research has on the academic mindset, what we (and others) call "upward drift" or downward tyranny.[24] This mindset leaves many academics repeating the mantra that research or *the scholarship of discovery* is the most prestigious and most important way to express the academic vocation (despite studies showing that a minority of faculty produce most academic journal articles).

Hundreds of colleges and universities, including many faith-based institutions, attempted to implement Boyer's ideas in the 1990s. Early in their efforts, they discovered that good intentions did not necessarily indicate how to assess the scholarship of teaching and the scholarship of application. In response to calls for help with assessment, the Carnegie Foundation published *Scholarship Assessed* in 1997. Boyer contributed to *Scholarship Assessed*, but he died before it appeared. His colleagues on the project set high expectations for themselves and for all of us. They write:

> To give the four kinds of scholarly activities the weight that each deserves, they all must be held to the same standards of scholarly performance. The paradox is this: in order to recognize discovery, integration, application, and teaching as legitimate forms of scholarship, the academy must evaluate them by a set of standards that capture and acknowledge what they share as scholarly acts.

Unfortunately, faculty handbooks seldom highlight qualities and characteristics common to the different kinds of scholarship. Rather, current wisdom assumes that research, teaching, and applied scholarship—the kinds of faculty activities recognized for purposes of evaluation on most campuses—each has its own special yardstick.[25]

On the basis of their survey of hundreds of chief academic officers, publishers of scholarly journals, and funding agencies, the authors of *Scholarship Assessed* developed a set of six criteria, which, taken together, offer a single, very helpful yardstick for assessing any of the four types of scholarship distinguished by Boyer. At the end of a twelve-page discussion of the standards that they believe capture the character of scholarly work, the authors offer this summary, which we quote verbatim and refer to throughout the remainder of this book:

> **Clear goals:** Does the scholar state the basic purposes of his or her work clearly? Does the scholar define objectives that are realistic and achievable? Does the scholar identify important questions in the field?

**Adequate preparation:** Does the scholar show an understanding of existing scholarship in the field? Does the scholar bring the necessary skills to his or her work? Does the scholar bring together the resources necessary to move the project forward?

**Appropriate methods:** Does the scholar use methods appropriate to the goals? Does the scholar apply effectively the methods selected? Does the scholar modify procedures in response to changing circumstances?

**Significant results:** Does the scholar achieve the goals? Does the scholar's work add to the field? Does the scholar's work open additional areas for further exploration?

**Effective presentation:** Does the scholar use a suitable style and effective organization to present his or her work? Does the scholar use appropriate forms for communicating work to its intended audiences? Does the scholar present his or her message with clarity and integrity?

**Reflective critique:** Does the scholar critically evaluate his or her own work? Does the scholar bring an appropriate breadth of evidence to his or her critique? Does the scholar use evaluation to improve the quality of future work?[26]

*Scholarship Assessed* provides helpful commentary on how to document that one's service, teaching, research, and integration efforts have, in fact, met the six criteria. We believe, with the authors of *Scholarship Assessed*, that "the campus community must be confident that the institution honors the range of scholarship that supports its mission and that appropriate standards are in fact used."[27] An institution may wish to revise the above list of six criteria, but we view it as a beginning framework within which to work and assess the domains of scholarship at any Christian college. We discuss that work and its assessment in the next three chapters.

*Scholarship Assessed* has not been the last word in the conversation Boyer began in 1990. Hundreds of articles and books on the topic have appeared since 1997. Two noteworthy contributions to the conversation appeared in 2002 in answer to a question not addressed by the authors of *Scholarship Assessed*: what activities count? The authors of that title, *Institutionalizing a Broader View of Scholarship through Boyer's Four Domains,* discovered through a survey of hundreds of campuses that many administrators and faculty would deepen their understanding of Boyer's framework if they had examples and illustrations.[28] They provided pages of such examples. Also that year, Robert Diamond offered an easily modified, descriptive list of criteria for determining and documenting scholarly activities: "An activity or work will be considered scholarly if it meets the following criteria:

- It requires a high level of discipline–related expertise.
- It is conducted in a scholarly manner with clear goals, adequate presentation, and appropriate methodology.
- The work and its results are appropriately and effectively documented and disseminated . . . a reflective critique. . . .
- It has significance beyond the individual context.
- It breaks new ground or elaborates on previous work.
- The work . . . is reviewed and judged to be meritorious and significant by a panel of one's peers."[29]

In 2005, a noteworthy update on the state of the Boyer conversation appeared as *Faculty Priorities Reconsidered.* The authors of this work provide case studies from nine campuses, some public, some private, some large, some small, and one for-profit. These case studies offer insights into work on the ground and include helpful suggestions for moving the work along at the institutional level. In addition, a chapter late in the book provides a set of principles for those interested in continuing this reform agenda:

### Ten Principles of Good Practice for Encouraging Multiple Forms of Scholarship

1. Prepare faculty in graduate school for the variety of roles and types of scholarship in which they will engage.
2. Socialize new faculty to the broader institutional definition of scholarship.

3. Promote clear expectations for scholarship in promotion and tenure guidelines.
4. Do not expect or reward the "overloaded" plate.
5. Assess the impact of scholarship on multiple beneficiaries and partners.
6. Provide useful feedback to faculty during evaluation.
7. Support pioneers with resources—structural and financial, training and development, political and symbolic.
8. Encourage scholarly contributions that build on strengths.
9. Define and emphasize scholarship in the context of institutional mission.
10. Resist increasing research expectations to enhance institutional prestige.[30]

As with many general lists of good practice, some of the suggestions are painfully obvious. There was hardly a need for a national study to come up with those, but we do commend several as pertinent to faith-based institutions: (1) take into account the prevailing faculty load when determining research expectations; (2) encourage research contributions built on strengths; (3) define scholarship in the context of the institution's mission; and (4) please, please don't think that requiring more faculty to write a research paper will enhance institutional prestige. Our experience is that when this expectation is embraced with a narrow definition of scholarship, the results, at best, are mediocre. How such scholarship enhances an institution's image and prestige remains a mystery to us. However, research expectations that embrace the interests, abilities, and passion of the faculty member and take into consideration the mission of the institution and the context for faculty work can result in scholarship that is personally satisfying and helpful for colleagues, students, and the institution.

There is a sobering side to this report as well. The authors confess in the foreword that "these stories are real political struggles that are still going on," and they end that foreword by pointing out the difficult road ahead, particularly given serious pressures for change.[31] This pressure for change has several quite different roots, including these: the generational change among faculty; advances in technology; contributions from brain research; a pedagogical revolution due to emphasis on collaborative, experiential, and technology-assisted learning; alternative providers (for-profit); and corporate involvement in curriculum development and research priorities.[32] These pressures, as well as the unforeseen economic downturn of 2008, the arrival of MOOCs (massive open online courses), the continuing erosion of public confidence in higher education (which is viewed in several national capitals as part of the problem rather than part of the solution), the loss of faculty voice to administrative prerogative, and an incessant focus on the bottom line as the hallmark for institutional performance, lead many to demand to know why anyone would still be discussing the Boyer model at all.

Christian higher educators may find two very recent works on Boyer helpful. The Summer 2014 issue of the journal *Christian Higher Education* is given entirely to Boyer, his life, his faith, his legacy, and how Christian higher educators may find help in his model.[33] Also, Ernest Boyer's wife, Kathryn, has written *Many Mansions*,[34] her own reflection on Boyer's life and work. We recommend both these volumes for their perspectives on Boyer; the first provides a current appraisal of how his work connects with all our work as Christian educators, and the second paints an intimate portrait of Boyer from the person who knew him best.

As we draw toward the end of this introduction to Boyer's work, we recognize that higher education faces serious challenges, but we also point out the resilience of institutions of higher education. During the last eight or ten centuries, universities and colleges have survived other challenging times, including wars, depressions, disasters, inquisitions, hostile governments, and bad presidents. All institutions face real and honest challenges, but they have enduring missions and wise communities, too. Faith-based institutions have a deeper understanding about whose mission and work this really is, as well as a sense of the eternal implications of our work together. The challenges facing higher education generally, and the perspective we have as Christian educators, call us all to be at our very best. For institutions wanting to heed that call, the Boyer model helps institutions reconceive faculty roles and realign faculty rewards, making faculty scholarship more robust, coherent, enjoyable, and useful. This, it seems to us, is worth all the effort.

In the next three chapters, we turn our focus to teaching, research, and service, weaving together three conversational threads: Boyer's understanding of what scholarship means in that dimension, possible approaches to and meanings of faith and learning in that dimension, and the expectations of provosts, deans, and tenure-promotion committees in that dimension. Before we do, however, we want to discuss why we believe that the Boyer model can give life to a Christian college, assisting in a realignment of institutional mission faculty and support.

## The Boyer Model in Christian Colleges

One of the authors of this book (PA) remembers attending a national meeting in the early 1990s, which was examining Boyer's *Scholarship Reconsidered*. He remembers the excitement at the event. Yes, it really was an exciting event! After the keynote, professors from institutions large and small were taken by the idea that their work could honestly change, that someone had actually articulated their dream that the container in which they worked could better fit and support their own scholarly inclinations, aspirations, and gifts.

Boyer was a kind of wisdom keeper who spoke into desperate faculty lives. After hearing his ideas, many thought that perhaps being a professor could be different. Although many were hired as teachers, they soon discovered they were being evaluated as researchers, a bitter case of bait and switch for many. It was particularly so for those who taught in professional fields (business, education, nursing, engineering, etc.), relative newcomers on the liberal arts scene. Although they were hired for their experience and expertise in their respective professional fields, they had encountered the expectation that they would do original research for promotion and tenure. This, for some, came after they completed their doctorate because they had "only" a masters degree and twenty years of professional experience. It was as if they had been told to do their work, but in another language with different work rules. The reconsideration of faculty work according to Boyer's framework brought much hope to those present.

The Boyer report spoke into an unrealized, unspoken aspiration: to be able to do meaningful academic work using one's gifts with a sense of calling and purpose. As we have recounted here, these conversations have continued, with some success, in institutions of all types. But Boyer also touched an establishment nerve. The Boyer understanding of scholarship requires a reorientation of faculty work and a realignment of institutional rewards; a reorientation from the professor to the student, from the guild to the institutional mission, from research to scholarship, from IRS to TSS (teach, shape, and send). Boyer pointed the academy back to the future.

Unfortunately, in many institutions, those who benefit most from the current system are unwilling to change it. Complicating matters further, some universities are so large that it is difficult to start a serious conversation about anything, let alone reorientation and redistribution of rewards. Deans who try to initiate such conversations are often thought to be "soft on scholarship," certainly no way to get promoted to the provost's office. Thus, at the very least, realizing Boyer's vision has been—and will continue to be—a prolonged, uphill battle.

But for faith-based institutions, this need not be the case. We openly affirm that we are not R1 institutions, nor do we aspire to be. Honestly, most Christian colleges do not have the resources or expertise to make that happen, even if the trustees decided to try. Instead, almost all faith-based institutions are T1 institutions, devoted to the development and transformation of students. This is something that research institutions simply do not know how to do very well. When it comes to formation and moral development, students at R1 institutions are left largely to their own resources. Yet, this is what Christian colleges do best! And the Boyer model is ideally suited for faith-based institutions that point to the transformation of students as their primary mission. Boyer's framework not only allows for but actually insists on scholarship being an essential aspect of every professor's portfolio, but the Boyer framework views scholarship in four dimensions rather than only one. In short, this model gives space for different intellectual gifts and interests, bringing scholarly habits of mind to teaching, research, and service. Truly, it can give life to those who feel they do not fit into the research paradigm that has exercised hegemonic control over academe for over a century.

But the Boyer model takes some work if we want it to function effectively in any given institution. Remember, real political struggles go on here, too. In a poll by the authors of twenty provosts serving at faith-based institutions, all twenty indicated they were familiar with the Boyer model, and eighteen said their promotion/tenure expectations either reflect or are influenced by the Boyer model. It is encouraging to know that the Boyer model is being discussed and used.

But while the model is familiar to many institutions, we are concerned that it often provides only an umbrella of sorts for the promotion process and lacks specificity about how colleges and their committees should evaluate and how professors should document each dimension of scholarship. For example, faculty members sitting on promotion and tenure committees often confuse the act of teaching with the scholarship of teaching. Every provost surveyed confessed that more work needed to be done to bring more precision to scholarship expectations on his or her campus, particularly so given the new economic realities colleges now face.

In the next three chapters, we provide specifics about how the Boyer model applies in the teaching, research, and service dimensions of faculty work. Again, we believe that the Boyer model is uniquely suited for faith-based institutions, and such institutions can be helpful models for the rest of the academy. In 1994, Boyer articulated his vision for the New American College, a place where "teaching is powerfully affirmed, research is selectively supported and . . . the Scholarship of Integration and Application come alive and take on a new vitality."[35] If one did not know better, one might think that Boyer had faith-based institutions in mind when he made that bold claim. Perhaps he did. And when you add to his vision a vibrant Christian faith at the very center of the mission, higher education has the potential to take on new vitality.

## Chapter 5

# The Scholarship of Teaching

Since Boyer first published *Scholarship Reconsidered* in 1990, a robust and at times controversial discussion has developed related to the scholarship of teaching. Without doubt, this aspect of Boyer's proposal has garnered more attention and caused more frustration than any other dimension. Although participants in that discussion have agreed on much, they have had difficulty agreeing on a precise definition of the scholarship of teaching itself.[1] Surprisingly, this is due in part because Boyer himself wrote and spoke so little about it. In *Scholarship Reconsidered*, he devoted just six paragraphs to his proposal to expand the traditional understanding of research to include aspects of teaching (or to view teaching as a form of scholarship) and to revise the accompanying reward system for promotion and tenure. Sharing his bold vision and high hopes for scholarship in the academy, he ended by writing:

> Here, then, is our conclusion. What we urgently need today is a more inclusive view of what it means to be a scholar—a recognition

that knowledge is acquired through research, through synthesis, through practice, and through teaching. We acknowledge that these four categories—the scholarship of discovery, of integration, of application, and of teaching—divide intellectual functions that are tied inseparably to each other. Still, there is value, we believe, in analyzing the various kinds of academic work, while also acknowledging that they dynamically interact, forming an interdependent whole. Such a vision of scholarship, one that recognizes the great diversity of talent within the professoriate, also may prove especially useful to faculty as they reflect on the meaning and direction of their professional lives.[2]

His inclusive vision of scholarship continues to this day to generate and energize conversation about the nature of faculty work. But the conversation related to Boyer's conception of teaching has often been confused and troublesome. On many campuses, there are actually two conversations. One conversation rejoices and marvels at the wisdom of Boyer's call to expand how we understand scholarship. Such expansion makes perfect sense (why not focus on improving teaching and student learning outcomes?), it is life-giving (it lets faculty focus on what they feel called to do), and it addresses the dramatic misalignment that so many faculty members feel (they are hired to teach but need to publish to get promoted). Expanding the concept of scholarship to include teaching makes particular sense in colleges and universities that identify themselves as teaching institutions.

The other conversation runs along these lines. "We all teach something, and we are expected to conduct research, particularly if one wants to be promoted—and certainly if one wants to be tenured. That's the way it was when I faced the committee. We had real standards back then, and quality and rigor, too." On this view, to talk now about counting the scholarship of teaching for promotion and tenure both conflates the two functions of a professor (and we know which one carries the prestige and rewards), and it waters down the expectations for promotion and tenure, a view caught in comments such as "You can't get promoted here for just working to become a better teacher. We are all expected to do that!"

Thus, even while the scholarship of teaching continues to develop into a rich and dynamic field of study, faculty conversations continue, and individual faculty members' concerns continue to percolate. We have heard these very conversations and complaints on more than a half dozen campuses in the past eighteen months, and we suspect that they are present to some degree on most campuses. Two decades after its release, *Scholarship Reconsidered* continues to produce both heat and light. In this chapter, we hope to shed some light for those working in faith-based institutions.

Some have wondered about the timing of Boyer's proposal. Would it have been better to wait to advocate for an expanded view of scholarship until more detailed definitions and explanations could be developed and a consensus achieved as to how to proceed with the conversation? Why rush the report to market, particularly by someone who was so careful with words? Looking back with hindsight, we agree. If his intent was to start a robust conversation, then he certainly succeeded. The conversation continues. However, if his ultimate objective was to achieve a radical change in the way the academy does business, that simply has not yet happened. Of course, there are many impeding factors: the economy, campus politics, and good old resistance to change, to name just a few. However, the Boyer report launched a reformation effort without providing a clear roadmap for the journey. Over two decades later, we are still trying to operationalize Boyer's proposal and find our way. On a brighter note, the continuing confusion and frustration about the scholarship of teaching give us the opportunity to include this chapter in this book. For that, we are indeed grateful.

In this chapter, we will try to clarify and advance the conversation about the scholarship of teaching. Every provost we know is familiar with the Boyer model, and most faith-based campuses have been influenced by Boyer's proposal in some way. Almost every university has a teaching center for excellence (by some name) or a faculty member or dean dedicated to the task of improving teaching and learning, but much institutional confusion remains—and this confusion flares up too often during the promotion and tenure process, often leaving the applicant for promotion or tenure smarting and wounded. Essentially, it boils down to three questions: What does the scholarship of teaching look like? What counts and what does not count as credible scholarship for promotion/tenure? Who gets to decide?

Before specifically discussing the expectations of provosts, deans, and tenure-promotion committees, we will make a clear distinction between effective teaching and the scholarship of teaching, the source of much confusion. We will end the chapter by offering some possible approaches to faith/integration that support the scholarship of teaching.

## Effective Teaching

### Learning to Teach

Learning to teach effectively is a bit like learning how to swim. Your brothers row you out to the middle of the lake and throw you in. That is certainly the quickest way to learn to swim. Really, it isn't too difficult—once you get your hands untied. Bah-dah-boom! That old joke resonates with many of us who learned to teach on the job, and that includes almost all of us. During our first year of teaching, most of us felt like we had been thrown into the middle the lake and had to work very hard just to get our hands untied. We were afraid of the water. Learning to use different strokes or volunteering to be a lifeguard took years. To this day, many of us wish we could go back and apologize to those students who endured our first semester of classes. We owe them so much for their grace and patience with us. There is no way around it. Learning to teach effectively is simply hard work, and it requires time on task.

But why is that so? Why is learning to teach such a difficult task? After all, most of us were very good students and loved the entire teaching-learning process from classroom to dissertation. Yes, we were very good (and even gifted) learners. That's the point. While teaching and learning are certainly related activities, in graduate school we become proficient learners but typically remain novice teachers.

In actuality, most people see far too few positive teaching role models and too many negative ones. (*When I get a faculty position, I won't teach like that!*) And teaching remains one of the most privatized professions in the western world. As professors, we go into the classroom and close the door. We are solely responsible for design and delivery of the course and for the evaluation of the students. In many cases, we also carry sole responsibility for the course contents. The last thing we want to talk about when we get to faculty lunch is the effectiveness of our teaching, and we certainly don't want to share our struggles as we try to become a more effective teacher. Sadly, unless students complain to the department head, the novice teacher marches steadily on though the first semester and rarely gets any feedback whatsoever until the student evaluations come back— usually well into second semester or even the following summer! In many ways, our academic systems are not designed to give adequate and timely feedback. It is as if novice teachers were on life support, needing only a pulse and some oxygen.

## *The Wisdom of Practice*

Of course, colleagues are always ready to give some advice, some of it sage and some not so much. "Students won't care what you know until they know that you care." "Teach the students you have, not the ones you wish you had." "Do not assume that all the students will be like you—they do not love physics." "Have high expectations and provide high support." And perhaps our favorite, "Give hard tests and do not be friendly—it's all about rigor." To be fair, of course, some colleagues will give good advice (and some of the above comments contain grains of wisdom).

There is an accumulated wisdom of practice that develops in a faculty— derived from experience, and it can be shared. But you have to be careful. As Maryellen Weimer points out, there are problems with leaning heavily on the current wisdom of practice: it is often not tied to theoretical or conceptual frameworks or to empirical outcomes; it is not generally situation specific; it often lacks historical perspective; and it is usually devoid of assessment techniques and approaches.[3] Simply put, the wisdom of practice could be greatly strengthened by a robust scholarship of teaching, precisely what Boyer called for. We will say more about this later in the chapter, but to conclude this part of our argument, let us say that graduate school did not prepare most of us well for teaching; even though we may have been strong learners, the private nature of teaching makes it difficult to observe and be shaped by effective models, and when we rely on the local wisdom of practice, the results may not be as satisfying or helpful as we would like or need them to be. Learning to teach effectively is hard work and takes time.

## Some Encouragement

It is not the purpose of this chapter to discuss effective teaching or how to develop it in great detail. There are literally hundreds of books, journal articles, conferences, websites, and handbooks dealing with this topic, and your campus most likely has a teaching center or dedicated professionals committed to improving teaching and learning. Our task in this chapter is to discuss the scholarship of teaching, point out ways you can work with your local promotion/tenure committee, and offer several approaches for bringing faith to bear in ways that could support your work.

Before we move on, however, several comments are in order. First, we do wish to be encouraging—effective teaching can be learned, and almost all of us are better teachers now than when we first began. Ronald Smith adapted the work of Dreyfus and Dreyfus to outline five stages of development toward becoming an expert teacher: (1) novice—relies on rules and checklists; (2) advanced beginner—recognizes when things go poorly, then uses rules to react; (3) competent—chooses to focus on certain goals, then follows rules; (4) proficient—intuitively recognizes entire situation and develops alternatives; and (5) expert—intuitively recognizes situations, draws on past experience, and adapts without apparent thought.[4] As you can see, the novice teacher moves from following rules and checklists to using experience and intuition. Smith concludes by arguing that if you teach, you ought either to be an expert or be well along the road to becoming one.[5] The assumption is, of course, that developing your expertise in teaching is a process and you can become an expert teacher!

Second, we now have available a large body of thoughtful scholarship on teaching and learning, including pedagogical knowledge; curricular knowledge; brain research; research on cognitive, moral, and faith development; and much more. In short, if you want to learn about teaching and learning, you have your choice of shoulders to stand on and do not need to develop your practice alone.

Third, for many faculty (including us), teaching is the most satisfying aspect of the professor's role. You get to know and care deeply about students; you receive instant affirmation in extraordinary and unexpected ways; you get to see and be a critical part of the formation of gifted individuals; and you serve as part of an organization with a rich heritage and honorable mission. As one of our colleagues loves to say, "And they pay us for this? Do not tell the administration, but I would do this for free!" You get to be a part of something much larger than yourself and more important than your own career: a wisdom community with a rich history, deep moral commitments, and clear intentions, dedicated to teaching, shaping, and sending students. It does not get any better than that!

We conclude this introduction by quoting Ernst Boyer on effective teaching and great teachers:

> All of us have been influenced by an outstanding teacher. What is it that makes these teachers great? Every great teacher has four characteristics: first, they know their subject; second, they know their students; third, there is active participation; and finally . . . they are honest and authentic human beings, that is, there is an integrity in what they say and how they live that gives power to their message. I absolutely believe that the value system of a school or college is sustained, in the end, not through the curriculum, but through the integrity of great teachers.[6]

Boyer has said this well, and we agree with him. It seems to us that the first three characteristics (subject knowledge, student knowledge, and instructional knowledge) can be learned. For that, we are grateful, and to that we are committed. The fourth characteristic, "an integrity in what we say and how we live" must be practiced. Indeed, as we noted in Chapter Two, faithful presence, and graceful, grace-filled practice are necessary conditions for faith-learning integration. We will say more about embodied teaching in the final chapter. For now, we simply recognize that to live a life of integrity takes the very rawest kind of courage, but the influence of a life well lived before and with students is beyond imagination. To live as a faithful presence among students is a high calling, indeed!

# The Scholarship of Teaching

## Narrowing the Vision

Let us be clear. Effective teaching and the scholarship of teaching are *not* the same thing—they are related and mutually supportive activities, but certainly not identical twins. The academy has made that very clear—you cannot get tenured solely of the basis of good teaching in any institution we know. It just will not happen. However, when Boyer began envisioning change in higher education, he favored a much higher and more encompassing view of the role of teaching. In a speech to the Association of American Colleges in 1988, two years before the release of *Scholarship Reconsidered,* he made the following comment:

> I'm suggesting that there is an enormous ambivalence within American higher education about the division between teaching and research. Somehow, we need to look beyond the "teaching vs. research" cliché and ask the more provocative question, What does it mean to be a scholar?[7]

He closed his comments that evening by suggesting that we should not only recognize teaching as a form of scholarship, but that we should recognize *advising and counseling students, too.* Perhaps he meant this suggestion as only a trial balloon, something that he had been thinking about since writing in the mid-1980s about the undergraduate experience. He knew then that many academics were not proficient at the scholarship of discovery, and it made little sense to him to make all professors jump through the same promotion and tenure hoops. Whatever else it was, his suggestion certainly was provocative. We know of no evidence that he persisted in his argument to include advising and counseling; it was a bit too much.

In 1994, four years after the release of the report, Boyer spoke at the Emory Symposium. There, continuing to advocate for the scholarship of teaching, he stressed that teaching sustains scholarship—if publishing in a journal is a form of teaching, so, too, is giving a paper at a conference. Perhaps revealing a level of frustration with both the continuing resistance to his proposal and the lack of substantial progress toward revamping the professorial reward system, he confessed to being deeply troubled that the academy viewed giving a paper at some major hotel in a distant city as so much more valuable than teaching undergraduates back home. He wanted to know why we give such high honor to the printed page but so little to our work with future scholars in our undergraduate classrooms. "Even the language we use is revealing. We refer to research *opportunities*, and to teaching *load*."[8] Words do matter.

A year later, at the 1995 ceremony where he was inducted into the American Academy of Arts and Sciences, Boyer gave one of his final speeches. He continued to advocate for the idea of embracing the scholarship of teaching as a legitimate form of scholarship, as much needed and even noble work. Scholarship, he argued, is always a communal act, and no one should receive tenure for research alone. In his view, tenure is granted for research and publication. One must be able to communicate with others to be tenured. He remained troubled that the classroom still did not count as a legitimate context for that kind of communication, at least for the purposes of tenure.[9] Ultimately, although Boyer's own public definition of the scholarship of teaching narrowed considerably, he continued to persist in pushing for a wide embrace of much of the teaching role as legitimate scholarship even while many in the academy persisted in holding the idea at arm's length.

After Boyer's death, it would be left to others to move the conversation forward, and the conversation has proceeded—sometimes forward and sometimes in circles. For an industry dedicated to learning, higher education can show remarkable resistance to change. There is a lesson in Boyer's story for all academics. He had a prophetic voice with access to the main stages in higher education, yet his ideas have never gained real traction despite the fact that—to this day—almost every academic administrator is familiar with Boyer's ideas, which remain a subject of discussion on almost every campus. During Boyer's life, the academy needed a better understanding of what the scholarship of teaching would look like and what kind of infrastructure would support it. That need for understanding remains. On any campus, seeing what needs to be done, having a clear consensus on how to move forward, and possessing the means to move remain essential. Vision and task are two sides of the same coin, a pair of terms we will return to in Chapter Nine when we discuss some concepts useful to those who would become productive academic writers.

## Scholarly Teaching

Learning to teach, moving through the stages of effective teaching—from novice to advanced beginner to competent to proficient to expert—allows faculty to move steadily toward the scholarship of teaching, but even reaching the expert stage does not meet the criteria for the scholarship of teaching as Boyer conceived of it and as we use the phrase here. Expertise usually implies that one is becoming a scholarly teacher, bringing the mind of a scholar or scholarly habits of mind to bear on the work of teaching. But the scholarship of teaching implies more than that. It certainly includes expanded instructional and disciplinary knowledge, thorough understanding of assessment, and a repertoire or even an arsenal of skills in course design and delivery; but, in Boyer's terms, scholarship is still more.

Expertise in teaching almost always entails becoming scholarly in one's teaching, using one's scholarly knowledge and skills to improve instruction and student learning, and becoming deft at critical analysis of and reflective critique on teaching. You are closing in on expertise in your craft. At this level of expertise you might begin to develop your own scholarship of teaching and begin to contribute to the field of teaching and learning. That is, movement into the scholarship of teaching occurs after one becomes a scholarly teacher.[10] We have seen novice professors misunderstand this process, causing complications in the promotion and tenure process.

## Beyond Expertise to Scholarship

Two scholars who had worked with Boyer and continued his work after his death, John M. Braxton and Marietta Del Favero, make a helpful distinction between scholarly activities (part of the work of an expert teacher) and scholarship. For them, a variety of scholarly activities require both disciplinary knowledge and pedagogical knowledge meant to improve classroom performance. Of course, these scholarly activities are vital. However, according to Braxton and Del Favero, scholarship must meet three additional major criteria: it must be public; it must be subject to critical review; and it must be useful to the scholarly community.[11] They add that it must result in either unpublished or published scholarly outcomes.

Considering "unpublished outcomes" legitimate catches many people off guard, including, we suspect, some of our readers. Braxton and Del Favero insist that unpublished scholarly outcomes can be a form of scholarship as long as they meet the major criteria for scholarship, especially appearing in some publicly observable form.[12] Making that happen takes some creativity and explanation given that most tenure committees view unpublished outcomes with suspicion. To help make the distinction, Braxton and his colleagues developed a list of examples of scholarly activities, unpublished scholarly outcomes, and kinds of publications for all four dimensions of the Boyer model (discovery or inquiry, teaching, service or engagement, integration). For illustration, we list below a few of their examples related to the scholarship of teaching:

- Scholarly activities: directed student research projects, preparation of a new syllabus or course design, construction of an annotated bibliography for course reference, or development of a new set of lectures for existing or new courses. (Note that the focus is on one's own teaching and students.)
- Unpublished scholarly outcomes: presenting new instructional techniques to colleagues, experimenting with new teaching methods or activities, employing a new instructional practice and altering it until it is successful, or creating an approach or strategy to help students to think critically about course concepts. (The faculty member must also make these activities accessible to the scholarly community in some way—a conference presentation, workshop, mini-course, etc.)
- Publications: publication on the use of a new instructional method; publication reporting about a new teaching approach developed by the author; or publication of examples, materials, class exercises, or assignments that help students learn different course concepts.[13]

We recommend the work of Braxton and his colleagues to all our readers, especially those who have come to the academy from clinical or professional practice and whose patterns of work may involve substantial public but unpublished work.

Ronald Smith suggests that "the essential difference between being a scholarly teacher and a scholar of teaching (at any level of development) is the degree of interest in the wider implications and impact of the results into one's practice."[14] In other words, what Pat Hutchings and Lee Shulman call "going meta" (which we distinguish from going over the top):

> A scholarship of teaching is *not* synonymous with excellent teaching. It requires a kind of "going meta," in which faculty frame and systematically investigate questions related to student learning—the conditions under which it occurs, what it looks like, how to deepen it, and so forth—and do so with an eye not only to improving their own classroom but to advancing practice beyond it. This conception of the scholarship of teaching is not something we presume all faculty (even the most excellent and scholarly teachers among them) will or should do—though it would be good to see that more of them have the opportunity to do so if they wish. But the scholarship of teaching is a condition—as yet a mostly absent condition for excellent teaching. It is the mechanism through which the profession of teaching itself advances, through which teaching can be something other than a seat-of-the-pants operation, with each of us out there making it up as we go. As such, the scholarship of teaching has the potential to serve all teachers—and students.[15]

Note that not all excellent or scholarly teachers are or should be engaged in the scholarship of teaching. An expert teacher knows his or her field and is able to promote real learning, focusing on improving student learning outcomes. The scholarly teacher goes the additional mile to seek out peer collaboration and invite peer review, bringing a degree of critical reflection and assessment to the teaching and learning process. Those joining the scholarship of teaching community must go even further. Laurie Richland suggests that the scholarship of teaching involves composing "selected portions of the scholarly investigation and findings into a manuscript to be submitted to an appropriate journal or conference venue."[16] In essence, the scholar of teaching submits work to a second peer-review process. Richland thus distinguishes the scholarship of teaching from mere teaching by including peer review and public dissemination of the scholarly work. Hutchings and Schulman conclude that it is a missing aspect of most teaching.[17] This is certainly a sobering appraisal of a situation that remains, in our view, largely unchanged today.

The good news is that there is a strong and growing infrastructure in place to support the scholarship of teaching. Today, we speak of the scholarship of teaching and learning, often abbreviated SoTL. In part, this phrase completes a circle by including the learner as the central focus of teaching activity; it helps remind us that getting through the material means nothing if our students do not learn. And both governments and accrediting bodies increasingly insist that institutions of learning have assessment structures in place and can demonstrate that students are learning. Higher educators have become increasingly aware that teaching, while vital, is intermediary. It is not an end in itself. We study teaching in order to improve learning.

The scholarship of teaching and learning (SoTL) is a robust and recognized field of study, sustained by a growing knowledge base, mounting institutional support, and increasingly robust scholarly infrastructure. Scholars of teaching and learning share their work in peer-reviewed journals, regional and national teaching and learning conferences, and disciplinary meetings and publications. The National Science Foundation, the Carnegie Foundation for the Advancement of Teaching, the Society for Teaching and Learning in Higher Education in Canada, the American Association of Colleges and Universities, the Fund for the Improvement of Postsecondary Education, Lilly, and many other funding agencies and foundations have sustained efforts for reform. Most campuses now have teaching and learning centers (by some name) or professionals dedicated to the task of improving instruction and student learning outcomes, and graduate programs now provide expertise and research to support the field (some with reticence). Scholarship in related fields, such as brain research, moral development, and stages of faith formation, have contributed greatly to the tapestry of the discipline.

Finally, some have divided SoTL itself into subsets related to the other three dimensions of Boyer's model—discovery, integration, and engagement.[18] In short, anyone wishing to develop a scholarly agenda related to some aspect of teaching and learning will find infrastructure in place to support and sustain that work. Such was not the case in 1990 when *Scholarship Reconsidered* was published. Although Boyer did not live to see the flowering of the field of SoTL, he deserves credit for having drawn attention to the need to focus scholarly attention on teaching and to recognize teaching as scholarship. SoTL remains hard work, but it is good work, too.

The bad news related to SoTL is that this hard work may not always be recognized and rewarded. To quote Richland again, "the sad truth is that many departments and institutions do not count pedagogical scholarship as part of the faculty member's scholarly production."[19] Or if they do, such scholarship is granted less credit than the scholarship of discovery or integration. This sobering reality is true for some faith-based institutions, too, but we believe there is a way forward. We will provide some insights and strategies about developing a scholarly agenda related to the scholarship of teaching and learning. If you choose to make some aspect of SoTL your scholarly emphasis (or if it chooses you), you can take concrete steps to ensure that it receives the recognition it deserves in the promotion and tenure process. We will turn to these steps now. Then, to conclude this chapter, we will explore several connections between faith-learning integration and SoTL that we believe can help sustain Christian college faculty in their work.

## Promotion and Tenure Expectations and the Scholarship of Teaching

In 2005, Mary Taylor Huber, Pat Hutchings, and Lee Shulman, all expert teachers and well-respected scholars of teaching and learning in higher education, characterized the state of the scholarship of teaching and learning in this way:

The placement of the scholarship of teaching and learning in the academy is very much at issue now. Its genres, topics, and methods are being invented even as we speak; its role in academic careers is being written case by case; new practitioners announce themselves everyday, and they are just beginning to seek each other out. Institutional realities and disciplinary styles are influencing the way scholars approach teaching and student learning.[20]

We want to highlight five aspects of this important assessment before offering some strategies for you to use on your home campus.

## Five Current Realities

First, the place of the scholarship of teaching and learning in the academy remains uncertain, and this uncertainty also affects many faith-based campuses. Faculty cannot assume that pursuing some aspect of the SoTL will automatically be embraced as a legitimate form of scholarship on campus, or that colleagues will give SoTL the same weight as the scholarship of discovery if they do accept it. We are not saying that such reticence to recognize SoTL prevails in every institution, but we are saying that our readers must recognize that SoTL remains uncertain ground and proceed accordingly. In many cases, an individual faculty member who has engaged in SoTL will have to make a case for its credibility. Fortunately, making such a case is possible.

Second, SoTL remains in relative infancy as a field of academic inquiry. It lacks a long history and has few established norms and precedents; scholars of teaching and learning regularly introduce new genres, topics, and methods. In these nearly building-the-plane-as-you-fly-it conditions,[21] individual faculty may have to make up their own rules about how to do their scholarship, figuring out as they proceed answers to questions such as: With whom do I collaborate? If and where do I publish or make my work public? How do I invite and document critical review and from whom? Building the plane while flying it can be exhilarating, but it can also leave one's promotion committee scratching their collective heads, trying to figure out how to evaluate scholarship that refuses to fit nicely into established scholarly categories.

Third, the role of the scholarship of teaching and learning in academic careers is being written case by case; we currently have few role models or established professional patterns to point to or emulate. Of course, this can be liberating for the faculty member who enjoys being on the cutting edge. But it adds a level of difficulty to the work of deans and tenure committees who want to understand and act justly as they evaluate that faculty member's work, especially when they are charged with determining if the institution should offer that faculty member a lifetime contract. In cases that deans and committees may view as unique, the individual faculty member must take care to map out clearly his or her academic career track.[22]

Fourth, fiscal realities have huge implications for how institutions view teaching and SoTL, particularly so since the economic downturn of 2008. Institutions must respond to continuing calls for accountability and affordability from parents, accrediting bodies and government agencies, and the general public. They deal with the continuing loss of faculty voice to administrative prerogatives. They face new and increasing competition from not-for-profit institutions and the business sector, from the growth in online learning, from the movement toward testing-out and certification on the basis of demonstrated skills,[23] and even from the public pronouncements of tech billionaires who ask "what's the point" as they boast about having dropped out of Harvard. These realities put the future of tenure at risk on some campuses, and they raise the stakes for granting tenure at almost all institutions. Many trustee boards now wonder if tenure remains viable given the new economic constraints within which higher education must now function. In such environments, professors in nontraditional academic career tracks will very likely face closer scrutiny in retention and tenure processes. We apparently are not in academic Kansas anymore.

Finally, we must consider disciplinary styles and approaches; all disciplines do not approach the scholarship of teaching and learning in the same way. Each faculty member must understand how his or her own discipline understands, approaches, and appreciates SoTL (or, soberingly, does not). In the promotion/tenure process, faculty will increasingly need to be able to document and articulate that they are working in concert with the best practices of their respective discipline. And they will need to document and articulate that work to make it accessible to and persuasive for promotion-tenure committee members who represent other academic disciplines.

In 2011, Hutchings, Huber, and Anthony Ciccone highlighted continuing progress for the institutional acceptance of SoTL as a legitimate movement but also noted that promotion and tenure evaluation practices, particularly when applied to individual cases, "have miles to go before they adequately acknowledge the scholarship of teaching and learning in any of the traditional categories of faculty work."[24] Two steps forward, one step back. The sad reality is that many faculty members who engage in SoTL feel unsupported by their institutions, and much of their work "gets done under the radar of formal faculty evaluation."[25]

We do not wish to burden our readers unduly with such sobering information, but we do hope to convey the seriousness of the times in which the academy has found itself. Jesus claimed that his burdens were light; the academy made no such claim. If you decide to become a serious scholar of teaching and learning, do not be naïve. There will be additional hurdles to clear in the retention and promotion evaluation process, so you must prepare for that reality. But do not be afraid, either. There is a way forward.

## Steps to Move Forward

Without criticizing high levels of teaching expertise, we must note two important benefits of walking what we have described as a tough road. The scholar of teaching and learning will ultimately teach more effectively than the mere expert. And, because he or she builds links between teaching and research, the scholar of teaching and learning will achieve more of the professional integration that Boyer identified as his fourth category of scholarship. Having said that, we note these important details about the way forward for the faculty member wishing to engage in SoTL.

**Step One.** First, get assurance that the scholarship of teaching and learning will be accepted and counted as a legitimate scholarly activity by both your institution and your department. If at all possible, get it in writing. And if you do receive such assurances, ask about specifics regarding your particular scholarship agenda. Do not rest on global assurances; talk about the realities of your specific work. On the other hand, if your institution will not accept SoTL, then we suggest that you either change your scholarly agenda or find somewhere else to work. You cannot fight City Hall on this one. Spending several years arguing for acceptance of work that your institution does not value usually bears very little fruit, and most of that is bitter.

**Step Two.** Talk with past and present members of the promotion and tenure committee. Find out how the committee discusses and evaluates a faculty member's scholarship portfolio. Unlike many R1 institutions, most faith-based institutions do not use a numerical evaluation system, determining which of your publications and presentations count and assigning points to those that do. In these systems, your point total must reach a certain predetermined number to be eligible for advancement. In many faith-based institutions, your scholarship is judged in a more generous, but less specific, way. However, most deans and committees still operate with some conception of critical mass in mind. While this threshold usually resists quantification or definition, these words keep surfacing in relevant discussions: "too lite,"[26] "too thin," and "too scattered."

The judgment that a scholarship portfolio is "too lite" implies that while the scholarship presented may be acceptable, the faculty member has simply not done enough to represent three or six years work in that field. The work does not represent a critical mass, an *oeuvre*, a term we return to in Chapter Nine. Exactly what constitutes a critical mass certainly differs from discipline to discipline and by the composition of the portfolio itself (what volume and what mix of journal articles, book reviews, conference presentations, books, book chapters, encyclopedia articles, workshops, etc.), but the committee will always take into account the amount of scholarship presented. One or two publications may be adequate in one department but not in another. Usually, departments have a pretty good sense of what is expected by their colleagues on the promotion/tenure committee. The burden to do due diligence remains on the individual faculty member; he or she must find out as much as possible about what counts as critical mass in his or her particular setting.

A scholarship portfolio judged to be "too thin" likely includes a substantial number of entries, but committee members view it as lacking depth of scholarship. Perhaps the portfolio is comprised primarily of published book reviews and presentations on campus. While counted as scholarship, these do not represent a sufficiently serious or deep foray into scholarship. We claimed above that SoTL remains in its infancy. Given that, faculty presenting a portfolio on the scholarship of teaching carry an extra responsibility to demonstrate depth in their scholarship. Even in settings where a committee views SoTL as legitimate scholarly endeavor, that work will, in essence, be discounted to some degree (at an unpublished rate). That is to say, the committee will count it but not at full value. Faculty members who will face such a discounted assessment of their work must fortify their portfolios with a substantial number of entries. Thus far, we have described *too thin* and *too light*; two concepts that are actually first semantic cousins.

A scholarship portfolio judged to be *too scattered* denotes a portfolio that lacks a scholarly agenda, a clear focus, or a cohesive plan. It is, to use a phrase we heard a dean use just this year, "all over the place." Serious scholarship is signaled by a consistent focus over time, allowing for a critical mass of scholarship to develop of sufficient depth and quality, which brings us to our third step.

**Step Three.** Be able to articulate and document a scholarly agenda. We cannot emphasize enough the importance of this step. We stress this not only because we believe that focus and time on task pay huge dividends in the promotion and tenure process, but also because we believe that Christian faculty (in both faith-based and public settings) do the work they do because they have heard a call, a voice. They have not only a job—they have a vocation. And in their lifelong response to that vocation, they will build a body of work, an *oeuvre*. We may be stretching the meaning of Hebrews 11 a bit too far when we make this claim, but we believe a cloud of witnesses does the happy dance when they see Christian faculty members succeed in focusing their scholarly programs and having those programs recognized by their institutions.

## Required Criteria for Documenting SoTL

In Chapter Four, we outlined the six standards for scholarship proposed in *Scholarship Assessed*. We affirmed them as excellent criteria for understanding and documenting scholarship, and we do so again here, particularly in light of the concerns raised in this chapter about presenting SoTL as a serious form of scholarship. In our view, any scholarship portfolio or essay discussing one's own scholarship should address these six dimensions, and we believe it is fair game for any evaluation committee to insist that they be addressed:

- **Clear goals.** Is the basic purpose of your work and how you go about it clear? Do you have a plan? Is it realistic and important to the field?
- **Adequate preparation.** Do you have the skills and necessary support to do this work here, and do you understand the existing scholarship in the field?
- **Appropriate methods.** Do you use methods appropriate for the scholarship at hand, and are you able to adjust as circumstances demand?
- **Significant results.** Have you worked your plan and achieved your goals? Has it contributed to the field and opened up areas for additional study?
- **Effective presentation.** Have you used appropriate venues to effectively communicate your work to peers and other audiences?
- **Reflective critique.** How do you evaluate your own work, and how have you reflected and responded to the critical critique of your work by others in the field?[27]

We believe that faculty can help themselves meet the critical mass test and avoid the characterizations of too lite, too thin, or too scattered by carefully and thoroughly addressing these six dimensions—both when developing their scholarly agenda and when building the case for their scholarship of teaching and learning. However, we note that faculty must bring a substantial body of work to the tenure-promotion table. There is no way to make work that really *is* too lite, too thin, or too scattered look otherwise. In light of that sobering fact, we invite our readers to view their academic work as a gift from God, as a way to realize their vocation, and as a channel by which God means to bless the world. Again, we want our readers to experience career success in their respective workplaces—and we believe that framing your work in terms of gift, vocation, and blessing will help you achieve that success and so much more.

## The Scholarship of Teaching and Learning and Christian Faith

Remember that becoming an expert teacher, a scholarly teacher, or a scholar of teaching and learning takes practice, and you get better at it over time. It is a developmental task. So, too, is faith integration. It may seem a bit strange to hear "time on task" applied to faith integration, but there it is. We believe faith integration is a wisdom practice, and that sort of knowledge and embodiment do not simply appear overnight. So, where to begin?

Let us begin with this question: is there a distinctly Christian approach to the scholarship of teaching and learning, something that only a Christian can do? Probably not, but being a Christian certainly does matter. Madeleine L'Engle, a most gifted American writer, when asked for advice on how to become a Christian writer, answered this way: "If you are truly and deeply Christian, what you write will be Christian whether you mention Jesus or not. And if you are not profoundly Christian, then your writing will not be Christian, no matter how many times you mention Jesus."[28]

The starting point, then, as Richard Hughes suggests, is to simply confess: "I am a Christian. That fact places other scholars under no obligation whatsoever, but it places me under a profound obligation. Indeed, that fact must inevitably lend shape and texture to all that I do."[29] We agree. Our faith does lend shape and texture to our approach to scholarship in several important ways: approaching the scholarship of teaching *with* faith, approaching SoTL *about* faith, and approaching SoTL *in* faith.

### *Approaching the Scholarship of Teaching and Learning With Faith*

If teaching can be an act and expression of faith, and we believe it is, then the scholarship of teaching can also be a means by which we act faithfully and express faith. We come to our scholarship as faithful persons, bringing a faith that has been shaped, formed, and informed by our convictions and practices. Although there are many ways that faith brings texture to our work, we want to highlight four: our understanding of vocation, a sense of wonder, an honest humility, and a faithful presence.

**Vocation.** Robert Nicholson, president emeritus of Anderson University, was fond of saying that the place to find God's will for your life is at the intersection of your abilities and your opportunities.[30] He had in mind something much larger than just discovering "the color of your parachute;" he saw that intersection of gifts and opportunities as a calling from God, as our vocation. Viewing our scholarship as a calling lends a certain steadfastness and focus to our work, providing a deeper significance than just something to do in order to get promoted. Honestly, there is a very short shelf life to that approach. Rather, if you are truly called to the scholarship of teaching and learning, it becomes for you a sacramental act, a very real and deep expression of your faith, a life-giving linkage between your work and your worship. There may be times when this realization alone will sustain you.

Having a deep sense of calling can texture your work in other ways, too. For example, you might feel called to a certain institution or a certain fellowship rather than to the academy. If so, there is likely to be a sacrifice in terms of compensation. In higher education, most professors trade money for time. That is, very few get rich, but one is granted a good deal of discretionary time . . . time needed for scholarship, reflection, and discourse. All of us are thankful that we do not punch a time clock. But in most faith-based institutions, it seems like less time is granted (higher teaching loads) for less money (lower salary scales). Many faculty members in faith-based institutions joke that they are doing missionary work. In some ways, of course, this is true and not a joke at all. We know of colleagues who answered a deep and real call to a specific place of service only to discover that they did not have the support and resources in place to do the kind of research they were prepared to do. So, believing deeply that they were in the right place, they shifted their scholarly agenda to the scholarship of teaching, richly contributing to their discipline while traveling a different road than what they had originally envisioned. When we approach the scholarship of teaching as an act of faith, it can be both a serious response to a sense of calling and an answer to earnest prayer.

**Wonder.** The wonder that comes with faith can also lend texture to the scholarship of teaching. When we embrace the reality that God is the creator and sustainer of all that is, and is still present and active, how else can we approach learning except with a deep curiosity and a reverent wonder about how things work, how things are connected, and how we live and learn and make our way together on this earth? Wonder compels us to approach our scholarship with care, and with a sense of mystery and majesty—a "Holy Wow—isn't that cool!" Wonder pushes us to ask honest questions—why is it that way, why didn't that work, and what if we tried this?

Wonder prompts us to ask ultimate questions, too, embracing the mystery and paradox of life together. Wonder ushers in the reality that we are about something far bigger than a job or the lesson of the day, that we are somehow tending a holy garden. When we pursue the scholarship of teaching and learning with wonder, it brings an added dimension of depth and significance to our work.[31]

**Humility.** We know that humility is far easier to write about than to practice. Recently, we heard a friend say, "I have been working on my humility, but no one noticed so I quit." Sadly, he wasn't joking. We see far too many Christian scholars working on their résumés rather than their humility; it is easier to get noticed. And of course what we might call the cognitive infrastructure of the academy—the ways we think—seem to promote self-promotion. We all know of colleagues who constantly promote their own work. They usually become a joke on their own campus, and their behavior sometimes borders on incivility. Perhaps we know of colleagues who find devious ways to take credit for their students' work as well, inflating their CVs, but at the cost of both their reputation and their character.

It is far better to let your work speak for itself. Nathan Hatch cautions that scholars are particularly subject to two deadly vices—autonomy and pride—and he observes that academe suffers greatly as a result.[32] If Christian scholars have anything to contribute to and model for the larger academy, it should be humility. As the Jacobsens note, "Christian scholarship, according to Boyer, is at its best when it is humbly and almost invisibly immersed within the larger academy."[33] We agree.

Humility improves the scholarship of teaching and learning in at least three ways. First, we must confess that we do not know everything; we all have so much to learn. That knowledge pushes us to keep asking questions about learning and presses us for improvement, to bring our scholarly habits of mind to the instructional task. There is always much to learn and understand. In other words, humility can contribute to a posture of lifelong learning. Second, humility permits us to see and learn from our neighbor, what many call *the other*.[34] It is so easy to develop a kind of superiority complex, becoming isolated inside our own little fellowship or circle. We stop asking for help or seeking new perspectives. Humbly recognizing that we can learn from those who do not believe and live as we do can be liberating, opening up new worlds of knowledge. It is truly a thin place where humility and grace walk hand in hand. Finally, humility adds texture to the scholarship of teaching and learning when we acknowledge that we might be wrong and someone else might be right. We approach our critique of the work of other scholars with respect and grace. It permits us to approach scholarship as a mutually beneficial discourse rather than as a competitive, winner-take-all game. Civility grounded in humility makes us better scholars and teachers—and gives life to the department, too.

**Faithful presence.** As persons of faith, we do at times bring a perspective to scholarship that others do not have, and this perspective can make a real contribution to the scholarly process. For example, one of us recently reviewed a book containing a chapter on Ernest Boyer's work and life. Surprisingly, the chapter omitted to mention his personal or public faith; perhaps the author simply ignored Boyer's faith or judged it to be inconsequential to his public work. Honestly, the chapter was well written and heavily documented, but it remains an incomplete piece of scholarship.

A Christian scholar could make three helpful contributions to this scholarship, starting by simply pointing out that the chapter makes no mention of Boyer's personal faith, an element you believe is important in understanding Boyer's public life. Without such acknowledgement, the work is, at best, incomplete. This step would take courage, to be sure, but it could be done in humility and with civility. Second, you could go further, explaining how Boyer's convictions, deeply grounded and rooted in his faith, influenced his understanding of learning, public service, and the connection of all things, among other elements. In other words, you could not only critique the scholarly work, but also expand and strengthen it.

Finally, you could work to strengthen scholarly practice by arguing that a person's worldviews and visions of the good life, particularly as they involve education, should be examined in any profile of a life of public service. We are not promoting reductionism here, where everything gets reduced to one's worldview, but we believe that without understanding a person's ultimate frames of reference, the portraits we paint will always lack depth and perspective. People of faith bring to their scholarly tasks a keen awareness of how perspective influences thinking, particularly that of critical theorists, some literary critics, and many social scientists. Attuned in this way, people of faith can make legitimate contributions to the scholarship of teaching and learning.

## Approaching the Scholarship of Teaching and Learning About Faith

We approach the scholarship of teaching and learning not only with faith, but also to learn more about faith. We learn about how faith develops, how instruction influences faith development, and how learning is promoted or inhibited by faith. There has been an energetic discussion about faith and learning over the past several decades, but participants have focused more on faith than on learning, and recently more on teaching practices and influences than on student learning outcomes. That's where the scholarship of teaching and learning comes into play. Recalling the difference between scholarly teaching and the scholarship of teaching, SoTL moves beyond teaching tasks to bring scholarly habits of mind to bear on the teaching process, habits that are public, peer-reviewed, and helpful to the academic community. We suggest that bringing the scholarship of teaching and learning to bear on the faith-and-learning discussion will push the conversation forward in helpful ways.

In 2002, Arlin Migliazzo and associates brought forward a wonderful book, *Teaching As an Act of Faith: Theory and Practice in Church-Related Higher Education,* offering insights into the faith-and-learning process in fourteen college courses.[35] We recommend this book to professors who want to see examples of their colleagues who bring faith to the academic disciplines in the social sciences, natural sciences, fine arts, and humanities, focusing in each case on what we call faithful teaching. In every chapter, we see scholarly opportunities to push the conversation further, not only to address the art and craft of teaching, but to ask questions about the impact of pedagogy on faith development and how to measure it, on what approaches produced intended results and why, on what approaches improved learning outcomes, and how they did so. In other words, this book, written by faithful expert teachers, could be the stepping-stone for the scholarship of teaching in a particular academic discipline.[36]

Faculty can also introduce spiritual formation practices in the classroom as ways to bring faith to bear on teaching and learning. In *Teaching and Christian Practices,* ten teachers tell how they incorporated Christian practices in their courses and the results they saw. The intent was not to focus on empirical validation or to develop generalizable data but to focus "upon 'thick' narratives and thoughtful connections between practices and pedagogy—our intentional aim from the outset was to illuminate and explore possibilities and potential."[37]

The next step, of course, is for scholars of teaching and learning to move the conversation forward with generalizable data and empirical validation. The introduction of spiritual formation practices in the classroom is an area ripe for bringing faith and scholarship together, an area needing both models for faith-integration and reportable results. For an example of how to advance pedagogy to the level of scholarship (peer review, critical critique, and usability in the academic community), see how K. Jo-Ann Badley and Ken Badley employed *lectio divina* (Latin for divine reading), a traditional Benedictine practice including reading of Scripture, meditation, and prayer, in the classroom (expert teaching), and then published the results (scholarship).[38]

We are suggesting here that much fertile ground remains for approaching the scholarship of teaching and learning with faith in mind as part of discussions about faith integration that take place daily in the various university disciplines, in the application of Christian practices in the classroom, and even in those instances where the call is to take a postmodern stance and look beyond integration.[39] This dimension of academic work offers an open venue for helpful and hopeful scholarship that is public, critically reviewed, and effectively presented.

### Approaching the Scholarship of Teaching and Learning in Faith

We have discussed coming to the scholarship of teaching and learning with faith and offered some strategies for pursuing scholarship about faith. We end this chapter with a few comments about practicing scholarship *in* faith. Jacques Maritain described a professor's role as that of a "ministerial agent in the learning process."[40] We like that characterization very much. Being a professor is a ministry, a vocation, a calling. And part of the professorial role is to be a scholar, implying that our work be public, be open to critical review, and be useful to the academy. We trust that we have provided a way forward if you choose, after moving from being an expert teacher to a scholarly teacher, to make the scholarship of teaching and learning your scholarly agenda. As we noted earlier, there is a way forward, and higher education desperately needs dedicated scholars who come to their profession with purpose and faith, and who have the skills and inclinations to study about faith.

So, what does it mean to come to your work in faith? In *Scholarship Assessed,* Charles Glassick, Mary Taylor Huber, and Gene Maeroff suggest that there are three essential qualities of a scholar: integrity, perseverance, and courage.[41] We find this trilogy particularly fitting for those who work in faith-based institutions. Our faith calls for integrity that is both personal and professional. It calls us to be truth-tellers, to act with humility, and to serve with passion. It calls us to work with the long view in mind, to persevere and lean into the prevailing wind, because we serve with a sense of calling to a special task and to a particular place. We know that there are eternal aspects in our work, too—we are about something far greater than working to pad our own résumés. That gives us hope. And when we have an eternal perspective and when we sense a true calling in our work, we find that—along with faith—comes the courage to be who we are called to be, the courage to know that we are all wounded, and the courage to follow and flourish where we are called to be. Like Abraham, we obey and go, even though we do not always know where we are going.[42]

Integrity, perseverance, and courage. These three virtues sustain our work as scholars, even as they are made evident in the daily practice of our faith in the One who calls us.

# The Scholarship of Discovery and Integration

While looking at data from national faculty surveys from the 1970s and 1980s in preparation for writing *College: The Undergraduate Experience in America,*[1] Boyer became convinced that something was wrong in the academic guild and something needed to be said about it. As president of the Carnegie Foundation for the Advancement of Teaching, he was certainly in a prime position to do so. First, he found a good deal of confusion about research and scholarship. Were they, in fact, the same thing? Could a professor be accepted as a legitimate member of an academic community, that is, promoted and tenured as a scholar without being a researcher, too? If so, how? If not, why not? Should tenure be reserved only for original researchers? Does the academy have a place for scholars who put the research of others into some broader context or synthesize findings from disparate disciplines?

He concluded that the "professoriate [was] a profession of many cultures" and that it was time to recognize and reward these cultures differently. He concluded that "while not all professors are or should be publishing researchers, they, nonetheless, should be first-rate *scholars*."[2] And he argued then that to reflect the reality of practice, the definition of and support for scholarship needed a radical expansion.

This confusion, Boyer came to believe, fed into a much larger problem—the pervasive discouragement of the faculty. In his view, renewal was sorely needed. Nearly half the faculty surveyed by the Carnegie Foundation in 1975 and 1984 said they would consider leaving the profession if they were offered another job outside the academy.[3] Sadly, decades on, we have no reason to believe that the percentage would be any lower today. In fact, this figure might be higher today, given the impact of the economic downturn of 2008 (particularly the dramatic decline in the public's willingness and ability to pay for higher education and the downsizing of full time faculties in many institutions), the growing public criticisms of higher education, the increase in competition from within and without, and the pressure to incorporate new technologies and modes of instruction.

Boyer became convinced that the time had come to reconsider scholarship and realign the reward and recognition structures in higher education. In his view, such reconsideration and realignment, if achieved, would give new life to the professoriate and the academy. Thus, he wrote *Scholarship Reconsidered* in 1990, arguing for recognition of the scholarship of integration, application, and teaching in addition to the scholarship of discovery (research). We addressed the scholarship of teaching in Chapter Five and will consider the scholarship of engagement (service) in the following chapter. Here, we focus on the two traditional forms of research—discovery and integration. We will say more about the scholarship of integration, particularly as it relates to promotion and tenure decisions, because discovery is such a dominant mode of inquiry in higher education and much has been written about this type of scholarship (research) and Christian faith. Integration receives less attention than any of the dimensions of Boyer's conception of scholarship, and a large cultural divide remains to be bridged.

## The Scholarship of Discovery

Considering the scholarship of discovery, on Boyer's account, research not only adds to the stock of human knowledge, but it also enriches the instructional environment of the university (a claim forcefully contradicted by a major meta-analysis, as John Hattie and H. W. Marsh found "zero" connection[4]). This debate continues. Boyer himself traces the introduction and subsequent narrowing of the term *research* between its introduction in the 1870s and 1990, the date of his landmark publication. Boyer and those who have followed in his tradition have concerned themselves with the tendency of the academy to define scholarship in terms of research alone, as if the two were coextensive.[5] Boyer sees this equation producing "a more restricted view of scholarship, one that limits it to a hierarchy of functions. Basic research has come to be viewed as a first and most essential form of scholarly activity, with other functions flowing from it. Scholars are academics who conduct research, publish, and then perhaps convey their knowledge to students or apply what they have learned. The latter functions grow *out of* scholarship; they are not to be considered a part of it. But knowledge is not necessarily developed in such a linear manner."[6] If this citation were to appear in next week's *Chronicle of Higher Education*, few readers would respond with "that sounds dated!" In other words, the problem Boyer identified still warrants discussion.

Of course, Boyer was not opposed in any way to the scholarship of discovery. It is significant, and in fact, essential—something for which higher education is held in high esteem. Discovery and originality bring a status and standing to the faculty member, too—as they should. There is genuine excitement associated with discovering and presenting something new, and this excitement is contagious, energizing departments and institutions. For this reason (among others), the academy has long granted "high value to originality in scholarship."[7] Some faculty in all types of institutions should pursue discovery scholarship, Boyer argues. However, it is clear that research activity and productivity vary across academic disciplines and types of institutions—being well-suited and supported in some, but less so in others. For example, in the humanities and in professional programs, the focus on research as original discovery can be disturbingly limiting, leaving little room for work in interdisciplinary areas or at the edges of the disciplines. And obviously, originality (in the fine arts, for example) implies much more than simply discovering something new.

Unfortunately, such work can be devalued or ignored in the promotion and tenure process, particularly in a one-size-fits-all evaluation system.

The support for doing original research in R1 institutions is much more abundant than in most teaching universities and community colleges. In fact, the resources and support structures are purposely aligned to promote discovery. It is unnecessary and certainly unfair to evaluate every scholar, regardless of discipline, assignment, and institution by the same restrictive discovery standard. It is this misalignment of expectations, resources, and rewards that Boyer sees as problematic.[8]

## The Scholarship of Integration

Boyer's concern for the renewal of the professoriate and his belief in the connectedness of all things drove his call for the academy to reconsider and expand the definition of scholarship, particularly to include integrative scholarship. In his view, we have found ourselves in the midst of an intellectual sea change as dramatic as the nineteenth-century shift in which science displaced philosophy at the top of the hierarchy of knowledge. "Today, interdisciplinary *and* integrative studies, long on the edges of academic life, are moving toward the center, responding both to new intellectual questions and to pressing human problems," he wrote. "As the boundaries of human knowledge are being dramatically reshaped, the academy surely must give increased attention to the *scholarship of integration*."[9]

Boyer underscores the need for faculty who "give meaning to isolated facts, putting them in perspective . . . making connections across disciplines, placing the specialties in larger context, illuminating data in a revealing way, often educating non-specialists, too."[10] Integrative scholarship also involves doing research at the boundaries, where disciplinary divisions make no sense. Knowledge is much too complex to be neatly organized into discrete neighborhoods. Rather, we need to view knowledge as located in the public square, accessible from many avenues. And finally, the scholarship of integration implies that faculty work to fit their own intellectual work and the work of others into larger conversations and intellectual patterns, serving as an antidote to narrowness and overspecialization. For Boyer, "those engaged in discovery ask, 'What is known, what is yet to be found?' Those engaged in integration ask, 'What do the findings *mean*? Is it possible to interpret what's been discovered in ways that provide a larger, more comprehensive understanding?'"[11] Obviously, Boyer argues, these questions call for critical skills in scholarship and should have their own legitimacy. On his account, scholars who engage carefully in the scholarship of integration move naturally "from information to knowledge and even, perhaps to wisdom."[12] That, for Boyer, is education's pearl of great price.

## A Profession of Many Cultures

When Boyer described the American professoriate as a profession of many cultures (in 1987), he no doubt was thinking about C. P. Snow, a British scientist-turned-author who in 1959 described his experience with scientists and writers as follows:

> There have been plenty of days when I have spent the working hours with scientists and then gone off at night with some literary colleagues. I mean that through living among these groups and much more, I think, through moving regularly from one to the other and back again that I got occupied with the problem of what, long before I put it on paper, I christened to myself as the "two cultures." For constantly I felt I was moving among two groups—comparable in intelligence, identical in race, not grossly different in social origin, earning about the same incomes, who had almost ceased to communicate at all, who in intellectual, moral and psychological climate had so little in common that instead of going from Burlington House or South Kensington to Chelsea, one might have crossed an ocean.
>
> In fact, one had travelled much further than across an ocean—because after a few thousand Atlantic miles, one found Greenwich Village talking precisely the same language as Chelsea, and both having about as much communication with M.I.T. as though the scientists spoke nothing but Tibetan."[13]

Tibetan, indeed!

It is plausible to think that this "two cultures" problem might be improving due to our use of technology but, if anything, the problem seems to be getting worse. Technology, with its connective properties, has allowed us to become even more isolated; we talk almost exclusively to those who already speak our language.[14] The lyricists and the empiricists remain siloed. We apparently need better translation software. Ken A. Dill argues that for interdisciplinary cooperation to succeed, researchers in different fields need to recognize and respect each other's differing cultures.[15] It is difficult to respect what one does not understand . . . or what one does not know exists. Two scholars in the molecular medical field point to Snow's attempt to diminish the misunderstanding, mistrust, and miscommunication between writers and scientists, saying,

> One of his aims was to promote cooperation between these two cultures in spite of their different perspectives and values. Forty years later, when molecular biology has come to full fruition and molecular medicine has begun to blossom, it is not too much of an exaggeration to speak in a similar way of the "two cultures" of doctors and laboratory scientists, MDs and PhDs.[16]

C. P. Snow identified the problem of academic silos; today we have silos inside silos. We need Boyer's call for integrative scholarship more now than ever.[17]

In fact, we can speak of two cultures on our campuses in many ways—sciences and humanities, professional programs and liberal arts, natural and social sciences, junior and senior faculty, graduate and undergraduate faulty, faculty and administrators, and students and faculty to name just a few. And, of course, the two cultures (or many cultures) become evident during promotion and tenure committee deliberations. The results can be confusing and hurtful to those under review. We will focus on promotion and tenure committees in the next portion of this chapter. Here, we simply note that we earnestly believe the whole academy needs to recognize and affirm the different cultures that thrive on our campuses. As Snow cautioned, "Closing the gap between our cultures is a necessity in the most abstract intellectual sense, as well as in the most practical. When those two senses have grown apart, then no society is going to be able to think with wisdom."[18] We paraphrase Snow this way: if we do not respect the other cultures on our campuses, we will not be able to think with wisdom or treat others with grace and dignity. We will lose the pearl of great price.

## The Scholarship of Confusion

The work of bridging the cultural divides on our campuses is neither for the timid nor the tired, and some in academic circles have never accepted Boyer's vision of scholarship. Note, for example, this 2002 title, "Is Boyer Misguided or Misused? The Scholarship of Confusion."[19] Alan Rubin, the author of that article, believes that it is a bit of both. He worries that the four dimensions of scholarship are easier to define than to understand and apply, and those who use a Boyer approach to support their scholarship for review will face questions of validity and reliability. Rubin gives three reasons for this concern: (1) the fear that in a Boyer framework everything will be offered as scholarship; for example, advising a student group or chairing a convention gathering will become the scholarship of engagement. (2) The overlapping nature of Boyer's four dimensions could result in trying to fit a square peg in a round hole; for example, if advising a student group does not count as the scholarship of engagement for the tenure committee, maybe it will be offered instead as the scholarship of teaching. And even more distressing to Rubin: (3) departments and committees may just look to see if the work offered fits into one of Boyer's categories while omitting to assess the quality, impact, and value of the scholarship.[20] He offers an example of a department that argued a candidate for tenure had nine publications when, in fact, the faculty member had written an op-ed piece in a local newspaper that was later republished by eight other newspapers![21]

The Boyer model of scholarship, argues Rubin, "creates problems of consistency and quality of expectations as guidelines may occur for reasons other than quality (e.g., such as by contending that a publication record is a true example of the Boyer model rather than focusing on the quality, significance, and impact of the work contained within that record)."[22] When this happens, criteria and justification become uneven at best, and could lead to renaming questionable research activities with labels such as "public scholarship" or the "scholarship of practice."

Rubin concludes that "all this leads to *the scholarship of confusion*. It fosters the potential for superficial work, isolation and division, and the lack of common or shared values, as faculty and units are unable to explain, support, understand, or appreciate each other's definitions and criteria of significant and productive scholarship. If universities choose to go the Boyer route without careful implementation and application of consistent standards of assessment, scholarship and faculties will be of uneven quality and substance, creating a mosaic of shattered tiles."[23]

We quote at length from this article because it illustrates so well the concerns that people express when different cultures collide on campus, even on faith-based campuses, particularly during the promotion and tenure review process. In the next portion of this chapter, we will present some strategies to address questions and concerns regarding the Boyer model in general and the scholarship of integration in particular. We move to the next section without wanting to minimize the concerns Rubin and others have raised; their concerns are real (but not new). Academics have always disagreed about what counts as scholarship and what is superfluous. Colleges always deal with fears that some departments are weak or devious, and faculty inevitably find themselves suspicious that a few colleagues are cunning, sneaky, incompetent, or just plain lazy. Yet, in thirty years, we have found this to be the case rarely, and we believe that grace is a great leveler.

The Boyer model will not make suspicion, fear, or incivility go away, but it does provide a way forward for those who honestly and earnestly desire to see a university or college fulfill its teaching mission. We do agree with Rubin that the best prescription for the scholarship of confusion is the "careful implementation and application of consistent standards of assessment."[24] In fact, such implementation and application could be a large part of the cure.

# Promotion and Tenure Considerations

## *Committees*

As a faculty member, you should keep in mind that promotion and tenure committees usually have your best interests in mind. They are not the enemy. Of course, there are stories of feuds, fears, and fights during tenure deliberations, but they are honestly rarer than what hallway mythology might lead you to believe. However, academics love to regale their colleagues with these kinds of stories, and they become larger than life.[25] It is always good to ask, "Now, when did this happen?" However, in fairness, peer committees (and sometimes deans and provosts) can lack a certain sophistication and understanding of integrative scholarship, even though they may be supportive of integrative efforts. A faculty member submitting integrative work needs to approach the review committee with a disciplined strategy, one that has been sustained over time and that demonstrates that the portfolio is all of a piece, that it represents the current state of a lifetime's *oeuvre*. In other words, the faculty member cannot hatch a portfolio a week or two before submitting the materials for review.

Peer committees for tenure and promotion are comprised of colleagues from different academic disciplines, particularly on smaller campuses with smaller raw numbers of faculty. Most campuses have committee selection criteria in place to ensure that various academic divisions and schools are represented on the committee, guaranteeing voices from across the faculty. Perhaps unfortunately, these criteria also guarantee that few of the committee members may be knowledgeable about your scholarly work or your approach to it. The process will require that you not only explain your vita, but also your scholarly agenda, how you go about doing your scholarship, the impact and importance of your work, why you devote your time to it, and what steps you will take next. The committee will not figure these answers out by themselves, so the faculty member must tell them precisely what they need to know to judge the portfolio soundly.

Such detail and clarity are especially imperative when the faculty member takes an approach to scholarship that may be less familiar to committee members, such as the scholarship of integration. When uncertain, committees often fall back to a more general means of assessment, focusing on the concept of *sufficient momentum,* even though they may know very little physics. An explanation is in order. Review committees first work to satisfy themselves that a scholarly vita represents sufficient mass to be considered acceptable for advancement. In physics, mass = density × volume. Committee members must determine that, taken as a whole, the scholarship presented has enough density (concreteness, gravitas, substance, content) and in sufficient volume (appropriate for that discipline) to be judged adequate for advancement.

But there's more. Momentum = mass × velocity. In other words, a mass has momentum when it is moving—going somewhere. The committee will want to see that the applicant's scholarship not only has mass, but also has velocity, that it is moving in a specific direction, a sustained scholarly agenda, if you will. Taken together, a scholarship portfolio needs to document density, volume, and velocity—indicating *sufficient momentum* to convince a peer committee of nonphysicists that the faculty member has planned, prepared, and completed his or her work effectively.

It is best to assume that the review committee is unfamiliar with the scholarship of integration, and there may be a skeptical member or two. The key, according to Cole Dawson, a senior academic officer, is to "document, document, document. I've reviewed promotion portfolios that contained literally hundreds of pieces in this category."[26] Now, we're not certain that hundreds of pieces are needed (we do not advocate the Mongolian Horde approach to documentation and caution against including thank-you notes from students as evidence), but Dawson's advice is spot on. How, then, does one document the scholarship of integration?

### Documenting Integrative Scholarship

A good place to start is to consult John H. Braxton, William Luckey, and Patricia Helland's *Institutionalizing a Broader View of Scholarship Through Boyer's Four Domains.* They provide a number of examples of the scholarship of integration, making the helpful distinction between unpublished scholarly outcomes (a talk on a current disciplinary topic given to alumni, a high school, a service organization, or a local television station) and publications (books, literature reviews, or journal articles on interdisciplinary topics).[27] And Carole Barbato offers these examples of integrative scholarship. We quote:

- Refereed journal articles synthesizing/interpreting literature in a specialized area of communication (including meta-analyses).
- Scholarly books or book chapters synthesizing and integrating scholarship in a communication area or linking it to findings in another discipline.
- Classroom textbooks that serve to explain original research or theories bringing new insights or perspectives to others.
- Nonacademic publications in trade magazines that provide interpretations of research to non-specialists.
- Videotape or computer materials to explain the synthesis or integration of theory in a classroom, workshop, or training setting.
- Interdisciplinary courses or workshops.
- Convention papers/panels that cut across divisions or special interest groups.
- Campus-wide colloquia. Interdisciplinary conferences.
- Invited presentations/keynote addresses because of one's reputation in the scholarship of integration.[28]

Note that in addition to the standard fare of scholarly books and refereed journal articles, Barbato includes textbooks, trade magazines, convention papers, presentations, and colloquia as fair game. Particularly with work appearing in this latter list, the committee will need to see documentation if they are to give full consideration to your integrative work in these venues. You must explain why that scholarship in such venues is important.

When documenting the validity and value of integrative scholarship, the faculty member must understand the means by which it will be evaluated. If your institution does not have published evaluation criteria, we suggest providing them with Barbato's recommended evaluation criteria for integration:

### Criteria for Integration

- Book or article
- Adequate synthesis of literature
- Adequate educational background
- Appropriate methods and results
- Effective presentation
- Meta-analysis or convention paper
- Thorough review
- Appropriate statistics and follow-up tests
- Other materials
- Peer review of goal attainment
- Reflective essay[29]

It is perfectly appropriate for a faculty member to suggest the criteria by which his or her scholarship should be evaluated (like others in the same field of work), then make the case that the criteria have been met. Do not leave it up to the committee to connect the dots. Draw them a picture.

Some committees also use a "significant results" standard, meaning that the scholar must demonstrate or document that her work has produced just that: significant results. Mordechai Gordon offers three helpful criteria (questions) for determining significance: (1) To what extent is the status quo shaken by raising questions and challenging old assumptions? (2) Is the scholar's perspective particularly interesting and helpful? and (3) Does the work make informative and useful connections across disciplinary boundaries? While not specific, these criteria do offer a way to discuss your work's strengths with the review committee and/or dean. Gordon believes that significance is documented as long as the faculty member has met one of the three criteria.[30]

We recommend that, even if not required, you should prepare a portfolio of your integrative scholarship. This will force you to think about how to organize and present your work to the committee most effectively.

Anne Hofmeyer, Mandi Newton, and Cathie Scott suggest that health sciences scholars develop a five- to eight-page portfolio with four sections: (1) philosophy and goals; (2) how your work contributes to the scholarship of integration and application; (3) critical reflections and scholarly assessment; and (4) supporting documentation and appendices.[31] This outline certainly has applicability outside the health sciences. In some settings, the portfolio must adhere to a stipulated template. In others, faculty members may craft their own portfolio according to the structure of their choosing. In those cases, we recommend creativity.

## Closing Comments

Before moving on to a discussion of how Christian faith can be brought to the scholarship of integration, several comments are in order. First, we believe that the scholarship of integration (or interdisciplinarity) is critical because it best responds to the complexity we see in our organizations and communities today, and it serves as a counterbalance to the pervasive narrowness we see in disciplinary specialization today. We highly recommend Marcia Bundy Seabury's thoughtful and inspiring article "Interdisciplinarity: Some Possibilities and Guidelines"[32] to anyone interested in the scholarship of integration. Advice, insight, and encouragement are all there.

Second, it is important to develop and sustain a meta-rationale and strategy for your integrative scholarship. Such a strategy must start years before any formal review for promotion or tenure. Integrative scholarship is a marathon, not a dash. Looking at a portfolio of "last minute scholarship," one review committee member commented, "Big hat, no cattle." Such critiques can be avoided with planned, sustained scholarly effort. Again, this approach to scholarship has at its foundation a view that an academic career is not only a career, it is a vocation, a lifelong response to a voice. Many academic workers talk about vocation. For those who name Christ, academic work is a way to respond to God's voice. For the Christian faculty member, writing essays and assembling a portfolio for tenure and promotion can become a time of reflection and celebration of continued—indeed, lifelong—work and participation in God's work of blessing the world.

Finally, if you are drawn to the wonder of the connectedness of all things (as was Ernest Boyer), then you will find the pursuit of the scholarship of integration to be motivating, nourishing, and sustaining. With Paul, we believe that in Christ all things hold together (Col. 1:17), not just the physical universe but the academic universe as well. To note the work of Reformed scholar, Herman Dooyeweerd, the academic disciplines represent the many aspects of the world God made (chemical, biotic, number, etc.) and of human society (social, psychological, economic, etc.).[33] If either Paul or Dooyeweerd has it right, to engage in integrative, academic work is to engage with—and wonder at—the very fabric of what God has made.[34]

## The Christian Faith and the Scholarship of Integration

Throughout this book, we have noted the variety of models and understandings of the integration of faith and learning, suggesting that there is no one best way or only way to do so. Ultimately, we have come to believe that faith-learning integration is a local, particular undertaking, and we will say more about that undertaking in Chapter Ten. Much has been written about scholarship and faith or *Christian scholarship* over the past two decades,[35] so we will not attempt to re-create that conversation or critique it here other than to say that it has been a yeasty conversation, focusing largely on traditional forms of research. Because much less has been written about faith-learning integration and the scholarship of integration, we will focus our remarks here on how those who name Christ can faithfully approach that mode of scholarship. As one of our students put it, "This is not rocket surgery!"

The Gospel of John speaks of the incarnation, telling us that the Word became flesh and dwelt among us, full of grace and truth (John 1:14). Of course, we all desire that our scholarship will be incarnational in some way; that the spirit of our work will find places to dwell and be taken seriously.[36] We pray that it will be full of grace and truth, too, and we are thankful for the knowledge that it has been done before. From John's writings, we lift three themes—light, majesty, and awe—and we use them to frame some thoughts about faithfully engaging in the scholarship of integration.

## *Light*

A light shining in the darkness brings hope. Recall how bright a candle looks in a dark room, and remember how much we appreciate a flashlight when we make our way along a path in the woods on a dark night. Light is good. We suggest that the scholarship of integration can be a light of sorts, too. When you work at the edges of your discipline or across disciplinary boundaries, you travel in remote, unknown, and uncertain territory, often in the dark. Integrative scholarship sheds light and brings attention to aspects of the disciplines (both persons and ideas) that are out of the way; it builds bridges between isolated territories where there has been little interaction. It is a conversation starter. Such work should not be underestimated, and the Christian scholar does not need somehow to throw Jesus into the mix to Christianize it. He is already there. Bringing light to dark places, making connections, starting conversations, highlighting the good work of others on the margins, and developing new understandings is holy work, full of grace and truth. If you faithfully use your gifts, opportunities, and insights to bring light and life to those who journey with you, faith integration is happening. So, do your very best work and let your light shine.

We do not mean to say, however, that you have to be silent or secret about your faith. As you bring light to your discipline, let your faith dwell there, too. At times and in certain instances, those who claim Christ see and understand things differently to be sure, and Christian faith can certainly guide a person's decisions about what scholarship to pursue, why to pursue it, and what to say about it. It is perfectly appropriate to do so. The key, we believe, is to be full of both truth and grace. Living a grace-full life shapes us and demands a deeper humility. As Christians, we have confidence that we see and we know, but we must humbly confess that we see and know only in part (1 Cor. 13:12). Letting your light shine means that one speaks in faith, with faith, and about faith . . . with humble confidence. The rub in the guild (and even more so on our own campuses) is that some Christians speak with intolerant, absolute certainty, diminishing or ignoring other voices, even other Christian voices. Such intellectual intolerance is just a sophisticated form of meanness.

## *Majesty*

We have suggested that integrative scholarship can bring light and life to the margins of a discipline and forge new connections between apparently incongruent areas of study. As new connections are made and new ways of understanding become obvious, both the academy and the world around it can see more clearly the connectedness of all things (to use again the phrase that Boyer loved). Each discovery and insight pushes us toward a deeper appreciation for the majesty of all creation. There is so much we do not know, but the more we learn, the more we understand that things do knit together in a beautiful way. Oliver Wendell Holmes said that "for the simplicity on this side of complexity, he wouldn't give a fig, but for the simplicity on the other side of complexity, he would give a lifetime."[37] Of course, so would we, all of us. The scholarship of integration, at its best, brings clarity and simplicity to complexity and confusion, reflecting the majesty of God and all that is. Christians have every right to point this out.

## *Awe*

When integrative scholarship directs our attention to the majesty of God, how can we who name Christ respond? Certainly, we can respond with wonder, admiration, amazement, surprise, and astonishment, to name just a few possibilities. We can point out to our colleagues and our students that what we are seeing and experiencing is the unfolding of a divine mystery, and it is truly amazing! When we bring that sense of wonder into the classroom, it is inviting and contagious, a lesson remembered by our students long after the lesson of the day has been forgotten. And a sense of awe is also appropriate in our writing, too.

A second response to the majesty of God's creation is admiration, respect, esteem, and veneration. Beyond the "wow" is a very deep appreciation for the magnificent mind of God and a profound respect for what we find unfolding in our scholarly work. Good integrative scholarship provides a connection to things far beyond what we can fully imagine or explain, but it is real nonetheless. It is appropriate for Christian scholars to say that, too.

Finally, along with the holy "wow" and the awareness of profound admiration comes a certain reverence, a sense that the work you are doing is indeed holy. Your scholarship is a form of worship, bringing together your preparation, talents, inclinations, insights, and opportunities for the glory of God. It seems to us that this is faith-learning integration at its very best, being a faithful presence, doing what you have prepared and love to do, all with a sense of wonder, admiration, and reverence.

"But whoever lives by the truth comes into the light, so that it may be seen plainly that what they have done has been done in the sight of God." (John 3:21, NIV)

Integration, indeed!

## Chapter 7

# The Scholarship of Engagement

In 1990, when Ernest Boyer asked the academy to reconsider and expand the meaning of scholarship, he started a robust conversation, one that continues to this day.[1] In the intervening years, some colleges and individuals have put the policies and practices in place to realize Boyer's vision, but his ideas have met resistance, too, although much of it is passive opposition. What we have labeled a robust conversation could also be described as an ongoing battle, a cold war of sorts, with a broader understanding of faculty work at stake. Using that metaphor, the scholarship of discovery and integration reside in friendly and secure territory, while the scholarship of teaching remains in a demilitarized zone (DMZ), usually considered legitimate and mostly thought to be safe but still subject to an occasional sniper shot from one side or the other. The scholarship of engagement, unfortunately, exists in contested territory, with unpredictable local skirmishes and occasional frontal attacks. There is much more ground to gain, and Boyer's vision faces real resistance in this area.

Ninetta Santoro and Suzanne Snead studied faculty who came to academe from successful professional careers. If they held a doctorate (and most did not), they earned it in their 40s—in mid-career. Universities recruited them because they had much-needed field experience, and they came to teach and prepare professionals for that field. Many of them came with a very idealized notion of life as a professor on a university campus, one that involved walking through the quad, talking with colleagues in the coffee room, and meeting with students by a picturesque lake. Instead, they discovered a reward structure and promotion system not designed at all with career and clinical professionals in mind. They found they were expected to be researchers and felt totally ill-prepared for the task. The title of Santoro and Snead's article speaks volumes: "'I'm Not a Real Academic': A Career from Industry to Academe."[2] Even though this study comes from a public university in Australia, the sentiments expressed by the participants are very real to many faculty serving in faith-based institutions. People who are recruited for their field experience in a professional career, then arrive on campus to discover they are expected to perform research in order to be promoted can feel like they have been caught in a clear case of bait and switch.

Well, not exactly, but close. The good news is that there is a way forward. In this chapter, we will discuss the scholarship of engagement, a form of scholarship suggested by Boyer that clinical and field-experienced professionals are uniquely prepared to carry out. There are a few land mines to be avoided along the way, of course, but we will point them out. We will also suggest several ways to bring your faith to this domain of scholarship and talk specifically about strategies for promotion and tenure. We believe that, with persistent attention and care, you can successfully navigate the promotion and tenure process as a faithful, engaged scholar.

Those entering the university at mid-career, particularly in professional programs, can make an important scholarly contribution to the academy *and* be appreciated and recognized for doing so. The academy in general, and preservice professionals in particular, sorely need the experienced voices of such professionals. The challenge is to be faithful to your gifts and leverage your experience while attending to the concerns of your institution. This can be done.

## The Idea of an Engaged Academy

In 1990, when Boyer called for the reconsideration of scholarship to include the scholarship of application (he later adopted the term "scholarship of engagement"), he pointed to the long-standing tradition of public service in universities and noted that providing service to society by applying knowledge to real-world problems was one of the original arguments for including professional schools in the university. For Boyer, theory and practice renew each other, and the university needs both if it is to fulfill its mission and public commitments. He lamented that this tradition of linking theory and practice has declined, and professional schools have in large part taken on the prevailing culture of the academy—using research productivity as the means to demonstrate academic quality and credibility.

For Boyer, the scholarship of engagement meant "connecting the rich resources of the university to our most pressing social, civic, and ethical problems, to our children, to our schools, to our teachers, and to our cities."[3] To avoid irrelevance, campuses needed to be "staging grounds for action"[4] and always "directed toward larger, more humane ends."[5] Interestingly, Boyer did not envision that every faculty member (even all those in professional departments and programs) would necessarily focus on the scholarship of engagement. Rather, he envisioned that each department would become a rich "mosaic of talent"[6] with every faculty member working with his or her own set of gifts, skills, and interests in one of several scholarly areas. Boyer offered a broad vision of an academic community, engaged and focused on the most pressing social needs to create a better life for all.

Some in the academy have found his vision compelling. Obviously, others have not. Boyer considered the scholarship of engagement important because for him it held a promise to re-energize the university for the common good. After his death in 1995, others continued to advance his vision of the engaged campus. For example, Robert Bringle, Richard Games, and Edward Malloy paid tribute to Boyer while presenting their vision for colleges and universities to be thought of and to act as citizens, working to improve relationships between campus and communities.[7] A robust scholarship of engagement would certainly support such a vision.

At the same time, Boyer hastened to add that the scholarship of engagement is much more than just doing good, as important as that is. "To be considered *scholarship*," he insisted, "service activities must be tied directly to one's special field of knowledge, and relate to, and flow directly out of, this professional activity. Such activity is serious, demanding work, requiring the rigor—and the accountability—traditionally associated with research activities."[8] Simply put, engagement that would meet Boyer's criteria would entail more than leading a workshop or doing some consulting and calling it scholarship. Just as the scholarship of teaching flows from teaching but involves activities and reflection beyond the classroom, so too, the scholarship of engagement flows from service but has dimensions beyond specific acts of service. This is an oft-confused distinction—but a critical one. Consulting and serving on university committees, for example, are legitimate forms of professional engagement (service) and sorely needed professional activities, but they are not scholarship. Service (or engagement) and the scholarship of engagement are not the same thing; the scholarship of engagement is significantly more involved.

This distinction continues to confuse many faculty members. If service is different from scholarly engagement, how is it different? Glassick and his colleagues observe that "service no longer conjures up the image of the scholar in shirtsleeves, meeting the intellectual challenge of using the most advanced knowledge to address complex social and technical problems. Today service has become equated with committee work on campus or in professional associations, or volunteer work in the community."[9] Such activities are to be listed on the résumé under service, and all faculty members are expected to serve in such ways. Every promotion process we know of looks at instruction, research, and service (IRS) elements, but service is the least of these. Promotion committees view the absence of any service in a faculty portfolio as problematic, but in most settings a little service seems to go a long way. We report this without cynicism, but service rarely becomes a critical factor, mainly because almost any academic worth their salt can assemble an acceptable list of service activities, particularly given that just about anything seems to count.

The scholarship of engagement, if one pursues it, does not fit under the service category in the portfolio. It is a scholarly act, meeting certain specified criteria. In *Scholarship Assessed*, Charles Glassick and his colleagues surveyed fifty-one granting agencies and a host of publishers, as well as reviewing dozens of college and university policy manuals on hiring, promotion, and tenure to distill what scholarship—any form of scholarship—meant. They identified six essential characteristics, which we have mentioned at several points in this book and repeat here because they address such a fundamental issue for the scholarship of engagement: (1) clear goals, (2) adequate preparation, (3) appropriate methods, (4) significant results, (5) effective presentation, and (6) reflective critique. The authors of *Scholarship Assessed* wrote (in 1997) that these six criteria, when taken together, "provide a powerful conceptual framework to guide evaluation. Their very obviousness suggests their applicability to a broad range of intellectual projects."[10]

These six criteria still apply today; many institutions have adopted this list or a derivative of it for the evaluation of scholarship for promotion and tenure. In particular, state universities with missions devoted to service to state and nation have moved ahead in recognizing scholarship of engagement in service learning and extension work, and clearing houses have been established to assist in the evaluation of engagement scholarship. Although we began the chapter by noting that the scholarship of engagement remains in contested territory, the rudiments of a supportive infrastructure have begun to emerge.

But what does the scholarship of engagement look like on faith-based campuses, and how is it different from service? To address these questions, Braxton and colleagues provided a helpful distinction between scholarly activities (service, not scholarship) and scholarly outcomes (either published or unpublished—but documented and made public in some way) and listed some examples of each:

- **Scholarly activities for service:** service on a departmental program review committee or a university-wide curriculum committee; a study conducted to help solve a departmental problem or formulate a departmental policy; engagement in consulting off campus, or serving as an expert witness.
- **Unpublished scholarly outcomes:** development of an innovative technology, conducting a study for a local organization or governmental agency, or conducting a study to help solve a local or state problem.
- **Published scholarly outcomes:** an article that describes new knowledge obtained through the application of the knowledge and skill of one's academic discipline to a practical problem, an article that applies disciplinary knowledge to a practical problem, or an article reporting findings of research designed to solve practical problems.[11]

As with the scholarship of teaching and learning, the scholarship of engagement requires a second-level activity beyond the actual act of service. For example, if a management professor consults with a local organization to improve employee productivity, it is not, in and of itself, scholarship. It is service. However, if the professor utilizes a certain motivation theory, obtains and measures results in some way, reflects critically about those results, devises or confirms a theory to explain what happened, and makes the work accessible to the academy in some way (a published case study, white paper, or conference presentation), then it becomes an act of scholarship. The faculty member must bring disciplinary knowledge and skills as well as scholarly habits of mind to the issue. It is both a procedural and a cognitive step beyond service.

The same would be true for a nursing professor volunteering in a local clinic serving the homeless. It is certainly a generous and much-needed community service. The faculty member could reflect on the pattern of needs represented at the clinic and then write and present a paper suggesting ways for organizations to prepare better as they establish clinics in other communities. In this instance, the volunteer service is grounded in and an expression of pre-existing scholarship (professional nursing knowledge); it is the field test site for an emerging, scholarly hunch or idea (organizations should prepare in these ways); and it inspires the kernel of further reflection and scholarship (presentation, article). Similar examples could be provided for professors in a variety of professional programs: engineering, education, physical therapy, athletic training, journalism, and many others. The key to transforming service into the scholarship of engagement is to bring scholarly habits of mind to bear: make the work public, subject the work to critical review and reflection, make the work accessible and usable to the academy in some manner.[12]

This should come as good news for faculty members serving in professional programs who were hired for their clinical experience but who can relate to the article title, "I'm not a real academic." Well, you are! In fact, professional program faculty bring connections and resources to the scholarship of engagement that some in the academy must work without. Their field experience, knowledge, and skills give access to organizations, associations, and projects that both desperately need their help and welcome scholarly intervention. Such engagement provides a way to do good and to produce scholarship. And faith does not have to be left out of the process. In the next portion of this chapter, we will discuss some of the implications for pursuing the scholarship of engagement when it comes to institutional decisions about promotion and tenure. We will close this chapter by suggesting some ways that faith and scholarly engagement go hand in hand.

## The Scholarship of Engagement and the Promotion/Tenure Process

We start with the recognition that the scholarship of engagement is not for everyone, nor should it be. It is always important to consider how your scholarship agenda fits with the direction of your department or institution. Many departments attempt to demonstrate scholarship in all four of Boyer's dimensions or to specialize in just one. They view scholarship as a corporate activity. Far too often, faculty members act as though the department (or institution) were created solely for them, to support them in their singular work. This is rarely, if ever, the case. Scholarship is a team sport, not an individual running event and, as we have noted already, certainly not a sprint.

The scholarship of engagement (SoE) is hard work, a two-step process that combines expertise and application in the field with scholarly habits of mind and participation in recognized academic venues for sharing and peer review. It is not the easy way out to pad a résumé. And the scholarship of engagement can be political. For example, Amy Driscoll, a true pioneer in service learning and an able scholar, confesses that she is concerned for junior faculty "and their lack of ease and security about pursing the scholarship of engagement, even on campuses with revised guidelines for promotion and tenure." She continues, there is "an unspoken lack of credibility for alternative forms of scholarship . . . an unspoken message that these products and results must be accompanied by traditional refereed publications to be rewarded as scholarship"[13] If Driscoll is right, faculty may want to embrace the scholarship of engagement only after being promoted and tenured; it remains too risky for junior faculty.

So, where does that leave us? Are we suggesting that you avoid the scholarship of engagement until you are a tenured senior faculty member nearing retirement and in need of a hobby? Not at all, but we want to be clear that you have to come to the scholarship of engagement with serious intent and expertise—and with eyes wide open. We asked some key academic administrators in faith-based institutions these questions: (1) does your institution recognize the scholarship of engagement for promotion and tenure; and (2) what advice do you have for faculty pursing the scholarship of engagement? Their answers follow.

### Linda Samek, Provost, George Fox University[14]

**Does SoE Count?** I would like to think the answer is *yes*, but I think it is actually *sometimes*! I think it is appropriate for consideration if the faculty member not only "brings scholarly habits to bear" on practice but also synthesizes theories that are generalizable or applicable beyond their own practice and shares that synthesis in a public forum that is recognized and valued by the community of practice.

**Advice?** That professors should keep extensive "field notes" when practicing that are above and beyond just a chronicle of the practice. He or she should think deeply about the impact of the practice and how it changes the community with which it connects. The professor should engage the practitioners from the field in the scholarly work, encouraging them to share in the generation and the evaluation of the scholarly presentation.

### *Linda Mills Woolsey, Dean of the College and Vice President for Academic Affairs, Houghton College*[15]

**Does SoE Count?** Houghton College has often considered use of expertise in service projects (which may include consulting), particularly in business and education. We are currently at work on handbook revisions that would clarify the parameters of this sort of scholarship, and we are basing our work on the Boyer model. Generally, where the faculty member is doing paid consulting, we would expect some result that could be incorporated into teaching or reporting to disciplinary peers.

**Advice?** We think it is important that, for consulting to be considered as scholarship, it needs to be framed in a way that enables the faculty member to advance his or her own knowledge (collecting data while consulting, building case studies that can be used in presentations or teaching) or to involve students in collaborative research or service learning. There may be a fine line between simply moonlighting and doing consulting work that represents learning to be shared with students and peers.

### *Doyle Lucas, Director, DBA Program, Falls School of Business, Anderson University*[16]

**Does SoE Count?** AU does consider the scholarship of engagement, as you described, as appropriate for promotion and tenure. I think the best example of this would be a marketing professor (name omitted) who brings his research and scholarship to the table in his "consulting" with many organizations within the Mennonite church hierarchy. He has conducted analyses using survey data and statistical processing to provide valued information in his role as consultant to that particular group. This kind of "scholarship" is also something we discuss in our DBA (doctor of business administration)  program as a possible avenue for our grads to consider as they develop their path toward "professional development" as business faculty members.

**Advice?** I think a key here may be to demonstrate scholarship in terms of fully investigating the industry that the firm is a part of and that firm's particular role within that industry. This would point somewhat toward a "literature review" if you will and provide the "consultant" (researcher) with a broader scholarly perspective than simply addressing a particular issue or problem that the firm wants him or her to investigate. Of course I would also encourage formal analysis, whether quantitative or qualitative, rather than an anecdotal approach to the problem.

### David Clark, Vice President and Dean, Bethel Seminary, Bethel University[17]

**Does SoE Count?** Now the three schools (undergrad residential, seminary, adult programs) work these criteria out in slightly different ways based on their distinct missions. So for adult programs, the kind of practical/applicational approach to scholarship that you describe would be viewed positively—it would "count." In undergrad, it would likely not count. (Other examples of unique application of these universal, general criteria: Teaching effectiveness means different things for 18-year-olds vs. midcareer adults. "Integration" means integration of faith and learning for undergrad, but integration of theology with character for seminary. Service in adult programs means service to a profession; in seminary, it means service to church.)

**Advice?** The diversity of specifics in how the five university-wide criteria are applied is based on differences in the missions of the three schools. So one idea might be to build a case for the kind of scholarship you're working with in light of the different missions of the units you have. It might make sense to talk about a rubric like I've described to both unify the criteria so there's no question that you're completely out in left field, and also to get around a traditional, R1 view of scholarship. Otherwise, your seminary and adult program faculty will be working with criteria, as they are actually applied, that are not helpful (at best) or completely irrelevant (at worst), given the power of the traditional scholarship mode.

## *Jonathan Parker, Provost, California Baptist University*[18]

**Does SoE Count?** We do consider the scholarship of engagement as "counting" for merit and promotion and tenure. The tricky part is teasing out what counts for "scholarship" and what counts for "service." With some consulting gigs the scholarship is so intertwined with the actual consulting it's difficult to see it for what it is.

**Advice?** A couple of pieces of advice that I would give to professors who do this sort of scholarship would be: (1) make sure up front that the institution and supervisor "count" this type of scholarship for merit and promotion and tenure; (2) be very explicit in identifying the scholarly elements in any consulting gigs; (3) be sure to engage in some "scholarship of discovery" and/or "scholarship of teaching" in addition to engagement scholarship.

## *What Can We Learn?*

What can we learn from the comments of these seasoned and respected academic administrators? First, the scholarship of engagement usually counts for scholarship in promotion and tenure decisions, but not always. Establishing criteria for scholarship is a local activity, and therefore somewhat the responsibility of the individual faculty member. Second, even when it does count, different parts of the institution may well view it in different ways. Different schools and departments have their own sense of mission, and different ideas about legitimate scholarship. Third, promotion and tenure committees do not always give the scholarship of engagement the same weight as they give to other forms of scholarship, requiring the faculty member to provide additional explanation or documentation. And finally, different institutions look for different aspects of scholarly engagement to be present—a review of the literature, documented enhancement of personal professional knowledge, extensive field notes, critical reflection, peer review, connections with other forms of scholarship, or collaboration with other scholars.

These comments from chief academic officers make clear that each institution is different, which is, we believe, as it should be. Expectations for scholarship should be aligned to reinforce the specific mission of each respective institution, but this range of expectations adds difficulty for faculty members seeking the smoothest path forward. In order to come to the scholarship of engagement with eyes wide open, we suggest the following discernment process and action plan: (1) clarify institutional and departmental expectations and outcomes early on; (2) dovetail your scholarship with departmental strategies and institutional expectations; (3) develop a particular and substantive scholarly agenda; (4) do the work of a scholar and develop a critical mass of scholarship; and (5) share your work and collaborate with other scholars in the field. We now expand briefly on each of these in turn.

**Ask for Clarification and Establish Expectations.** As Jonathan Parker writes, "make sure up front that the institution and supervisor 'count' this type of scholarship for merit and promotion and tenure." View this as sage advice from an experienced provost. If your preferred approach to scholarship does not count, then you need to move on, figuratively or literally. Either work to develop another form of scholarship amenable to your department and institution or work to find another institution. And if engagement does count, ask for clarity about how and by whom it is viewed and evaluated. Is it, for example, given the same weight as discovery, or will you have to submit additional work samples, documentation, or explanations to demonstrate the fit and credibility of your work?

**Articulate Your Scholarship with Departmental Strategies and Institutional Expectations.** Even if you get signals from the dean and provost that the scholarship of engagement has credibility at your institution, you must agree with your department chair on at least two counts. First, will the department (and the chair) support the scholarship of engagement? Even if high-level academic administrators indicate that you are on the right track, you have to walk with your chair and work with your departmental colleagues every day. If they do not support or respect your scholarly work, you will be isolated at best, and possibly deeply disappointed in the promotion/tenure evaluation process. Department chairs have a great deal of influence with evaluation committees, and promotions rarely happen without their support. The second question is this: Does the department have a strategy related to scholarship? Some departments, particularly larger ones, may work to represent all four scholarly domains, while others specialize in one or two domains. Sadly, some departments have no strategy at all. It is important, of course, to know if the department has a strategy and how your scholarly work can contribute to it. It is always a good idea to have your department members view you as a supportive and contributing departmental colleague.

**Develop a Particular and Substantive Scholarly Agenda.** Once you ascertain that the institution and your department support the scholarship of engagement, you must develop a particular and sustained scholarly agenda. By *particular* we mean an agenda that fits you—one for which you have the knowledge, skills, interest, and support to embrace. In other words, do something that you can do where you are located with the resources you have. Many faculty, for example, work in relative isolation on smaller campuses located in smaller towns and have to choose carefully their engagement strategies. We say, without joking, that you would be wiser to consult on timber usage if you are working in the Northwest rather than working thousands of miles from the nearest stand of timber. And by *sustained*, we mean developing a focus to your scholarship that you pursue over time. We have seen scholarship portfolios come up short simply because they lacked a sustained effort in any one direction or in any one area of expertise. No one wants their scholarship criticized as "all over the place." This criticism usually results when faculty members work to add items to their vita without any plan other than trying to get their scholarship to "count" any way they can a year or so before their next review. As we have noted several times already, faculty members who view their academic work as their response to a divine call to participate in God's work of redemption in this world enjoy life more and worry about their résumés less. Working to build a focused *oeuvre* rather than working to enhance a CV ultimately gives weight and credibility to your scholarship because each particular project rests on previous efforts, providing rich opportunities for collaboration and critique with colleagues and friends in that specific academic sector or specialty.

**Do the Work of a Scholar and Develop a Critical Mass of Scholarship.** There is no substitute for hard work. Of course, it helps immensely if you love the work you do, but even then—even for those who have heard God's voice—days will come when you must simply keep your oars in the water and pull. It is critical to schedule your time in such a way that you have a certain rhythm to your week, month, or summer. Unfortunately, many faculty are as accomplished at procrastination as are their students. In Chapter Nine, we consider in detail some of the typical characteristics of productive writers. Almost universally, whether they work in the academy or not, productive writers view their writing simply as *their work*. Certainly anyone wanting to embrace the scholarship of engagement will need to adopt that view. Such a person would never consider not showing up for a prearranged consulting meeting with a corporate client or taking a skip on a speaking engagement. Being a professional demands that we show up. The scholarship of engagement also demands that we show up to do our writing, that we take the same attitude toward the writing appointments we make with ourselves that we take toward our commitments to others. Strong words? Yes, they are.

**Share Your Work and Collaborate with Other Scholars in the Field.** Many faculty in professional disciplines consult, speak, and lead workshops but never devote the time and energy to push that work to the scholarship of engagement. Even those who do move past engagement into the scholarship of engagement sometimes fail to share their work or collaborate with other scholars in the field. We lament this because such collaboration can bring depth and joy to a scholar's work. Having partners and colleagues who both encourage and push you can give life, and working collegially also makes you a more careful scholar. We know of faculty who, in the name of Christ, seek partners for collaboration and work to help other scholars move ahead, finding both added joy in their work and greater success in promotion and tenure processes. This second result—success in tenure and promotion—surprises some people because they believe shared authorship and shared credit, which run counter to their vision of the autonomous and solitary scholar, dilute an individual's accomplishments and record. This is rarely the case. Sadly, with the mindset that "it's all about me," some faculty members grasp for more work opportunities and the corollary credit (more lines on their résumé, so to speak), lose the joy of sharing, and still do not get promoted faster than they might have been had they worked collaboratively.

## The Scholarship of Engagement, Scripture, and Christian Faith

Like good stewards of the manifold grace of God, serve one another with whatever gift each of you has received. (1 Peter 4:10)[19]

How do we bring our faith to the scholarship of engagement? To allude to Paul (2 Cor. 6:5), what on earth does Jerusalem have to do with our consulting for a corporation, speaking at a service club, or advising a nonprofit? Does the Bible really offer direction to us as we consult, speak, and work in the field?[20] Clearly, it does. Scriptural writers call us at several points to be good stewards of our gifts and to serve one another in love. In doing so, we steward or appropriate various forms of God's grace. Our service, in other words, becomes a sacramental act, an act of worship. We want to highlight a faithful understanding of the stewardship of gifts, humility, and neighbor.

### *The Stewardship of Gifts*

We believe that all academic gifts come from above (James 1:17; Ps. 85:12; John 3:27; 1 Cor. 4:7; Eph. 4:7). Given the intellectual requirements for faculty work, we believe that Jesus's parable of the talents applies as well (Matt. 25:14–30). In the terms of that parable, we must not—as individuals—hide our intellectual gifts, but we must invest them wisely so that they bring maximum benefit to the One who gave them to us in the first place. In this context, it is important to understand and appreciate our professional experience as a gift, too. We are to leverage it for the Kingdom.

But we do not teach and study only as individuals; faculty work has an institutional aspect as well. We believe the parable indicates that any college or university and its respective departments should work diligently to help faculty identify their gifts and should ensure that faculty work in the areas where their gifts are expressed and realized most fully and authentically, a conclusion we believe fits with Boyer's distinction between the four kinds of scholarship—particularly for the scholarship of engagement. The formal and organic structures in place in any department or school should neither deny the exercise of gifts nor ignore the possession or sacredness of them.

In three different letters, Paul offered lists of what he called spiritual gifts (Rom. 12; 1 Cor. 12, 14; Eph. 4). Peter also provides such a list (1 Pet. 4). Paul mentions some gifts that have obvious relevance to our work in higher education, such as wisdom and knowledge (1 Cor. 12:8); teaching (Rom. 12:7; 1 Cor. 12:28; Eph. 4:11); discernment (1 Cor. 12:10); and leadership (Rom. 12:7; 1 Cor. 12:28). Because faculty learn, teach, and work together in community, and because we all carry heavy burdens, gifts such as generosity and cheerfulness (Rom. 12:8) or hospitality (1 Pet. 4:9) deserve our attention as well.

Paul does not simply list these various gifts. Because the actual churches to which he wrote—in Rome, Corinth, Ephesus—had the same kinds of people in them that our colleges and universities have (people like us), Paul also outlined principles for how people were to think about their gifts and use them within the community. He says we are to consider our gifts and our place in the larger community with sober judgment (Rom. 12:3), which we interpret to mean we should think our own gifts and abilities are worth neither less nor more than they actually are. We do not all have the same gifts or do the same work; we carry out different functions in the community (Rom. 12:4–6, 11; 1 Cor. 12:4–6). Paul describes the Christian community as one where we are actually "members one of another" (Rom. 12:5; 1 Cor. 12:12–26). In that kind of community, we do not use our gifts for our own advancement, but for the good of the whole group (1 Cor. 12:7, 14:26; Eph. 4:12, 16). We know that Peter and Paul did not agree on all points, but on this point they do, for Peter says that those who would exercise their gifts must do so for the glory of God (1 Pet. 4:11).

Our description of Paul's high ideals for community fit in a general way with Boyer's distinction between the four kinds of scholarship, especially for the scholarship of engagement. Boyer saw the connectedness of all our gifts and did not see the need to have all professors pressed through the "discovery" sieve. But we wish to note several of Paul's instructions that go beyond Boyer. In 1 Corinthians 12:23, he writes that "the members of the body that we think less honorable we clothe with greater honor." Given the current hierarchy of values in the academy—research, teaching, then service—in Boyer's terms, that instruction implies that we should elevate teaching and service, returning them to places of honor.

Paul continues by saying that "our more respectable members do not need" to be so elevated (1 Cor. 12:24). Paul speaks a prescient truth here about the academy today; we know that personnel committees do not single-handedly elevate gifts of scholarship; most members of the academy accord more honor to those who publish. Interestingly, Paul next notes that "if one member suffers, all suffer together with it; if one member is honored, all rejoice together with it" (1 Cor. 12:26). From this passage, we might take direction regarding our need to help our colleagues succeed within the reward system in place (while we work to realign reward structures), and we also might hear Paul's words as an exhortation to celebrate more openly when our members succeed. Perhaps we are called to be humble about our own work—and lavish about that of our colleagues.

### Humility

We believe that we should do all our scholarly work—research, teaching, engagement, integration, but particularly engagement—in a spirit of humble service, a posture Jesus embodied in his own life. Paul described this posture in Philippians 2:5–11 as a denial of the prerogatives of office. Witness Jesus washing the feet of his disciples (John 13:1–11), engaging the marginalized in conversation (Luke 19:1–10; John 4), and rebuking his disciples for arguing about who would get the place of honor in the Kingdom (Matt. 20:18–28). In a particularly blunt part of that passage, he notes how some love to lord it over others (v. 25) and makes clear that those who follow him must be servants. A bit later, Matthew records Jesus's disapproval of those who love to be called by their titles and who love the place of honor at banquets (Matt. 23:7–8). We assume that demanding the best presentation slot at a conference fits Jesus's intention here, as does waving our doctorates around. He notes that we have only one teacher and that we "are all students" (v. 8), a humble posture indeed, and one in accord with Carl Rogers's idea that the teacher's posture toward students should be that of a co-learner.[21]

In fact we believe that any professor adopting such a posture may end up at odds with the values of the larger academy. Jesus has harsh words for those who want their "deeds to be seen by others" (Matt. 23:5). But is it not essential for academics to publicize—to make public—their ideas, creating a problem for anyone wanting to remain humble while engaging in academic work? Bluntly, scholarship requires making ideas public and, we assume, wanting others to receive those ideas because they are good ideas.

In "Humility and Truth," Deirdre McCloskey hints at a fundamental problem for some academics that arises in part out of being stewards of our academic gifts and thus being called upon to tell what we have learned or discovered, that is: to talk about our accomplishments.[22] Her brief historical survey, which includes such diverse figures as the author of the Proverbs, Thomas Aquinas, George Fox, and Roman Catholic activist Dorothy Day, leaves us in a tension. On her account, as it did to our forebears, humility calls us to listen. Perhaps the central aspect of research—the need to make it public—is fundamentally at odds with the values of the Reign of Christ. At the very least, it challenges us to think carefully about how we practice humility on our campuses and in the academy. A good start would be to listen first, then talk—but only as needed.[23]

Drawing from this broadly Christian heritage, we argue that professors in faith-based institutions ought to give special consideration to Boyer's scholarship of engagement—to service. In 1990, Boyer nuanced his concern with these questions, "How can knowledge be responsibly applied to consequential problems? How can it be helpful to individuals as well as institutions? Can social problems themselves define an agenda for scholarly investigation?"[24] For example, education faculty should find Boyer's questions particularly germane at this time, a claim we illustrate with reference to just three current issues: (1) school districts everywhere face deep fiscal difficulties; (2) an alarming percentage of induction-phase teachers leave the profession; (3) schools and teachers struggle to know what to teach and how to teach it as they find themselves working in a culture of assessment and testing. Perhaps more than at any other time, education faculty have an opportunity to serve educators and students. Were Boyer rewriting *Scholarship Reconsidered* for education faculty today, we believe he would say that the time for the scholarship of engagement is now and the place is any school or school district. We believe this truth holds for any clinic, community organization, business entity, church, or field-based ministry. If it does hold for that variety of settings, then all faculty have the responsibility to ask what are the consequential questions in their fields. And they all have the opportunity to serve God and the world in those fields.

So, recognizing that our professional expertise and *entre* into fields of service and areas of need are truly spiritual gifts for which we are accountable, and we are called to approach our scholarship with humility—listening before talking—how do we proceed? The answer, we believe, lies in our understanding of *neighbor* and how we are called to serve.

## Neighbor

In the gospel of Luke, we find the story of the Good Samaritan (Luke 10:29–37). After giving correct answers about how to obtain eternal life (love God and neighbor), the lawyer asks Jesus to define "neighbor." In response to his question, Jesus tells the story of the Good Samaritan. We assume you are familiar with the story. If not, we commend it to you as a remarkable story in which Jesus dismantles cultural and social barriers by making the Samaritan the hero, with full knowledge that Pharisees not only oppressed Samaritans but despised them, too. They were considered to be dirty and treated as invisible. Jesus used this parable to challenge the religious leaders of the day to live out their faith in tangible ways rather than working to keep their hands clean and their résumés impressive.

This parable is troubling not only because of the violence done to a traveler (he ends up beaten and left in a ditch), but also because the Jews in high position were more concerned for their own purity than for the pain of another. The parable asks us to grapple with the reasons this despised, hated, and unclean Samaritan would show such compassion and take care of a stranger. It is a story in which the hated enemy becomes the hero—a story turned on its head, and demonstrates with clarity that entering into eternal life and experiencing God's Kingdom may require going against our own cultural and social values. What seems right and comfortable is turned upside down, too. Love is no longer just for our family or those like us, but also for those who are despised and oppressed by society, or simply invisible. And Jesus concludes this story by giving a compelling command, "Go and do likewise" (Luke 10:37).

So, how do you go and do likewise as a professor serving in a faith-based institution? As Peter suggests, you steward the gifts you have received in service to others in need, to your neighbors (1 Pet. 4:10). And who are your neighbors? Regarding the scholarship of engagement, we suggest that you look in the ditch by the side of the road. In other words, look for organizations that are low-profile, suffering, or left for dead. They need your assistance. Truly, your gifts, abilities, and knowledge can be grace for them. And it is one way to negotiate the tension between the call to humility (to listen) and the necessity to make your scholarship public. Make these organizations visible, too.

Another way to bring your faith to the scholarship of engagement is to seek out the stranger, to move outside your own comfort zone. The Greek word for hospitality is *philoxenia*, which literally means love (*philo*) of the stranger (*xenos*). Why not use your professional expertise to associate with and gain access to an organization that is a complete stranger to you, not in your usual professional circles? You can work there as a faithful Christian presence, and let your life and convictions speak much like Ernest Boyer did throughout his career. He did not chase his peers around with a big Bible and a condemning spirit; rather he intentionally and humbly lived out his faith in their midst by serving. Ultimately, it made a profound difference. The scholarship of engagement is a wonderful way to work among strangers and organizations that are on the margin, invisible, or in the ditch. In doing so, your faith and your learning will be integrated, made whole.

## Chapter 8

# In Word
# and Deed

## Assessing and Reporting Your Work

We have noted that new faculty often end up scratching their heads when trying to understand what the Christian colleges that employ them mean by *faith-learning integration*. Some veteran faculty do the same. What do these colleges want professors to do or not do? How are professors to articulate their understanding of being Christian in an academic workplace? We have explored Boyer's framework at length in an attempt to help faculty assess and describe their scholarly efforts in the domains of teaching; of discovery, inquiry, and integration; and of service and engagement. As we noted, Boyer had deep faith. We have outlined how his faith informed all his academic work in winsome and inviting ways. At several points, we have suggested ways that Christian college faculty might realize in practice the educational ideal of faith-informed scholarship.

How do professors articulate their understanding of faith-learning integration, and how do they assess and describe the steps they take to realize that understanding? What language should they use? What beliefs or practices do they point to? These questions give rise to our chapter title,

"In Word and Deed." We thank the biblical writers who bequeathed us this language.[1] Specifically, Paul instructed the Colossians: "And whatever you do, in word or deed, do everything in the name of the Lord Jesus, giving thanks to God the Father through him" (Col. 3:17). Paul used similar language in his letter to the Romans, as did Luke in both his Gospel and in the book of Acts. We use this familiar duo of words to introduce a framework for assessing faith-learning integration that entails both *articulation* (words) and *realization* (deeds), at both the institutional and individual levels.

A phrase closely related to our chapter title, *walk the talk,* has become more popular in recent decades. Rightly so. To our point in this book, Christian colleges and the students who attend them want faculty to walk the talk. But when they prepare essays for a tenure or promotion review, and even when they answer students' questions about what faith might have to do with this or that topic in a course, professors also need to know how to talk the walk, how to explain and articulate what they think and do. We have repeatedly noted Christian educators' love for the language of *faith and learning integration.* We have observed the dearth of attention scholars have given to some of the ambiguities involved in using that language. We have reported on the growing chorus of voices suggesting that Christian higher educators abandon integration language. When we turn to assessment, we discover that despite wide usage of this phrase, only sparse attention has been paid to the ways we might assess whether we have achieved the ideal of bringing faith to bear on our work of teaching, service, and research. We will turn our attention to that matter, offering a framework we think will aid individuals and institutions to tackle this important question, but first, we will address an even more fundamental question—can we actually assess faith and learning?

## Assessment of Faith and Learning: *Sic et Non*

Should we even be talking about assessing faith and learning? Some respond to this question with a visceral response akin to that of the Robin Williams's character, Mr. Keating, in the famous *rip it* scene in the movie, "Dead Poets Society."[2] The point Mr. Keating underlines with his senior secondary English class is that the quality of poetry cannot be measured as easily or mechanically as his students' assigned textbook suggests. He insists that his students rip the offending pages from their textbooks; in fact, he instructs them to tear out the whole introduction, written by the (fictional) textbook's author, J. Evans Pritchard. For some, matters of faith are similarly resistant to measurement. Can a department chair or dean assign one professor a score of 60 percent on her efforts to integrate faith and learning while another professor gets 90 percent for her effort? Mr. Keating, were he the dean or department chair in a Christian college, would answer with a definitive *no*.

Does not any such assessment presume that we can know the interior state of another person when all we can observe is that person's behavior? Jesus himself warns us about the risks of judging other people (Matt. 7:1, from the Sermon on the Mount). For some, the desire to assess someone else's success at thinking, teaching, researching, or serving as a Christian veers dangerously close to the territory Jesus warned us to avoid. In other words, a rather persuasive argument could be mounted that we should proceed with caution—if we move at all—in assessing faith-learning integration or anything to do with the inner state of another person who names Christ. In their essay, "Assessing Ineffable Outcomes," Arthur Chickering and Marcia Mentkowski review several aspects of this question, using as a definition of *ineffable*, "incapable of being expressed in words."[3] They conclude that colleges can assess student growth in such areas as authenticity, spirituality, purpose, and meaning. They also note a feature of this question that bears on our question of integrating faith and learning: higher educators are still trying to get used to the idea of assessment itself; assessing the ineffable will present even bigger challenges.[4]

Those arguing for assessment would likely counter that a faculty member's deeds day to day and year to year, as well as his or her portfolio essays, reveal that inner state. And those arguing for assessment might also note that Jesus warned us to be as wise as serpents because we are like sheep among wolves (Matt. 10:16). The context in which Christian educators and especially Christian colleges carry out their educational tasks offers two more perspectives. First, accrediting agencies, parents, and students all want to know if Christian institutions do what we say we do—if an education with us is somehow different from or more than an education at a public college or university, what many call the added value argument. Second, department chairs, deans, provosts, and members of tenure and promotion committees want to know if faculty understand and how they plan to implement their respective institutional missions.

In what follows, we assume that these various people, agencies, and committees have a legitimate interest in knowing if individual faculty members or whole colleges are delivering on their advertising. After all, people want to know if corporations, nonprofit groups, athletes, musicians, environmentalists, and a host of others are good for their word. Why would any Christian educator expect an exemption, especially with regard to such a salient aspect of Christian education?[5] In light of the debate about the appropriateness of assessing this dimension of our work, we therefore propose these simple scriptural categories: *words* and *deeds*.

## The Biblical Words and Deeds Framework

As have many of our readers, we have observed that professors' abilities to articulate Christian understandings of academic work run along a continuum, from low to high. Bluntly, some do better than others at articulating and describing their biblical foundations, ideals, frameworks, and understandings of their work in the academy. Some see, work within, benefit from, and can explain the overall coherence between their beliefs and the work they do day to day. Others struggle to find or explain such coherence. This is true of individuals, and it is also true of institutions. Some institutions seem more capable than others of understanding and describing how faith connects to the component parts and varied aspects of academic life. Of course, institutions do not really explain anything; people who represent institutions do. So our claim about institutions really implies that some academic communities succeed better than others at employing people who can articulate the connections between faith and their academic work.[6] They are better with *words*.

As a corollary to what we call the articulation continuum (words) we just described, another continuum runs from weak to strong realization of ideals. With many biblical authors, we label this with the ordinary word *deeds*. As does the articulation continuum, this *deeds* continuum applies to both individuals and to institutions. It has two aspects. First, can we enumerate and describe what we are doing to realize our ideals? That is, what are our plans, our approaches, our strategies, and our practices?

Second, can we assess how well we are accomplishing our goals? Do we have criteria to carry out that assessment? In short, can we measure the results of our efforts? We use the word *measure* cautiously because we know that the very idea of measuring our accomplishment of faith-learning goals may strike some readers as logically or theologically mistaken. Neither of us is a behaviorist, and neither is Dan Aleshire, a longtime leader in the Association of Theological Schools (ATS, the main accrediting body for seminaries). But, with Aleshire, whom we quoted earlier in the book, we believe that if we succeed at achieving our goals our success should, in some sense, be measurable.[7] We represent these two dimensions, articulating and realizing—words and deeds—in the diagram below. Any individual faculty member (and for that matter, any institution) will fall somewhere along the articulation continuum and somewhere along the realization continuum.

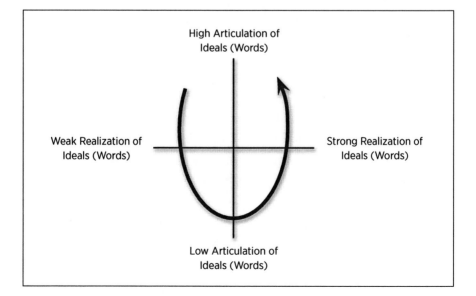

**Figure 8.1. The Axes of Words and Deeds**

We will briefly explore these four quadrants in turn, suggesting possible examples as we go. Beginning at the top left quadrant, we find faculty members who can talk the integration talk (or theological talk, or biblical talk) but do not walk the walk.[8] Typically, the top left quadrant would include people we call *hypocrites*. However, that cell might also include faculty who simply do not know how to realize in practice something they first heard about on gaining employment in a Christian college. Perhaps they just encountered the new language of faith-learning integration when they arrived at this workplace. Perhaps they previously assumed that loving Jesus, attending chapel, or praying for students might be the main distinguishing features of Christian higher education. On encountering this new language, they realize they have only a vague idea of what it means. We have met many such persons, and we do not criticize them for what they did not learn before taking up their new post. In fact, we have written this book partly to help them address this very lack of understanding.[9]

Moving to the bottom left quadrant of our diagram, we find faculty who lack the ability either to articulate or to realize the ideal of faith-learning integration. We know that for various reasons (for example, a shortage of qualified applicants for a position), Christian colleges do hire faculty whose articulation of a Christian conception of academic work is weak and whose realization of it is sketchy. As one dean said to one of us, "The ox is in the ditch, we need to get it out any way we can—and we don't have many options."[10] We do not criticize such persons, but we hope this volume helps them with both their words and their deeds.

The lower right hand quadrant of our diagram represents those whose articulation of a conception of faith-learning has gaps but whose lives exemplify what Christian colleges want to see in their faculty. There is no need here to enumerate all the possible reasons such persons cannot— or do not—articulate what they do, but their students, their colleagues, and their department chairs and deans know they are getting something right. Though she never worked in the academy, Mother Teresa of Calcutta might serve as a good example here. Her deeds spoke loudly and clearly of her commitment, obviating any need for explanation. In a twist that perhaps warrants critical examination, were Mother Teresa applying for promotion from assistant professor to associate, the relevant committee in most Christian colleges would still demand an essay. That is, her dramatically full realization of an ideal would not suffice. We would want her to describe and articulate her biblical philosophy and her approach to faith-learning.

The Teresa example certainly points up an irony, but in that irony lies a real tension for professors and for their colleagues who serve on promotion and tenure committees. Under the most common current arrangements, the ideal candidate for promotion or tenure is represented by the upper right quadrant of our diagram. That is, were she to apply for promotion or tenure, Mother Teresa's application really would come up wanting. Many faculty in Christian colleges may realize or incarnate in their day-to-day practice (we use *incarnate* in its nontechnical sense) the biblical ideals and published missions of those respective colleges. But they still need to *articulate* why they do what they do and explain how they go about doing it. Although in Chapter Ten we offer another approach, we will not question this set of arrangements in this chapter because we both expect that faculty in Christian colleges should be able to explain the Christian education difference. We will not defend these arrangements either; they are simply the typical arrangements that colleges put in place, and our job at this point is to help faculty articulate their practice.

On first glance at our diagram, some might conclude that the direction and movement of the arrow imply increasing approval. After all, no student or department wants to spend time with the hypocrite potentially represented by the upper left quadrant, the one who talks Christian faith but does not live it. And we are not sure if the individual represented by the lower left quadrant will even find employment—or should (unless the ox truly is in the ditch).[11] We trust a college that names Christ would demand high realization of some conception of Christian education from those who teach and steward the ethos of the institution. The lower left quadrant of the diagram represents the person who can neither articulate a conception of how faith bears on academic work nor show in practice that it does so. Whether such a person would be a worse or better teacher and colleague than the hypocrite of the upper left quadrant, we are not sure.[12]

Certainly, the two right-side quadrants prove the most interesting for both faculty and the members of committees who must evaluate their portfolios. Does it really matter if an academic Mother Teresa can or cannot produce a clear statement of her conception of faith and learning? Yes, in the Christian colleges we know, it matters. Should it matter? That is the question we said we would not address here. Our point is that the arrow in the graphic probably does indicate a preference, with those represented in the upper left quadrant the least preferred for tenure and promotion and those represented by the upper right quadrant the most preferred. The desire to grant someone promotion or tenure likely increases with the path of the arrow.[13]

Every word we have read by or about Ernest Boyer indicates that he consistently walked his talk and articulately talked his walk. He lived a life of excellence in faithful service (strong realization of his vision), and he persuasively and clearly explained his vision in both public and religious settings (high articulation). He thus serves as a paradigm exemplar of someone represented by our upper right quadrant. Presumably, colleges by the dozen would love to have offered Boyer tenure.

## A Cautionary Note: The Faith Piece

We have heard faculty in Christian colleges refer to the matter of faith-learning integration as the faith piece. A moment's reflection should reveal to most that such a phrase hardly catches the degree to which faith should inform and form the work of students and faculty in Christian colleges. It would be like an economics major saying that economics should take into account *the money piece*, or a coach referring to *the training piece*. In the first chapter of the letter to the Colossians, Paul identified Christ as the foundation of all things, as the person who holds all things together (Col. 1:17). In our conception of Christian education, faith is the integrating framework within which we do all our work. It is not a piece; it is the frame in which all the other pieces fit, not some kind of millimeter-thick laminate that goes on top of an otherwise-secular education. Throughout this book we have repeatedly warned against allowing sub-biblical understandings to shape our work as professors, and we have looked for winsome ways to characterize the foundational and all-encompassing place of faith in our work. With that caution in mind, we ask then how we assess the faith dimension of our work, not the faith piece, the faith dimension.

## Assessing Words and Deeds: Individual and Institutional Dimensions

Without presuming that Christian colleges should assess faith and learning integration, we simply recognize that they do and we want to offer a helpful framework within which faculty can think, work, and write: *words* (which we call the *articulation* of ideals) and *deeds* (which we call the *realization* of ideals).[14]

By *words* we mean simply that individuals and institutions should be able to list, describe, and explain their ideals. With *deeds*, we recognize the typical scriptural priority of deeds over words, and the reality that many *walk* like Christians regardless of their ability to talk that walk in theological detail. But our *deeds* label presents a small complication that the *words* category does not. Deeds denotes actions but leaves outcomes unspecified, reminding us to be humble because we cannot guarantee the outcomes of our work, but, we hope, not leading anyone to conclude they can get off the hook. No one is allowed to plea, "I taught it, but they didn't learn it." For the purposes of our discussion, we will restrict *deeds* to its narrower sense (actions planned and taken to realize our faith-learning ideals), recognizing that some might prefer our using a wider sense in which we also ask about outcomes.[15] One final note about Scripture before we begin to examine what we think *words* implies for faculty. We have no interest in setting up a false tension on this question of words and deeds, but Scripture proves interesting here. We claimed above that biblical writers generally give deeds the priority. Peter instructs the recipients of his first letter always to be ready to explain their faith (1 Pet. 3:15). Without wanting to approach that one verse too slavishly, we still must note the priority he gives to words. Arguably, Jesus himself admits the importance of words (Matt. 28:20; Mark 16:15–16).[16]

## Words and Deeds—Institutional Criteria

We present the following section with a mix of humility and trepidation. We have accepted that people need to assess faith-learning integration, whether or not they like the language and whether or not they accept the raw idea that this dimension is even suited to assessment. If we are to assess it, we will need criteria. Presenting criteria will not make all our readers happy, but trying to assess anything without criteria is like trying to make your way through a forest in the dark without map, guide, compass, or GPS. Better to have some idea of where you are and where you need to go than to try every pathway. They will all look the same.

**The Institutional Dimension.** Faculty work in specific settings; they have institutional homes. Given that particularity, they can do some kind of general faith and learning integration, but ultimately they must articulate and demonstrate having done so in specific institutional surroundings, what in Chapter Ten we will call wisdom communities. So, we begin our list of criteria with some institutional or corporate standards, for individual faculty must do their work within the contexts shaped by such standards. We suggest the following as a beginning criterion: *the institution must clearly and consistently articulate its corporate vision for faith and learning, Christian education, or whatever name it prefers.*[17] Venues for clarity and consistency include the language that appears in website announcements, institutional advertising, and faculty manuals, as well as the stories told at signature events such as convocations or student and faculty orientations. Obviously, that clarity and consistency should extend to reports submitted to accrediting bodies, government agencies, and granting organizations.

In light of all we have said in this book about the variety of ways faculty will conceive of the relationship between faith and learning, we immediately add a second criterion: *The institution articulates its aware-ness of the wide range of possible ways faculty understand and approach the question of living faith-fully in the academy.* That claim brings a corollary or perhaps implied condition to mind: those judging professors' realization of faith-learning integration also must recognize the difference between conceptions of integration and examples of practices meant to realize those conceptions. Recognizably, this claim implies that trustees may need in-service sessions about faith and learning. If nothing else, such education would grant them a better understanding of faculty essays. At best, in-service sessions would also encourage deep reflection on the institutional mission and provide a venue for conversation about that mission with faculty and students.

The third criterion focuses not on words, but on deeds: *institutions must offer adequate resources to support faculty in their efforts to understand and realize faith-learning integration.* We suggest such resources as the following:

- library resources related to faith and learning
- funds granted specifically to attend conferences that address questions of faith in the disciplines
- structures for faculty discussion about realizing faith in various aspects of academic work
- support for newer faculty mentoring programs
- time to reflect on the relationship of faith and learning and the frameworks within which to do that reflection. Individual faculty obviously must make their own time, but institutions can help create spaces for collective reflection in colleges, departments, or professional learning communities.

A fourth criterion also specifies deeds. The second criterion called for colleges to articulate their awareness of the varied ways faculty approach faith and learning. The fourth flows from that: *colleges must ensure that trustees, administrators, and tenure/promotion committee members honor in practice their understanding that faculty approach faith-learning integration in many different ways.* If our argument in Chapter Two holds any water at all, then institutional reward and recognition structures must reflect the reality that God has blessed different faculty with a variety of gifts and that God has led people to some dramatically different understandings of how faith bears on learning.

We have offered four criteria for institutions: two related to words and two related to deeds. The connections between them become quite apparent with this simple table.

| Institutional Criteria/Standards | | | |
|---|---|---|---|
| **Words** | | **Deeds** | |
| 1 | The institution articulates a vision for Christian education.[18] | 3 | The institution offers adequate support for faculty efforts to understand and enact the integration of faith and learning. |
| 2 | The institution articulates its awareness that faculty approach faith and learning in varied ways. | 4 | Institutional structures honor the fact that faculty approach faith and learning in many different ways. |

**Table 8.1 Institutional Words and Deeds**

This list of four criteria certainly does not exhaust all the possible standards we or you might ask our institutions to meet. But, if faculty could see their workplaces meet even these four standards, they would find their work lives deeply enriched. To our point, they would also understand their institutions' and their own conceptions of faith-learning integration much more clearly. So, we view these four standards as a starting point, but also—if any college were to meet them—as major steps in the direction toward deeply Christian higher education.

## *Words—Criteria for Individual Faculty*

Having noted these four institutional responsibilities, we turn now to the criteria by which we believe faculty should assess their own attempts to bring faith to bear on their tasks as scholars, in service, in teaching, and in research. We begin with three foundational conditions. First, based on responsible readings of Scripture, *the faculty member articulates a Christian foundation for his or her conception of how Christian faith bears on academic work*. Second, *the faculty member is able to work with relevant theological categories* such as special and general revelation, sin, redemption, common and special grace, the goodness of creation, the whole creation's being held together by Christ's creative power, the value of human work, and the humility of admitting that now we see only in part. These are samples—albeit very important ones—of the biblical themes and doctrines that should inform the faculty member's thinking and work. Third, *the faculty member is able to draw on the resources of Christian history and on Christian tradition to articulate the context for his or her own conception of faith-learning integration* (a matter we return to in Chapter Ten with reference to the particular wisdom communities in which we work). As we did for the institutional standards, we summarize these preliminary individual standards in a table.

| Words: Foundational Conditions for Faculty | |
|---|---|
| 1 | Faculty member articulates a biblically responsible, Christian educational philosophy. |
| 2 | Faculty member works with relevant theological categories. |
| 3 | Faculty member draws on Christian history and tradition. |

Table 8.2 Individual Words: Foundational Conditions

We offer those three foundational conditions as a beginning point. Building from there, what other conditions should an individual faculty member meet? Some might suggest that we take this approach: compare what students say they see in our classes to what we want them to see. For example, a faculty member might want students to see that she has a thoughtful and solid foundation, that she has specific ideals and intentions that flow out of and are consistent with that foundation, and that she has identified and implemented specific practices consistent with those ideals and intentions. Faith-learning integration aside for the moment, these questions figure centrally in how the best educators now understand assessment. Certainly, we could use such questions in our assessment of the connections we have articulated between faith and learning.

We would also ask, of course, to what degree students think we realized our ideals, how close we came to reaching our goals. Those who use assessment to full advantage, having assessed their degree of achievement, go back and adjust their practices accordingly. Recall what we called the CIA rope: curriculum, instruction and assessment work in a cycle. We do not plan, teach, assess, and then stop. We plan, teach, assess, and then revise. Assessment tells us how much our students learned, but it also tells us how well we taught; that is why we call the steps *the CIA rope* instead of *the CIA straight line*. The rope has and needs all three strands; they support each other.

In Chapter Two, we reviewed the various venues where integration of faith and learning might be said to happen: the curriculum, the student, the teaching moment, the professor's character, the whole institutional ethos. Obviously, someone focusing on professorial character would likely want to add some more conditions to our list. One might call these personal and spiritual conditions. For example, students or colleges might expect that a faculty member should show evidence of personal transformation of character through Christ and the Holy Spirit's work within the individual. We might ask that the faculty member engage in Christian practices in his or her own life, practices such as prayer and reflection, Bible reading, and church attendance. A college might expect students and colleagues to report having seen evidence of personal transformation of the professor's character. We provide these only as samples, but they do indicate a line of thought that might be detailed by those who view good faculty character as important.

Others who tend toward epistemological and curricular conceptions of faith-learning integration would list a criterion something like this: The faculty member articulates an epistemologically responsible model of faith-learning integration suited to his or her academic discipline. That standard likely implies three subcriteria along the lines of (1) a *breadth or coherence condition*, whereby a conception of faith-learning integration must furnish coherence to as much curricular material as possible; (2) an *external consistency condition* requiring conceptions of faith-learning integration to furnish coherence to a lesson, unit, course, or whole curriculum; and (3) *an economy condition* requiring that a conception of faith-learning integration must not be so unwieldy or complicated that only the brightest can comprehend it.

A college that has adopted Boyer's framework might require that a faculty member be able to articulate how his or her conception of faith-learning integration enriches the kinds of scholarship identified by Boyer: the scholarship of discovery, inquiry, and integration (research), the scholarship of teaching and learning, and the scholarship of application or engagement (service).

Recall from Chapter Two the view that classrooms and what happens in classrooms are the locus of faith-learning integration. People taking this view might suggest what we call pedagogical conditions. We ask if issues of faith are purposely introduced and discussed in the classroom. Did the class sometimes stop its daily work and discuss serious faith issues or campus or world events in light of personal faith? Can students point to specific faith-related teachable moments? On reflection, would they say that this course helped them to think more carefully and deeply about their faith and learning? As you can see, a variety of questions could be developed for assessment purposes.

Late in the process of writing this book, one of our librarians brought to our attention a resource that we think every faculty member in every Christian college could use. The Office of Faith Integration at Azusa Pacific University has produced *Faith Integration: Faculty Guidebook* and made it available online for all.[19] Clearly, those who produced this guidebook performed a great deal of detailed work that, to our knowledge, no one had done before. In short, after offering a definition of faith-learning integration, it addresses what shapes faith-learning integration might take for both teachers and researchers.[20] The Azusa Pacific (APU) writers differentiate a dozen models of what they call faith integration, some of which overlap with models we have described. They address departmental and individual responsibilities for integration, and they discuss its relationship to academic freedom. They examine the knowledge, skills, and dispositions related to faith-learning integration that a Christian might expect to see (and APU does expect to see) at five levels: novice, developing, proficient, advanced, and expert.

For those in the Wesleyan tradition, the APU guidebook offers an extensive bibliography related to faith and learning integration. For non-Wesleyans, the bibliography illustrates the kind of resource that would help scholars of any tradition who want both to understand and to work intentionally within their tradition. In Chapter Ten, we stress the importance of recognizing and embracing the fact that we work in particular traditions and in particular wisdom communities. It is not a "one size fits all" approach. We urge you, our reader, to find that resource, print it, and keep it in the front of your portfolio binder or annual professional binder. Absent your own college providing such a resource, we even recommend that you request that your dean or provost seek permission of Azusa Pacific

University to use this resource until your institution produces a similar high-quality guide.

## Conclusion

Should we assess faith and learning integration? Likely. Are we going to? For sure. Two or three decades ago, the faith-learning integration path had a few signposts and a few maps. Those were supplemented with dozens of college advertisements brimming with promises. Thanks to many people's hard work, a few more signposts now help the traveler on the faith-learning integration path. And a few cartographers of Christian education are committing themselves to the hard work of giving us the maps we need.

Colleges will assess faculty on this dimension of our work. Furthermore, parents, students, and accrediting agencies will assess colleges. If our marketing departments keep saying that we integrate faith and learning—or if we keep claiming to teach Christianly, to teach worldviewishly, to teach from a Christian perspective, or to be Christian scholars—then we should expect people to assess our work. Indeed, we should welcome such assessment because it will help us identify areas for attention and improvement. Let us welcome assessment as a needed examination of our work as Christian educators.

## Chapter 9

# The Productive Academic Writer

Throughout this book we have paid attention to the institutional settings within which we do our work as professors, and we have addressed the expectations that our administrators and colleagues have of us, which are, in fact, expectations that almost all faculty have of ourselves. In this chapter, we shift our focus to address some of the dispositions, concepts, habits, and support structures that typically characterize faculty who become productive researchers and writers. We know it is one thing to talk about different dimensions of scholarship in general and another thing altogether to talk about *your* scholarship. This chapter is about your work as an academic writer.

We should define *productive*. We equate productive and effective in some areas, accepting as givens that the productive (or effective) professor prepares for teaching, teaches well, and gets students' work back to them quickly and that the effective (or productive) professor also engages with and serves his or her university and the wider community. However, when discussing research and writing, we must distinguish between productive and effective. One could write productively—creating lots of words—but produce mainly garbage. Throughout this chapter, we want to assume that our readers wish to become productive academic writers with worthwhile things to say.

That clarified, the *productive* professor also engages in a program of research—the scholarship of discovery and inquiry—and systematically presents that research at conferences and publishes it in articles and books. In honesty, we and our readers know that not all faculty actually perform research, present papers at conferences, or publish articles and books, and most faculty do not achieve the ideal (R1) levels of research and writing to which the academy gives lip service. At several points we have noted that Christian colleges may have confused themselves about their mission, that perhaps we should leave most research and publication to faculty in those institutions whose mission is to do that work, that we should focus on teaching. Whether you agree with that view or not, you will agree that faculty members in Christian colleges typically find themselves pulled between the two ideals. For those who do need—and, we trust, who want—to research and write, we offer this chapter.

What follows reads at many points like a how-to guide. Although we tried our best to make it otherwise, the material repeatedly forced us back to this format, so we finally admitted what it was. We have organized it under these main points:

- the real tensions academic writers experience regarding research and writing
- typical dispositions of productive academic writers
- useful concepts for those wishing to submit more writing for publication
- several habits and strategies used by successful academic writers
- some tools, systems, and supports that productive academic writers typically use
- guiding questions for a writing/planning retreat
- some useful further readings about writing and vocation.

What follows is certainly not the last word on moving from stalled to *Send*. But we hope that what we say here will help the intimidated, the blocked, the busy, the hesitant, and the uncertain move into a more effective mode of research, discovery, inquiry, and publication. Becoming a productive researcher and writer requires a long-term program of reading and research that is reflected in successive professional growth plans; again, this program is about vocation, not conjuring up a portfolio. What we offer here will take more than a weekend to implement. But we have seen dozens of faculty move toward life-giving and productive rhythms of research and publication by adapting some of these ideas to their specific situations.

## The Real Tensions Academic Writers Experience

First, we should address the real tensions many faculty experience, especially when new to their jobs. We do so not because we have big news to break here, but because we want to set the remainder of the chapter in a realistic context, one that is packed with conflicting demands and expectations. All courses take work; we and our readers know that too well. In a normal term, preparation, instruction, grading, assessment, and course revision can easily fill a work week. That full-week calculation is without any department or committee work or the inevitable interventions of life, such as a child's dental appointment. For a new faculty member or for any faculty member with a new course, preparation—when done with integrity—takes more time. There, in one paragraph we have just filled the typical faculty member's week, without asking when she or he will do research or write. We consider that time crunch the number one tension for faculty: "How can I do research and writing when teaching and administration take that much time?"

Tightly connected to that tension, many faculty need larger blocks of time than they naturally get in a typical week of teaching and departmental work. Therefore, the obvious pattern for some is to view the summer term as a time to conduct research and complete writing projects. Some faculty follow this pattern successfully; others struggle to make it work because of tiredness, postponed projects at home, summer holidays with family, and so on.

Some feel a tension between what makes them passionate and their perception of what topics or writing genres academic journals prefer to publish. Some faculty—especially those freshly arrived in the academy from professional or clinical practice—tend to discount their own perspectives, knowledge, and experience. Somehow, the arcs of their own life appear to them illegitimate as sources of writing. As we noted in Chapter Six, interdisciplinary and integrative interests can generate their own doubts for faculty because of a well-founded suspicion that tenure/promotion committees and many academic journals prefer to publish work well bounded within disciplines.[1] Many faculty also believe that even if they succeeded at publishing an article in a journal, the peers who review their portfolio might look more favorably on a published article about a substantive issue within their respective disciplines than on an article that represents the scholarship of teaching within that discipline. The question of how to find the most appropriate journal for their work hobbles some academic writers.

Some faculty lack basic factual information about the writing and submission process. As far as they know, their institutions offer no formal venues for disseminating that information, and they may wonder how to revise work from their doctoral course papers or dissertation into a form appropriate for submission for publication. They may lack knowledge about the path to writing and submitting an academic journal article or even to publishing a book review, and that lack of knowledge undermines their motivation to complete the writing. Writing aside, they may wonder how to get a sympathetic hearing from the editors of whatever journal they might submit to if they were to complete a journal article and submit it. Not knowing the details of submission processes generates more apprehension.

Many faculty have a dozen or more ideas about what they would like to write (if ten assistants suddenly appeared in their life!) but literally do not know where to start. To be blunt, some faculty have a chaos of ideas, but these remain fuzzy and in the background because of the demands of teaching. Ideally, faculty with fresh graduate degrees in hand or those who have just completed two or more decades of professional practice and now face the expectation that they will teach and write, should perhaps be told not to worry about writing for a couple of years (which we suggested already, in Chapter Five), so that they can begin their academic career by growing into their teaching. Whether or not their institutions allow them that freedom, they will eventually need to transition from the rhythms of graduate school or professional practice into the rhythms of teaching, research, and publication.

We start with the real tensions that academic writers experience because we need to be candid: you will experience these tensions, too. So, don't be naïve. Writing is no ivory tower experience. If you desire to be a productive and effective writer, you need to understand the terrain and prepare for the journey. A good deal of writing is simply hard and honest work. But we also hasten to tell you that it is good work and can be part of a very satisfying journey. Do not be discouraged.

## Dispositions

Successful academic writers typically share several attitudes about or dispositions toward their research and writing. We view the dispositions we list here as typical of productive professors, not as necessary and certainly not as sufficient. We also think of them as a basket or package; an individual does not need them all to research and write productively, but we doubt anyone who lacks them all can succeed as an academic researcher and writer. Most people will need to possess several of these characteristics if they hope to work productively. We invite our readers to approach our list of dispositions as an invitation—that is, people can develop dispositions. In his *Ethics*, Aristotle argues that we can change our dispositions by changing our behavior. Regarding these dispositions especially, we agree with Aristotle. We believe that people can grow into these.

Recalling Chapters Four through Seven of this book, we urge our readers to consider again Boyer's argument that both institutions and faculty see the connections between all the domains of scholarship. Research and writing do not live in some silo that faculty get to visit if we ever have time; they run through all of our work. In view of Boyer, one does not produce articles and chapters to pass one's annual review, lengthen one's CV, or make one's department chair or dean happy. Rather, research and writing build a stronger foundation for one's teaching and service. They provide a means of reflecting on teaching and service. They become a venue by which we live into and out of our God-given academic vocation. And, we trust, they make the world a slightly better place. In other words, we have an integrated, Boyeuristic understanding of scholarship that includes research and writing, teaching, and engagement. We begin then by arguing that productive academic writers will be those who view all their work as scholarship and who view it as a whole, in the integrated way that Boyer described.

Second, many successful writers tend to love language. They love words and their origins. They love the sounds and rhythms of language, the aural or rhetorical qualities and cadences of written and spoken language. They look up unfamiliar words they encounter in their reading, perhaps adding them to a *new words* file on their computer or in a notebook. It is a truth universally acknowledged that they play with sentences and invoke images unannounced. The further readings we recommend at the end of this chapter include works by Stanley Fish and Stephen King, both of whom discuss this kind of delight in sentences and their construction.

Most productive scholars have an incurable fascination with finding things out. They find the whole world, whether natural or made by humans, amazing, and they live in a constant state of wonder (we noted this characteristic in Chapter Six as well). Doubtless, academics conduct and publish research for reasons ranging from wanting to improve the world (the noble), to getting promoted (the pragmatic), to demonstrating their brilliance to their colleagues or family (the less noble). Some of these motivations yield more joy than others. The plain old desire to find things out yields immense satisfaction to many researchers. They wake up in the night wondering "Why is that the case?" or "What would happen if . . . ?" They design and conduct research to look for the answer to their question and, when they get the answer (or find out they had asked the wrong question), they look for ways to tell the world what they have learned.[2]

Most successful academic writers build a corpus of work, an *oeuvre*, in the same sense that we speak of the body of work produced by J. S. Bach, Dorothy L. Sayers, or Frank Lloyd Wright. We have used this word throughout the book because we believe that, framed this way, the time and effort given to reading, researching, and writing for a particular article or chapter are in a very important sense given not only to this current project. Rather, they are invested in one's whole life work. Like some financial investments, these investments grow and can be drawn from later in life. The disposition here is not hard to identify: the successful academic writer views the current project not just as the current project but as the current installment in a life's work.

The view of one's work as a lifetime's work leads naturally to the next disposition. We have observed that most successful academic writers are disposed to view their academic work as vocation, another word we have used repeatedly. That is, they research and teach and serve in the academy because they have heard a voice; they work in response to a call. Christians find this language familiar, and many Christians in the academy work in response to what they believe is an actual divine call. Academic writers who conduct research and write in response to such a call sense they are onto something great. They do not say to themselves, "This is what I have to do to get promoted." Instead, they say, "This is what I get to do." They do not say, "This is what I get to do when I finish my work." They say, "This *is* my work." We will not repeat here what others have already written at greater length elsewhere, but we do recommend that readers interested in academic work as vocation see the books we have recommended at the end of this chapter under the heading "The Academic Vocation."

Recognizably, productive writers come to their work with dispositions other than what we have discussed here; and we remind our readers and ourselves that none of these is sufficient, and they are not all necessary. But we believe that productive academic researchers/writers will certainly possess some of these dispositions, and we remain confident that people can learn new dispositions.

## Concepts

Every faculty member views research and writing through certain lenses or within some kind of cognitive framework. That framework has in it ideas, distinctions, old sayings, social knowledge (what we call hallway mythology), stories from other academics or writers, memories, and even jokes. Some of this stock of taken-for-granted knowledge hinders academics from writing, and some of it encourages writing.[3] In what follows, we offer a dozen concepts that we hope will encourage you to write and will help you press *Send* sooner rather than never.

## The Long Haul

Our observation of the work of hundreds of productive academic writers reveals they consistently gain a measure of sanity from the concept of *the long haul*. We discussed already the related disposition of viewing one's current project as part of a lifetime's work, not just an additional entry on one's CV meant to satisfy a department chair or dean. In teaching, the new professor can look forward to improving, especially if he or she intentionally and systematically addresses matters of curriculum, instruction, assessment, and the ethos in which those occur, what some call the CIA rope.[4] We have already dealt with teaching and the scholarship of teaching at length in Chapter Five, but we note it again specifically with reference to this concept. As we write, both of us are in our last decade of our careers. And we both do our work better than we did two decades ago—or three. The same holds true in scholarship. Feeling the pressure to publish, new professors often adopt a kind of gotta-crank-it-out attitude, perhaps producing some work that they will later view as marginal and sacrificing too many of the good things of life along the way.[5] Many times reading becomes one of those sacrifices; the professor who would be productive over the long haul needs to read for the long haul. Viewed as part of the long haul, one's current project is not just a single project; it is both a dividend paid because of earlier investments of research and reading, and it is also a further investment in a lifetime's *oeuvre*.

## The Lousy First Draft

We take this second concept—*the lousy first draft*—from Anne Lamott's *Bird by Bird*.[6] Readers already familiar with her book know she uses slightly earthier language in her description of the first draft. Her point, and our reason for quoting her, is straightforward: we cannot expect perfection of ourselves in our first go at a piece of writing. Lamott directed *Bird by Bird* at fiction writers; we believe academic writers could benefit from her advice as well. Actually, we recommend that you read the whole book. We like Lamott's concept because it is both straightforward and powerfully liberating for writers. Too many writers have as their goal the quick and perfect expression of some idea, which, unfortunately, remains vague at the outset of writing. And too many writers worry about their voice in the early drafts.

Lamott advises, and we agree, that the task in the early drafts is to get ideas, themes, complaints, questions, insights, counterarguments, and the like, onto paper. Some kind of coherent order may begin to emerge only in the later drafts, sometimes in the seventh or eighth or later draft. The first numbered file might contain only some idea sparks, a summary of some reading, a piecemeal outline, or even a rant. In some cases, it might have less than that, perhaps only a quotation, a recollection of a cartoon, song, or movie scene, or an interchange at a conference. But the writer who succeeds is the writer who keeps working and playing with what is already in the file and who keeps writing new things down, including whole book or article summaries from a bibliographic database and even notes to self such as "see Morehouse, p. 19" or "get ref for this from JB." In other words, the early drafts are an evolving transformation of a set of notes and ideas on their way to becoming a coherent and structured piece of prose. The record for either of us is "draft 33" for one co-authored article. And our point is not that producing it caused pain (because it did not cause pain) but that the article is published, and it looks better now than it did when it was either "draft 1," typed as a rant, on a train, after a night class, or "draft 18," when the two authors were negotiating how to structure the main, central section. To be absolutely clear about drafts, the first draft is messy by intention. It is not just a work in progress, which it is; it is also the work site. Construction sites look messy, with building materials stacked and stored here and there; they are often strewn with packaging and garbage. Like construction projects, early drafts are messy. The landscaping comes last.

### Balance between Production and Perfection

The concept of the lousy first draft brings us to another powerful and related concept. A carpenter once told one of us that he always had to find *the balance between production and perfection.* Because he needed his shop to make a profit so he could earn his own living and keep his staff employed, he needed production. Any customer with unlimited funds and time could demand and pay for perfection, but most of the time that carpentry shop will need to find the balance. Writers also work in the tension between production and perfection. Of course we could improve our work if we held onto it a bit longer.

We have all read academic work that needed more thought and more editing.[7] In a sobering cartoon one of us had hanging on his fridge door for many years, the wife says, "There are so many bad books out there, sweetheart, surely you could write one." Agreed, many published works could have used more care before going to press, or perhaps they should never have gone at all. Putting such warnings aside for the moment, we want to encourage our readers that—in the name of publishing something—they should eventually press *Send*. As we mentioned in Chapter Three, Boyer himself pained over every word of every draft, often revising a document over 100 times before submission. Few of us have the luxury of that much time or staff support. But in the name of balancing perfection with production, we should keep the *Send* button in sight.

### Writing to the Word Count

Next, we offer *writing to the word count* as a simple but very powerful concept. We know some readers will find this idea counterintuitive, perhaps even distasteful. After all, should our writing not be driven by the results of our research or by some grand vision? Yes it should. But the person who does the writing, squeezed by time and quite possibly with paper and books stacked on every horizontal surface in sight, needs a concept that will liberate him or her to write *now*, for these few minutes. We know that our readers can do math, but we suggest this unpacking of the concept of writing to word count. A chapter or article typically involves writing 5,000–8,000 words, including references. Of course we do not know the appropriate structure for whatever specific articles or chapters you may be writing in your academic discipline, but for the sake of argument we propose that an introduction, at 10–15 percent of the overall length, will therefore run between 750 and 1,200 words. The writer writing to word count faces a different task from the writer writing to the research or to the grand vision. She no longer has to ask, "How will I ever find the time to write this 7,000-word article in this crazy semester?" Rather, she can ask, "Can I write a first draft of a nine-hundred-word introduction by Friday?" If she keeps Anne Lamott's concept in mind, she can change the question to, "Can I write a *lousy* first draft of a nine-hundred-word introduction by Friday?" Combined, those two concepts could help many faculty get past whatever blocks their writing.

We will return to the concept of writing to word count later in this chapter when we explore some of the habits of productive writers, but we want to point out one more benefit of it here: it allows the writer to work under imperfect conditions. One of us wrote the first draft of this chapter on a noisy train. The idea was not to produce the last draft of the chapter that would coherently bring together decades of writing experience and a dozen courses and workshops. The idea was to start a computer file with at least a thousand words related to useful writing concepts. The train ride lasted three hours. The first draft of this file had 1,700 words. It initially looked more like a messy construction site than a book chapter, but it constituted a start. Some of those initial words filled a much-needed gap in this chapter (and, appropriately, disappeared along the way). Others have remained in the file. We know that some writers sense a deep, visceral resistance to this word count approach. It may not be for all. But it works for us.

## The Appointment with Yourself

We tie writing to word count to two other concepts, *the writing block* and what we call *the appointment with yourself*. If you review the last month or so, you will recall that you made and kept appointments to take care of such matters as your health, your teeth, your hair, your car, your children's education or health, some gift purchases and social events, even perhaps your dog's license. Some of these might rank only as errands, but you ran them. Others required that you book and plan weeks in advance, in some cases arranging child care, class coverage, or alternate transportation. Our point is, you got there; you showed up. Could you make similar appointments with yourself for writing?

We do not ask our readers to think that three hours per day for writing will suddenly appear five times per week because you read this book. But what if you asked for fifty minutes one day next week? What if you booked such an appointment in your planner right now and treated it as if it were a dental appointment, one that you would keep, even if you could give more time to your classes and even if you have three hundred messages in your in-box when that time comes? What would that be like? Whether they use this or some other label, productive writers keep appointments with themselves, many while ignoring three hundred messages in their in-boxes. To quote Polonius, Yogi Berra, or Groucho Marx, they keep showing up for work. The appointment with yourself is a simple concept. Initially, it is very hard to put into practice because the habits entailed in *not* writing have such deeply furrowed neural pathways. Dental appointments have no such pathways, but we get to them. If we will make—and keep—such appointments for writing, those appointments will eventually form their own deeply furrowed pathways.

## *The Writing Block*

The *writing block* actually has two meanings. First, it is not what we typically call writer's block; it is something far different from that. The writing block is a time-planning concept. For many writers, the hour from 6:00 to 7:00 A.M. is a writing block. We both plan our writing time with such blocks.[8] The "results section" in a research article is also a writing block; this is the second meaning. Some academic writers write to the clock (or to word count, its cousin), and others write most productively to the section (another of word count's cousins). We do not recommend one over the other, but we do recommend that you try both and eventually adopt one or the other. The task—the chapter or article—is too big and intimidating a prospect for most of us. And, also for most of us, the time available—the semester, week, or even day—is too amorphous. But most of us can think about a nine-hundred-word introduction or the slot from 6:00 to 7:00 tomorrow morning.

Obviously, the block-as-section approach ties to outlining, and those who like to organize and outline their writing may therefore prefer this approach. One advantage of this understanding of block planning is that if you find yourself conceptually blocked in one section, you can go to another section and carry on working there. The time-scheduled block may be more suited to those who think the first real opening in their schedules will be in May of the year they retire. We do not want to over-simplify this concept, but it actually is simple; it entails (as a beginning) that you identify a fifty-minute block in your planner for some time in the next seven days, keep the appointment with yourself, and produce some words. Imagine the endorphin rush if right now you identified one block in the next seven days and kept that appointment with yourself—the start of a new neural pathway.

---

**Error Reporting**

# Time not found

The writing time you were hoping would appear in your schedule by Friday did not appear. Meetings, e-mail, and other urgent matters did magically appear. For next week, try blocking out that time in your calendar.

If you believe the lack of time for research and writing is ontological, check with God or Descartes. Otherwise, check your calendar to see if you blocked it out.

Cancel

---

### Unsubmitted Work Never Gets Rejected

Writing to the word count and keeping appointments with yourself lead naturally to another important concept. We both grew up where people play hockey: Michigan (PA), and Saskatchewan (KB). Hockey players and fans all learn that "you never miss the shots you do not take." We believe that saying has a sobering parallel in the academy: *unsubmitted work never gets rejected* and its corollary, *only submitted work gets published.*

The downside of never missing the shots you do not make, of course, is that you never score on those (non)shots either, just as unsubmitted work is never accepted.

We will not belabor the obvious importance of this concept. But we want to point out a kind of subterranean layer to it. When an article finally does appear, even after thirty-three drafts, and even if its author(s) had to revise and resubmit three or four times, to two or three different journals, readers will see only the article that finally appears (a tautology, we know). But let us emphasize: readers will read it and use it and perhaps quote it, but they will never know how many missed shots preceded it. They will know only that someone took the shot; someone pressed *Send*. We both know the fear of having our writing rejected, of having our work sent to reviewers who might fail to appreciate how insightful, funny and widely read we are. But the alternative—having our work never appear because we have kept it in The Computer Folder of Eternal Safety—drives us to press on and to press *Send*.

## Your Voice

As do writers everywhere, we examine the concept of *voice*. If you do a quick search on the Web, you will find several sites claiming you can find your writer's voice by following these steps or those steps. About as many sites will claim that voice comes naturally and you do not need to follow steps at all to find it. Like many writers, we believe you develop your writing voice mainly by writing. In view of that conclusion, we want to note one aspect of voice that academic writers in particular should concern themselves with. As we understand it, the point of academic writing is to say something, to get our ideas into view for the rest of the academy and, ultimately, for the public. To do that, we will need to develop a voice. *Develop* is the key verb in that sentence. To develop your voice you will need to write, and write, and write (unless the Websites claiming you can develop it without doing anything are correct). Because we believe that discussions of how fiction writers find or develop their voice also apply to academic writers, we list several worthy books about writing at the end of this chapter.

In academic nonfiction, voice has a corollary: *conversation*; as academics we need to locate our own voice in a wider conversation, one that started a long time before we joined in. We take this concept of conversation from Mortimer Adler's second volume in the Great Books series, *The Great Conversation*.[9] Whether or not you agree with the concept of great books or with the particular selections made by the Britannica editors for their series, you must agree that our job as academics always remains both to enter a conversation and to enter that conversation respectfully. That usually implies writing a responsible literature review or, in some fashion, attending to, honoring, and engaging with those who have engaged with each other—before our arrival—on the topic at hand. Having done that, we may then speak to that topic. We recognize that these two concepts of conversation and voice exist in a creative tension with each other. Faculty have graded students' papers that erred toward both extremes, some of them reading like a diary entry (on the too-much-voice end of the continuum), and others filled with stacked quotations (on the too-much-attention-to-the-conversation end of the continuum). Academics aim for writing that attends to the conversation but speaks something into that conversation.[10]

## Vision and Task

Most successful academic writers have found the happy meeting point between the grand vision and this week's and this day's tasks. These two words—*vision* and *task*—apply perfectly to scholarly writing and connect to the idea of an appointment with yourself. We borrow this duo of terms from the title of a book about Christian education written by some scholars at Calvin College.[11] On their account, a task without a vision is drudgery (need we explain?), but a vision without a task is simply a dream. Many faculty envision writing articles and books on important topics in their field. Perhaps in their most private and least humble fantasies, they become leaders in their field. But the envisioning, the vision, needs to be realized in action. So we ask not only what is the writing that you or we envision, but also what is the next task we need to do to fulfill that vision? We could make the point more precise by asking what is the one task you or we will work on before this Friday?

The best books about writing, Anne Lamott's *Bird by Bird* and Stephen King's *On Writing*, for example, tend to de-romanticize writing, viewing it as work, simple work. Patrick Kinsella, whose story *Shoeless Joe* became the basis for the movie, *Field of Dreams*, views writing the same way. He says writing is a "buns on the chair" activity.[12] Some might find Kinsella's observation simplistic. We do not. While it is sobering, the truth is that those who succeed in producing academic writing do so to a significant degree because they have learned the simple discipline of sitting at a desk and making words. In our decade, even more than when Kinsella wrote *Shoeless Joe*, that discipline likely implies that writers have switched off their e-mail. If Kinsella and King and Lamott are right, then we may legitimately extrapolate that the productive writer views *writing as a task like other tasks*. Writing is simply one of the things we do. It is not a prize that we get to claim when all our courses and administrative work are done or when everything else is in order. And it is certainly not a punishment because we happen to work in the academy.

## The Walled Garden

Finally, we introduce the concept of *the walled garden*. Most of the dispositions and concepts we have listed connect to habits. We introduce this concept last because it perhaps connects most closely to habits. Many successful writers protect their writing with the concept of a walled garden or something like it. A few of our readers may actually have the luxury of writing in a literal walled garden. Finances, children, urban noise, teaching, geography, and other of life's interventions mean most of us probably write in an office at home or in our departmental hallway (we hope not in the literal hallway). So the walled garden is less about a physical place and more about time and a mental frame for writing. In fact, this concept relates so closely to dispositions that perhaps we should list it there. Here are a few ways experienced writers carve out a walled garden—the time and a place for writing—in their busy work weeks.

- They set a timer for fifty minutes or one hour and do nothing but write until the clock rings.
- They go to a coffee shop or library to work for one hour.
- They turn their cell phone off and tell the department administrative assistant to hold all calls for one hour.
- They turn off e-mail. They note on scratch paper anything not related to their writing that comes to mind and check it later. They asterisk or highlight in their draft file anything related that needs checking online—and check later. This scratch-paper strategy is simply to help the writer stay off-line and thereby away from e-mail.[13]
- They usually write in the same physical place, for example, the dining room table or a simple desk somewhere other than the office desk where they do most of their administrative computer work. Some use a nook in the college library. Some literally build a simple micro-office under a staircase, thereby channeling Harry Potter, albeit not his author.
- They get up earlier or stay up later and call it their "writing time."

This list of typical characteristics reflects the truth that for productive writers the walled garden relates to both time and place. At the end of this chapter, we suggest several questions to lead our readers in a time of retreat or reflection on how to construct a walled garden for writing.

## Everyone Needs an Editor

We find a measure of liberation in the idea that *everyone needs an editor.* Not just weaker writers, but all writers need someone who will read our work and give us honest criticism. We recommend that you pay one commercially instead of asking a colleague. Do not use someone who loves you. Such people will worry about your feelings and then go too easy on you. You need a good writer, likely one trained in editing, who has the courage and the vocabulary to tell you the truth about your writing and who can make concrete suggestions for making it better. When contacting and querying potential editors, be sure to understand the differences between proofreading, copy editing, editing for syntax, and editing for structure and argumentation. These are four quite different levels of editing and if—like most academics—you want help with the middle two, then you would be wise to know what you are asking for. Many writers want the middle two or even the last three but make the mistake of asking someone who worries about their feelings and, in response, only proofreads the manuscript.

### Idea Sparks

Finally, we introduce the concept of twenty-five to 150 word *idea sparks*. These grow out of journal entries and begin as marginal doodles from meetings and conference papers. They originate in conversations, reading, and classes. For example, one of us recently wrote in a margin at an education conference, "This is so boring; drive the needle into my eye but please stop talking!! Why don't education professors follow their own advice about pedagogy? Why do they always lecture in their conference sessions?" Perhaps several years from now, this marginal note will lead to some formal exploration of the question (or at least a scintillating lecture). Meanwhile, it rests securely in a file called "Ideas May 2013." Given that all faculty members have such ideas and write notes to themselves, we need two things. First, we need a system to keep track of such ideas. Second, we need conversation partners to help us discern which sparks are worthy of research and continued attention. We will address both those needs in the next section.

## Habits, Strategies, and Systems

Successful writers do not all use the same strategies, nor do they all practice the same habits. But enough successful writers commonly rely on enough similar strategies and follow enough similar patterns that we will list some here. We noted already that we do not view this as a how-to chapter, but inevitably this section and the next one will strike some readers that way. We have met many faculty who want to know how to get a book to review, or how to find the time to write, or how to submit an academic article to a journal (or any number of other how-to questions related to academic writing), so we know many will value what we offer here, its how-to tone notwithstanding. If the map of the academy for new faculty has "Here be monsters" written anywhere, it would be in the region related to writing for publication.

## Tracking Systems

Most successful writers have *a system for tracking ideas and sparks of ideas*, whether they come from reading, conversations, dreams, long walks, conference sessions, or blinding flashes of light. Writers use journals and notebooks, index cards, e-mails to self, bibliographic databases, and a dozen more ways to keep track of ideas. We make only one recommendation here: devise a system. That system will offer you more if it helps you find out about and order relevant research materials, receive advance notifications of new publications, record references, and take notes that you can actually understand when you come back to them.

We do not consider ourselves techies,[14] but both of us prefer digital systems because those systems save us from having to type ideas or bibliographic details more than once. Some academics think of database software on a piecemeal basis. That is, they use the software to format the references and bibliography for the particular piece of writing they are working on at the moment, and bibliographic databases do format references simply and usually quite well. But we view the database as much more: it serves as the academic's personal library, the record of a lifetime of reading. Formatting references is—literally—the last thing you need from your bibliographic database.

To increase the utility of your database software, we recommend taking the extra few seconds required when entering a new record to type in five or six *keywords* in the keyword or subject field. All the recommended readings that appear at the end of this chapter are included in the bibliographic database of the author who first drafted this chapter, and all include the keyword *writing* in the database entry. We also recommend that you use *meta-tags* or the *groups* function in your database. We will not explain meta-tags here but will note that the recommended readings we list in this chapter have meta-tags tied to a course one of us teaches: 685W4P ("writing for publication"). Your campus librarian will happily explain the difference between a subject word, a keyword and a meta-tag. Our point is that you can tie a group of references to specific course syllabi and bibliographies or to specific writing projects; you can even use meta-tags to indicate an item's status such as "ordered for church library."[15] Ultimately, we tie this advice about keywords and meta-tags back to the concept of a lifetime's work or *oeuvre*. If you know that someday you will write about subject X and you come across something germane to it today, you can tell yourself that you will remember this reference when the time comes. Really? How about making the note, with a keyword or meta-tag that will still be there in fifteen years.

### Back-Up Systems

Nearly all successful academic writers have a *simple back-up system,* using either their campus server, a cloud service, or a flash drive. We will not explain this further, but we urge you to devise and start using a back-up system now. Do not make jokes about backing up your hard drive after you retire. You will lose too much work between now and then, even if retirement comes next year.

Most publishers and editors use *a draft numbering system,* as do many productive academic writers. We recommend that you adopt this practice. Very simply, every time you touch a draft, renumber the draft (one higher) and include the date in the filename. If you are writing with one or more other people, include your own name in the file name. Keep all your earlier drafts of any given project until the project is done. Why? Because storage is free, because accidents happen, because work gets lost, because computers crash, because we change our minds about what belongs and does not belong in a given piece of writing and do not want to give time to retyping or energy to regretting.

This paragraph, for example, initially appeared in a file called "productive scholar draft 4 Ken November 25." It will likely go to draft 14 or 15 before the book appears. The draft numbering system has a psychological benefit as well: every time you open a directory to retrieve your draft you see a visual record of your progress, a tangible source of encouragement for faculty who perhaps feel like they do not get to their writing as often as they wish.

## Word Count Strategies

Many productive writers habitually check the *word count*, which we also mentioned in the concepts section. Some set a word count goal for a given day or for a given time slot. When interacting more heavily with research materials, for example in the literature review section of an article, your typing rate will obviously be lower than when writing material with fewer references. Regardless of what you are writing at a particular time, we recommend setting a realistic word count goal. And whatever the goal—two hundred words in one hour or five hundred words in one day—we recommend writing to word count because it allows you to enjoy small celebrations for work completed.

One of us (KB) checks his word count approximately every fifteen minutes while writing. That will sound obsessive to some. The habit actually arises out of Mihaly Csikszentmihalyi's work on flow.[16] For those unfamiliar with Csikszentmihalyi's use of that word, he means roughly what athletes mean by the word *zone*. One of the conditions he names for flow states is consistent feedback. Runners wear smart watches to track their pace and their pulse. Parents measure their children's physical and academic progress. Writers celebrate incremental progress by checking word count.[17] Writing to word count may sound like a form of indentured servitude, an overly bold counter to the idea that writing requires inspiration, but it is actually liberating, especially for those whose habit of noting the growing number of written words flows out of the concept of writing to word count as we described it earlier.

Writing to word count also helps control verbal overruns. The disciplined author of a 900-word introduction knows she cannot give 250–300 words to a minor part of that section. She also knows that if she has only 900 words to work with, and her introduction must set up two major ideas and three minor ones (as well as include three or four sentences to start the whole article and a transition to end the section, the approximate word counts on all those parts become quite clear: 50–75 (start) + 250 +

250 (major ideas) + 100 + 100 + 100 (minor ideas) + 40–60 (transition to remainder of article). This may seem very mechanical to some, but, again, many productive writers work this way because they find it liberating. The author watching her word count while writing an introduction does not need to work for a year to set her project within the whole history of the universe. Rather she needs to write 60 words, or 250 words, or 100 words or, in the case of the final transitions in the introduction, something about the length of a brief e-mail.[18] Furthermore, if she has set her goal to produce only a lousy first draft by Friday, she may actually be able to complete one of those hundred-word sections before that student comes by. A hundred words—that's five sentences—two e-mails.

## Daily Writing, Reading Habits

Productive writers *write every day*, even if only for a few minutes. Some writers recommend that you write at the same time every day, and others recommend that you always write in the same location (the walled garden). Following both recommendations would help most writers construct their own walled garden. In discussing the concept of an appointment with yourself, we noted that our neural pathways either encourage or discourage writing. Thanks to advances in brain research, we now know a lot about the neurological dimension of habits. Writing and not writing are both habits. If one habitually does not write, for any of the dozens of reasons that non-writing faculty typically offer, how can one abandon the deeply rutted neural pathway called *not writing* and start to form furrows on a different neural pathway called *writing*? We will not repeat the literature here on the neurology of breaking habits and forming new habits, but we believe most of our readers can form the writing habit.

An obvious corollary to writing every day, productive academic writers *read every day*. We do not need to write a long commentary about this. Writing and teaching both require that we draw from a lifetime's scholarly investment. We must steward and nurture those investments. If we are to sustain a pattern of scholarship, we must invest continuously. We read because we must sustain the vocation we are following.

## *E-mail Habits*

Productive writers *control their e-mail*. Protections from e-mail range from simply not checking (although e-mail might be open, only a click away), to writing on a computer that is not connected to the Internet. We will not give advice here regarding the degree to which our readers need to protect themselves from e-mail, but we know that most productive writers do not attend to e-mail during the time slots they have blocked out for writing. At minimum, we believe the faculty member who wants to build regular writing into his or her academic week will have turned off the *Desktop Notifications*—which might as well be called *Writing Interruptions*—for e-mail. Productive writers open their e-mail intentionally at specific times and respond. Then they return to their writing.

## *Clean Submission Habits*

Successful academic writers habitually *submit clean manuscripts*, by which we mean manuscripts characterized by the complete absence of factors that repel editors. This claim has several aspects. First, the submitted work must fit the writer's best understanding of the journal's stated purposes and preferred genre or range of genres. If you are unfamiliar with a particular journal, we suggest that you read several back issues to get a clear idea of its purposes and preferences. Your library databases likely include such directories as Cabell's and Ulrich's, both of which index and provide key information about scholarly journals.

Second, the author submitting an academic article will not violate any of the submission protocols or advertised format requirements. These protocols can include not identifying the author within the article, always using inclusive language, following the journal's preferred style guide (Chicago, MLA, APA, etc.), and adhering to the preferred font and page or word count. Some of our readers may wonder (rightly) why we would need to offer this advice. We do so because editors send back a significant percentage of submissions because authors did not attend to these simple matters.

Third, the successful submission usually contains no grammar, spelling, or punctuation errors and no bad writing.[19] We know that few people achieve perfection easily in these areas, a reason we strongly recommend using an editor as well as taking advantage of the tools built into your word processor (which we discuss in more detail in the next section).

### Preferred by Journal Editors

There are some positive features that will encourage journal editors to seriously consider a submission, although we recognize that including a list of such features might cause writers to assume incorrectly the list is exhaustive and contains sufficient conditions. Let us caution: the list is not exhaustive, and these conditions are not sufficient. But they are typical.

**Clear and Interesting.** First, accepted articles usually have clear, interesting, and possibly even catchy titles, followed by absolutely clear and tight abstracts.[20] Editors take more seriously the article whose author has followed the clear title and abstract with a clear introductory paragraph that contains a clear thesis or statement of the research question being addressed in the article. Writers who work for magazines know they have only the first paragraph to hook the reader. Perhaps as academic writers we should work under the same burden.

**New Insight.** Editors are more prone to publish an article that contains some genuinely new insight or makes some new contribution to the field, even if it is a narrow and incremental contribution. Many editors look for articles that make connections between things that no one has connected before. We do not believe interdisciplinarity to be the "new black," and we noted our cautions about interdisciplinary and integrative work in Chapter Six. Those concerns notwithstanding, we believe that for scholars who believe the whole world belongs to God and that in the Reign of Christ the academic disciplines will all bow in allegiance to God, interdisciplinary scholarship is a field ready for harvest.[21]

**Good Writing.** Journal editors want to see competent writing at minimum, and they look with favor on the article that has at least some sections of good, memorable writing. On these pages we cannot instruct anyone on how to move from competent to good writing any more than we can show them how to drive better or play the piano better. But we do know that good writing almost always involves repeated editing by the author and at least one edit by an editor. We urge our readers to form the habit of editing at least twice by reading their writing aloud—from a paper version of the work—and listening for rhetorical, oral (aural) qualities. A sentence that will not work as speech will usually not work in print. Reading and editing aloud help most writers identify clunky syntax in their writing.[22] Not one word should sound like it originated in a thesaurus, even if it did. Again, we view meeting these conditions not as sufficient, not as guarantees of publication, but simply as necessities to get an editor even to look at your work and consider sending it on to reviewers.

## Conference Strategies

Even when facing shrinking professional budgets, faculty need to attend conferences and present papers. Given that pressure, our readers may consider this bit of advice odd, but we recommend that you habitually *attend fewer conferences but complete a 6000-word manuscript* as the foundation of your presentation. We say *foundation* because no one wants to hear a colleague read a 6000-word paper at a conference. But if you have created this foundation, immediately after the conference, even on your way home, you can revise the manuscript so that you can submit it quickly. Academics present literally millions of conference papers that never appear in print.[23] In general, we should perhaps give thanks for their absence. But, to our point here, some of that work—some of your work—needs to move ahead to publication. The writer who takes a completed manuscript to the conference is far more likely to submit an article than is the writer who plans to finish the paper afterward.

## Avoidance Habits

We want to suggest two *avoidance habits* that we consider key to success in meeting academic writing goals. First, and for the last time in this chapter, take serious note of what it may imply for your productivity that the seat, keyboard, and screen you use to write are likely the same seat, keyboard, and screen by which e-mail comes into your life. We will not complain about how e-mail functions in our lives; others have done that quite adequately already.[24] Rather, we will suggest a simple strategy. Plan a writing block of fifty minutes. Turn off your browser or e-mail for that block of time. To keep yourself off-line for the fifty minutes, note down on scratch paper any ideas, stray thoughts, or errands you remember during the writing block so that you can focus on writing for the fifty minutes. When the time is up, take an actual break from your chair, check e-mail, do what you like. If you need to take a more aggressive stance regarding your e-mail, learn to treat the subject lines in new e-mails, regardless of their actual wording, as if they said, "Stop being productive in this rare moment of writing, and look at me, look at me! Time to write will magically appear several times later today, but you may NEVER GET ANOTHER E-MAIL IN YOUR LIFE!" We apologize immediately for the sarcastic netspeak outburst, but we use it to help make the point.

Second, *avoid giving writing time to learning new versions of your software or hardware.* Productive academic writers tend to focus on their work and not on their tools. They change technology less often so they can use their time writing rather than learning new systems. Obviously some of the systems faculty use are beyond our control, but to the degree we can, we should focus on using our tools to produce clean manuscripts rather than on learning how those tools work. Remember Kinsella's comment, that writing is about staying in a chair and producing words.

## Tools and Supports

Productive writers admit they need help, and they draw that help from many directions, some human and some technological. Here, we describe a few of the tools that productive writers typically use and supports that they typically have in place.

### Technology Tools

Most word-processing systems offer an arsenal of tools for writers. Unfortunately, most writers do not know about the variety of tools available aside perhaps from the thesaurus and the spell-checker. We strongly recommend that you explore your word processor to find those tools and switch on those that would help you address your own writing weaknesses.

We also recommend that faculty spend the five minutes required to learn how to find books not yet published. Go to *Books in Print* through your campus online databases and select "Advanced Search." The advanced search screen includes a "Status" menu that includes "Forthcoming." Selecting Forthcoming will give you some sense of what books publishers plan to release in the next year or two. Amazon also has an "Advanced Search" screen that appears only after you have searched one book title. At the time we were writing this book, Amazon's advanced search allowed you to search any date range, including future dates. Searching both Amazon and Books in Print will produce lists with titles in common and some titles unique to each. Remember that Amazon includes many more self-published titles than does Books in Print.[25] Knowing what books will appear in the coming months will allow you to plan your reading, to order new acquisitions for the library, and to query editors about book reviews.

We recommend that you develop an über-organized directory structure on your computer. We cannot recommend exactly what yours should look like because your life and work are different from ours (and ours are different from each other's), but we know this truth: new sub-directories are free, and organized academic writers use them liberally.

## *Personal Supports*

All but a tiny minority of successful writers need people around them to encourage them to keep writing and to hold them accountable for keeping the appointments with themselves and actually producing words. We can identify no single pattern here. For some, it is a spouse. For others, a colleague or group of colleagues functions this way. Those colleagues can be from within your department or from across campus. In many cases, colleagues from other institutions, even on other continents, help keep faculty focus on their writing responsibilities. Such colleagues or writing partners serve several functions, the most important of which is to encourage writers to meet their deadlines. A book with a contract has its own deadlines, as do encyclopedia articles. But journal articles do not. A few academic writers have the internal resources to keep working on an article until they finish. The rest of us need help.

But writing and revising articles can be lonely, which is why we urge our readers to involve others in the process. Some professional learning communities (PLCs) that focus on writing devote meeting times to reading, others to status reports. Some divide the meeting time ruthlessly so that all members get equal time to present or discuss their work; others take a more relaxed approach, with each meeting taking its own course as individual members have more or less to report. Some meet monthly, and some meet weekly. Writers already pressed for time probably do not want to give up a potential writing slot every week to a meeting devoted to writing (we do not need to explain the potential irony in that pattern). Regardless of what structure would suit you best in your current circumstances with your specific goals, we urge you to join or form a group of colleagues who will serve as a writing PLC.

Neither of us is a behaviorist, but we want to recognize here that writing is partly about behavior. For anyone who still believes that writing is primarily about inspiration rather than perspiration, we recommend Paul Sylvia's *How to Write a Lot*, a book that takes an openly behaviorist approach to writing and the habits and structures usually associated with successful academic writing.[26]

Faculty who write also need help with finding sources. Obviously, researching one's area(s) is an individual task, perhaps primarily so. But we have found that colleagues with some awareness of our topics of interest often feed us references and ideas. We also recommend hiring a part-time research assistant. Many colleges provide student assistants to faculty for a few hours per week. Faculty can assign some research and writing tasks to their assistant, thus providing employment to someone who needs it, and leaving more time to writing the needed words for a given project. We expect that few of our readers are wealthy, but we recommend hiring a research or administrative assistant for a few hours a month out of your own funds if college money is not available. Even a budgeted amount of $100 a month will give you a few hours of research support.

## Pushing and Pulling

We distinguish what we call push and pull factors. For any kind of project to succeed, people need to be both pushing and pulling. Sadly for many faculty, much academic writing lacks pull factors, meaning, simply, that no one is asking or waiting for the work. If and when the faculty member completes a project, he or she can submit it. Until then, no one may be asking how the writing is proceeding or how close to done a particular piece is. A writing group may be established to work as a pull factor.

Although pull factors are largely absent from the academy, they are not entirely absent. An accepted conference proposal forces the academic to prepare—it pulls. Chapters in edited books as well as encyclopedia or dictionary articles have due dates and thus function that way as well. If pull factors function as importantly as we think they do, then academic writers should take steps to build them, whether that means forming a writing PLC or contacting an editor to gauge interest in an article or chapter, to suggest two examples. Rather than work in isolation until a project is done, why not nurture one's writing context and the interest of others along the way?

As we have noted several times, the faculty member who understands academic work as God-given vocation, who is responding to a call, will view academic work as spiritual and professional work. Inasmuch as it is professional, a professional coach might be able to assist the academic who wants to improve. Inasmuch as it is spiritual, a spiritual director might ask the right questions to help a faculty member view writing (or other aspects of faculty life and work) within the larger rhythms of life and as part of the overall trajectory of one's calling and life. You can find the names of both coaches and spiritual directors online. Staff at local churches may also know of spiritual directors. In both cases, quality varies, and faculty members wanting such support should feel free to search until they find someone they trust and who they believe can ask the right questions.

We have mentioned assistants and editors several times in this chapter, and we want to recommend again that you take advantage of such people to help you get your work done (in the first case) and to move it to a publishable standard of quality (in the second). Editors advertise on the Internet.

The administrative assistant or the director of any doctoral program will likely also know of professional editors who work with academic writers.

## Conclusion

We cannot make you write. In fact, no one can. But we believe that faculty who want to write can make a start. Those being compelled to write can make the same start. We made clear that productive writers typically possess some of the dispositions and typically work with some of the concepts we have explored in this chapter. They typically nurture the work habits we have listed and typically use some of the tools and build some of the support systems we have described. We can guarantee nothing.

But we urge you to consider the suggestions we have made. And we invite you to begin by taking a half-day writing retreat, perhaps using some of the questions we include below, and we certainly encourage you to read some of the materials we have suggested in the list below the retreat questions. To recall the cartoon again and twist it slightly, with so much bad writing out there, surely the world does not need yours. Actually, the world cries for good writing that tells the truth in love, and we commend the work of producing that good writing to you, our readers, and to Christian scholars everywhere.

## The Walled Garden: Questions to Guide a Time of Retreat and Reflection on Writing

Even though the writer's walled garden is not merely a physical space, take a moment to think about the features of walled gardens, most of which are carefully planned and structured by designers who incorporate elements to keep out intrusions and focus attention. You usually enter a walled garden through a gate. High stone walls or hedges reduce noise from the surrounding neighborhood. Benches and water features create still places and invite you to stop and enjoy some quiet.

Readers may want to extend the garden metaphor to their specific circumstances. What kind of intrusions do you need to protect your writing from for a single hour? Administrative intrusions? Self-generated emotional intrusions such as apprehensions about submitting your work?

Self-sabotaging behaviors such as checking e-mail? Who would you like to be in your walled garden with you? That is, who do you want to support you in your effort to write? Where is the secure place where you know you will write when you can get there? We urge our readers to plan a one-hour or half-day writing retreat, focusing on the concept of a walled garden. Spend a maximum of five minutes on the Internet (need we say, without checking e-mail?) to find a couple of photos of walled gardens. Reflect on those for a few minutes to calm yourself. Then ask, "If I were trying to find one hour a week to write for the next four weeks, what conditions would yield a walled garden for me?" Using the questions and ideas we have offered here, take a whole hour or a half-day to think about this. Then book the four slots in your planner.

Given the time squeeze that most academic writers experience, is it wise to take time to plan writing rather than simply writing? Periodically, yes. The structure of this chapter makes quite clear that, in our view, academic writing requires not just data and skills. It also requires dispositions, concepts, systems, habits, and supports. And it requires planning. The writing/planning retreat can serve powerfully to alter the faculty member's mindset regarding writing. Here are several questions, framed with first-person pronouns, to help guide a part-day writing retreat.

1. Would an *ideas file* help me, either in a writing journal or in a digital file? Could I e-mail ideas to myself and store the e-mails in a single folder?

2. How might a writing journal or diary help me? Could I use this as a venue for processing ideas and reflections, possibly by writing things here first and then checking later to see if they seem worth expanding into articles?

3. Would *database management software* help me if I built systems around it specifically related to my writing priorities, and my course syllabi? Could I put in the right kind of work and the right amount of work so that my database became not just a way to format references but also my actual resource cache, my library?

4. Could I learn how to use meta-tags in the keywords field of my database records of my books and articles to track reading status, location, and connections to projects and course bibliographies? Which words would be most useful?

5. Could I keep a digital *books to get* file so I do not lose track of any more titles that I come across or that people recommend to me? Could I integrate into this file a system for tracking the books I want to recommend or order for my university library?

6. Can I work *book reviews* into my reading, especially ones that I would read anyway? Do I know how to get the go-a-head on a book review? Do I know how to find out about forthcoming book titles?

7. How would I benefit from a *semi-annual retreat* where I reflect on my grand vision, my current faculty growth plan, and my writing priorities for the current semester?

8. What are *the resources I have* at this point in my life? What online and library resources do I have available? What colleagues would support my work? What do I know at this point in my life? What stage have I reached educationally, professionally, financially, and socially that makes writing easier to do now than it was before? (Examples: children now in school or gone; doctorate done; student loans reduced; years of work experience to draw on; signature courses in good shape.)

9. What connections can I make between my class contents and the research I would like to conduct? What do I need to adjust to make these links and to help me capitalize more on them?

10. How about *a review* of what I have completed recently, including notes about the circumstances in which the writing seemed to work?

11. How about *monthly writing/planning retreats*? Would those work for me? How about booking fifty minutes for writing

in the next seven days, and identifying who will ask me if I kept my appointment? Can someone e-mail me in the thirty-six hours prior to my appointment with myself to help me focus on that slot?

12. Could I find an *editing partner* or become part of a *writing group* (research/writing professional learning community)? Whom do I trust enough that I could make AA-type statements such as "I'm blocked on project X," and celebratory reports such as "Be happy with me because *The Journal of High Impact* just accepted my article"?

13. What times have I blocked out in my planner to work on writing in the next four to six weeks? To whom am I going to report? Who has agreed to read it for me?

## Recommended Readings on Writing

John Alexander, "An Intelligence Role for the Footnote," *Studies in Intelligence*, 8 no. 3, (1964), 1–10.

John Barth, "Writing: Can it Be Taught?" *New York Times*, (June 16, 1985, Late City Final Edition), 1.

Bruno Bettelheim, "Essential Books of One's Life," in Bruno Bettelheim, *Freud's Vienna and Other Essays* (New York: Knopf, 1990).

Louis J. Budd, "On Writing Scholarly Articles," from *The Academic's Handbook*, ed. by A. Leigh DeNeef and Craufurd D. Goodwin (Durham, NC: Duke University Press), 1995.

Gregory G. Colomb, Wayne C. Booth, and Joseph M. Williams, *The Craft of Research,* 3rd edition (Chicago: University of Chicago Press, 2008).

Stanley Fish, *How to Write a Sentence, and How to Read One* (New York: Harper, 2011).

William Germano, "Do We Dare Write for Readers?" *The Chronicle of Higher Education*, (April 22, 2013), http://chronicle.com/article/Do-We-Dare-Write-for-Readers-/138581/?cid=cr&utm_source=cr&utm_medium=en/.

Gina Hiatt, "Writing in Toxic Environments—7 Steps to Change," in *Tomorrow's Professor*, Stanford Center for Teaching and Learning." Retrieved from http://cgi.stanford.edu/~dept-ctl/tomprof/posting.php?ID=921/.

Gertrude Himmelfarb, "Where Have All the Footnotes Gone?" *New York Times Book Review*, (June 16, 1991), 1, 24.

John Irving, *A Widow for One Year* (New York: Ballantine Books, 1998). Some may mistake this for a book obsessed with sex, but it's a wonderful book about writing.

Stephen King, *On Writing: A Memoir of the Craft* (New York: Scribner, 2000).

Anne Lamott, *Bird by Bird: Some Instructions on Writing and Life* (New York: Anchor/Random, 1995).

Elmore Leonard, *Ten Rules of Writing* (full text available online), http://www.nytimes.com/2001/07/16/arts/writers-writing-easy-adverbs-exclamation-points-especially-hooptedoodle.html?pagewanted=all&src=pm/.

John McPhee, "Draft No. 4," *New Yorker* (April 29, 2013): 32–38.

Pat Schneider, *How the Light Gets In* (New York: Oxford Press, 2013).

# Recommended Readings on
# Vocation and the Academic Vocation

Tomie de Paola, *The Clown of God* (New York: Harcourt, Brace, Jovanovich, 1978).

Douglas V. Henry and Bob R. Agee, eds., *Faithful Learning and the Scholarly Vocation* (Grand Rapids, MI: Eerdmans, 2003).

James Hollis, *Finding Meaning in the Second Half of Life* (New York: Gotham/Penguin, 2005).

Richard T. Hughes, *The Vocation of the Christian Scholar: How Christian Faith Can Sustain the Life of the Mind*, 2nd ed. (Grand Rapids, MI: Eerdmans, 2005).

Parker Palmer, *The Courage to Teach* (San Francisco: Jossey-Bass, 1998).

Parker Palmer, *Let Your Life Speak: Listening for the Voice of Vocation* (San Francisco: Jossey-Bass, 2000).

Mark R. Schwehn, *Exiles from Eden: Religion and the Academic Vocation in America* (New York: Oxford Press, 1993).

Gordon T. Smith, *Courage and Calling: Embracing Your God-Given Potential* (Downers Grove, IL: InterVarsity Academic, 2011).

Barbara Brown Taylor, *An Altar in the World* (New York: Harper, 2009).

## Chapter 10

# Looking to the Future

## Reconceiving the Faith-Based University

We began this book by noting that Christian colleges expect new and continuing faculty to articulate clearly an understanding of the impacts that Christian faith has on their teaching, research, and service. They also expect their faculty to be able to assess and demonstrate that they are realizing this understanding in their ongoing work as scholars and teachers. Many faculty find this dimension of their work, often labeled *the integration of faith and learning,* confusing and difficult to practice, to assess, and to describe (Chapter One).

In Chapters Two and Three, we summarized the faith/learning discussion and noted the many different conceptions of faith-learning integration that faculty actually work with. We outlined the expectations for faculty that deans, provosts, tenure-promotion committees, and trustees typically have for faculty in Christian colleges. Then we introduced the highly regarded framework of Ernest Boyer and the Carnegie Foundation (*Scholarship Reconsidered*) and wove together three conversational threads: Boyer's understanding of what scholarship means in each of the domains of scholarship; the expectations of provosts, deans, and tenure-promotion committees in each respective domain; and possible models and meanings of faith and learning integration for each domain (Chapters Four to Seven).

In the final section of this book, we have presented both a framework for assessing faith-learning integration in the three domains of teaching, research and service; listed step-by-step instructions for reporting and describing the individual faculty member's approach and success; and described some of the typical dispositions, concepts, habits and support structures of successful faculty members in Christian colleges (Chapters Eight and Nine).

Thus, we have *looked back* at the ongoing faith-learning integration discussion for context, and we have *looked around* at current institutional practices for insight and assistance, but before we end our examination of the practical dimensions of the faith-integration discussion, we want to *look to the future* and offer another way to understand the challenges of teaching faith-fully for both the faculty serving in a faith-based institution and the wisdom communities that sustain them. To be blunt, we are asking this question: *Are we guarding the ashes of a very tired conversation or are we tending the flame of a vital aspect of our collective work in faith-based institutions?* We hope that what we offer will push this conversation forward.

## Two Challenges

A number of factors make faith-learning integration a challenge, but two quickly rise to the top of the list, one an individual concern and the other an institutional concern. The first is a general lack of theological understanding or sophistication on the part of many faculty members, making it difficult for them to place their faith journeys in a shared communal context. Faculty members often bring to their new post in a Christian college a deep faith in Jesus Christ and a passion for teaching, loving, and serving students; but they struggle when they need to describe and discuss their theological underpinnings in depth or even simply identify their own theological tradition.[1] Some do not even know about theological traditions. This lack of knowledge indicates clearly that many newer faculty have been shaped and formed in a post-denominational context. For example, it is not unusual for a faculty candidate, when asked by a provost during the initial interview process to describe their faith journey, to say something like this: "I attended a Methodist church after college, then switched to a Baptist one in grad school, then an Assembly of God church when we were married, then a Church of Christ close to home, then a Lutheran church, stopped out for a bit while the kids were very young, and we now worship at the Solid Rock because they are friendly and have a great children's program." Wow!

Such inability to reflect critically about one's own theological formation or to locate it within a larger theological tradition becomes a major impediment for faculty members earnest about faith-learning integration, especially so if the institution that has hired such faculty has articulated and attempted to realize (words and deeds) authentically Christian higher education. We believe a new entry strategy is required, a locally-focused inductive approach. Rather than starting with an orientation to the history of Christianity, fundamental elements of the faith, and foundational philosophical assumptions that inform the integrative task (deductive approach), we suggest an inductive approach, starting with the distinct beliefs, practices, traditions, values, and stories of a particular faith community. When a faculty member joins a faith-based institution, it is around these things that a covenant is made.

The second major factor that makes faith-learning integration difficult and confusing for some faculty members (particularly newer faculty) is the lack of alignment between institutional mission, reward structures, and expectations for faculty (which we mentioned at several points in Chapters Four, Five, and Six). Most faith-based institutions have a clear sense of identity; they know who they are, who they serve, and what they do well. Except for a very few cases (Notre Dame and Baylor to name two), most faith-based institutions do not describe themselves as R1 institutions, nor do they aspire to be. Their *raison d'etre* is not the generation of new knowledge. By their own admission they are not Stanford, and never will be nor should be. Faith-based institutions most often think of themselves as teaching universities whose primary mission is the transformation of students in service of the Church or Kingdom (hopefully both). In short, faith-based institutions are Transformational Institutions (T1).[2]

Yet the reward structures for faculty—promotion, tenure, release time, sabbaticals, faculty grants, and recognition—often convey the conviction that individual research remains the purest expression of scholarly work. Thus, while T1 institutions may pay lip service to service and to going the extra mile with students, those activities carry less weight when committees make decisions about promotion and tenure. Sadly, on over a half dozen occasions, we have heard promotion and tenure committee members tell their colleagues during new faculty orientation to avoid engaging too much with students or accepting any university assignments. Instead, if they want to get promoted and be taken seriously by their colleagues, the advice runs, they should stay away from campus several days each week to work on their own reading and research. In other words, while some colleges earnestly profess to be T1 institutions, they try to emulate and to borrow faculty reward and status structures from R1 institutions.

## Misaligned Mission, Rewards

This misalignment of mission and rewards—*the folly of rewarding A while hoping for B*—is a classic organizational problem.[3] And even when formal reward structures align with a T1 mission, the informal status system for faculty members often mimics the R1 world. The highest-regarded faculty members are those who do R1 work within the confines of a T1 world. No academic can miss the academy's hierarchy of deeds, with R1 institutions occupying the top rung and their values shaping the lives of all who occupy the rungs below. If we are to be a good institution, we must be like them—or at least have some faculty who are. And we highlight those faculty activities all the time. We even grant these "stars" release time away from teaching and students so they can do their special work among us. This orientation to faculty work starts in graduate school and never stops.

We believe that faith-based institutions are different—and should be. Christian colleges need to embrace unapologetically their T1 missions. They have no need to work from a deep and abiding sense of inferiority, leading to emulation of the worst kind. If colleges are creative and courageous enough to align their rewards with their mission, faith-learning integration will become a more understandable and attainable proposition.

A quick caveat: we are not suggesting that the scholarship of discovery and inquiry has no place in a T1 institution. On the contrary, research is critical to the vitality both of the individual faculty member and of the institution, but alignment is crucial. The key for faith-based institutions of learning remains to understand, articulate, and practice that which makes them truly distinctive—what they are to be *primarily* and what they are to be *in addition*.[4] The scholarship most valued at a T1 institution should be scholarship that engages, involves, and shapes students. For example, many undergraduate science departments do this very well, and we see this type of formative scholarship in doctoral programs in education and business, in biblical studies and psychology (grad and undergrad), and in the arts and humanities on our own campus.

## Embracing the Professorial Call: To Teach, Shape, and Send

The concern for community in higher education has come and gone and come back again and again. Parker Palmer reenergized the conversation and brought it into the national educational limelight some thirty years ago, and the discussion continues today. We now have learning communities, knowledge communities, covenantal communities, service communities, living-learning communities, local/global communities, and many others. Christians understand and appreciate the importance of communities of faith, and we are particularly drawn to the idea of a wisdom community as a cornerstone for a fresh and meaningful way for faith-based institutions to rethink and practice faith-learning integration.

### The Wisdom Community

David Hassel observes that students in higher education are rather transient; that is, they come and go.[5] They are after a *paideia* of knowledge, skills, and values, one documented by a credential and followed by a job offer. Of course, many students are interested in social and moral development as well, but it is usually of secondary importance, particularly so given the high cost of private higher education, the concerns brought by parents, and the press for employment outcomes.[6]

On the other hand, the faculty, as a body, is a more stable entity. Over time, at most faith-based institutions, a deep sense of community develops with shared values, understandings, hopes, and dreams about what faculty have in mind for their students, about what constitutes a life lived well as a Christian (the kind of things students hear at orientation, graduations, and other special events), about shared Christian practices and expectations, and about what commitments will shape life together as faculty and learners. In short, a wisdom community forms. We contend that this wisdom community ultimately shapes the educational experience for students, and each wisdom community has unique dimensions and characteristics. Wisdom communities do, however, share some essential elements. We will look first at these commonalities before discussing what practices and influences give shape to a particular wisdom community and the implications of those practices and influences for individual faculty members and the institution.

## Teaching, Shaping, and Sending

Apart from Boyer's framework, people commonly use what we call the IRS model to discuss the three primary dimensions of faculty work: instruction, research, and service. In this book, in fact, we structured the conversation about how to demonstrate and assess faith-learning integration using these categories (even while discussing Boyer's framework, Chapters Five through Seven). IRS remains the most popular way to think about faculty work in North America.

However, we would like to suggest another way, a T1 way. The three essential aspects of faculty work at a T1 institution are: *to teach, to shape,* and *to send*—and the local wisdom community largely forms the nature of the teaching, shaping, and sending at any given institution. In other words, faculty members teach, shape, and send to further the aims and essence of a particular wisdom community. Regardless of why students decide to attend, the identity of wisdom communities roots itself in instruction, formation, and vocation. It is truly a great challenge and high calling.

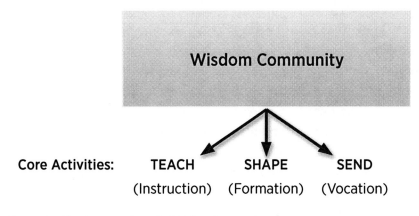

Figure 10.1. The Core Activities of a Wisdom Community

## *To Teach*

Each faculty member represents the wisdom community—inside and outside the classroom. It is easy to see how one can represent the faith commitments of the wisdom community in certain courses or when meeting with students for advising or prayer, but what about when teaching calculus or accounting principles? How does one bring faith to bear in such classes as these? Does one try to develop a Christian way to determine the area under a curve? Is Jesus hidden behind every debit and credit? Obviously, one cannot Christianize every lecture, nor should one try.

Rather, let us think of the wisdom community extending into the classroom. Whenever a professor enters the classroom, she has a dual task: to teach the lesson of the day and to represent the wisdom community. The first obligation is to teach the lesson of the day as creatively and effectively as possible. Sometimes the material and questions of the day are seeded with profound spiritual implications, making integration work easy. At other times, this is simply not the case. No apology is necessary. Students need to acquire essential knowledge and skills—so teach!

Just remember that a professor is also a representative of a particular wisdom community, and this role takes center stage in the most unlikely times and unusual places. A student has a death in the family, an effigy is hung on campus, a bomb explodes in Boston or Belfast, a student unwittingly asks a truly profound question in class (or asks why anyone would need to know this stuff), or a speaker in chapel suggests that gays might be Christians, too. When these teachable (wisdom) moments arise, professors speak not primarily as content experts, but as representatives of the wisdom community. And when they do, they are integrating faith and learning in a profound way, one of the reasons we suggest that our assessment frameworks may need to attend to winsome/offensive continuum and some kind of formal/organized—informal/organic continuum.

We know that professors approach the task of teaching in a variety of ways. Some lecture, some use small groups, some lead great Socratic discussions, and others engage students using self-directed or experiential learning. All these learning strategies (and many others) have merit, and all professors must develop their own unique, personal tool kit to be fresh and effective in the classroom.[7] However, we contend that the best teachers among us do something very special—indeed spiritual. They intentionally connect the lessons of the day to the wisdom community. They make their classrooms holy places because they are after something much deeper, something in addition to learning subject matter. As one professor told his provost, "Students think they're in this class to learn organic chemistry, but this is about their lives. There are big stakes here!"[8]

### *The Five E's*

Regardless of the particular pedagogical approaches they take, the best T1 teachers find a way to incorporate into them these "Five E's": *engage, enlist, enlarge, enable,* and *encourage.*

**Engage.** Simply put, they develop a deep connection with their students. The message is essentially "Hey, I'm here—all here. You need to be here, too!" As one professor we know puts it, "If you're going to be present, you might as well be present." There is no single way of doing this; sometimes it comes through the sheer joy and love for the subject matter, for learning, and for students. Sometimes it results from showing care or personal interest in students. Sometimes it grows out of provocative questions and honest discussions. Whatever the approach, students get hooked. They walk away from class thinking, "This is going to be really good. Not just a good class, but good for me." Without initial engagement, the class runs its course, but the wisdom community rarely makes an appearance.

**Enlist.** Not only do great T1 teachers engage their students, they also enlist them to become part of something much larger than a three-unit course. In essence, students learn that the success of this course (or venture or adventure) is really up to them. They need to sign up and commit fully to do their best. We know of faculty members who take time during class to calculate the cost of each hour of instruction, and challenge their students to get their money's worth—by working hard and by working the professor hard, too. It is a conscious and conscientious recruitment process. Without a professor's serious commitment to the course, the wisdom community seldom makes an appearance. Students simply will not care.

**Enlarge.** With students engaged and enlisted for the ride, great T1 teachers begin to enlarge their own vision for the course and their expectations for students, and even how students see themselves. Professors communicate that this time together is about something BIG and that students must be at their growing best.[9] Great teachers get more out of their students than even the students think possible. And, because they look into the future, great teachers see more in their students than students see in themselves. We consider it a profound act of grace to speak into students' lives, telling them that you know they are capable of better work, that you know they will succeed in the work world, that you know they would do well in graduate work, or that you are proud of how they have worked this semester. We can all point to influential teachers who spoke into our lives and the difference it made for us. It is a gift that costs nothing, but means everything to students. With an enlarged vision of the course and of the students who are engaged and enlisted, wisdom conversations begin to appear and take shape.

**Enable.** This is not rocket science, but providing an enlarged vision of the possible is not terribly helpful if you do not put some feet to the possibilities. The very best teachers first provide a vision of the possible (*words*), then work very hard (*deeds*) to make it happen. They come fully prepared for the lesson of the day every day, giving a constant nudge (*did you get that paper done or have you made an appointment yet*), making a call on a student's behalf, arranging a meeting with someone in the field, reading and editing an application, sending a résumé, or pushing the best students to do more than just get an A by providing additional out-of-class experiences. For many faculty, this truth seems obvious. If so, great! But for many it is not so easy to see. When we provide tangible ways for engaged and enlisted students to act on an enlarged vision of themselves and the course, we help reveal the wisdom community.

**Encourage.** Courage is perhaps the most precious gift that a student can receive from a professor. In fact, we could all use a courage booster shot now and then, and certainly just before the first class of a new semester. We find this true even though it may not be our first rodeo. Students often struggle to find their way even though they have the skills and abilities to do so. They need encouragement—to find the courage to lean in and keep going. We heard a great teacher, a biologist, explain that 4:00–5:00 P.M. was the holy hour for science students.[10] As the lab work was winding down for the day, a student or two would stop by his office and ask, "Do you have a minute?" The conversation usually started with a question about an assignment or lab, but often turned to questions about the future, about faith, and about fear. What those students needed most was to be encouraged—to have courage. When we frame such conversations in the values of the wisdom community, we see that such conversations have eternal implications.

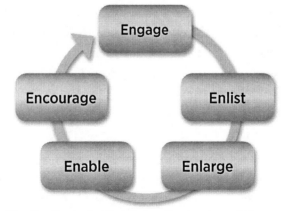

**Figure 10.2. The Five E's—Connecting the Wisdom Community and Classroom**

We want to note that these activities can take place in any class or laboratory in a variety of ways, and in addition to the lessons of the day. We do see a sequence to these five activities, but our experience tells us they can also sometimes happen out of sequence or even simultaneously. In essence, we have listed ways that the very best teachers enlarge their own task by working intentionally as representatives of the wisdom community. We are talking not only about loving students—although that remains an excellent starting point. We are arguing for the integration of the wisdom community and the classroom as an intentional, thoughtful practice of connecting faith and learning. When the wisdom community becomes alive and present in the daily classroom, faith-learning integration *is* happening. Would it not be interesting if faculty members were evaluated and rewarded on the Five E's of teaching in addition to the design and delivery of (and student satisfaction with) the lessons of the day?

## To Shape

The second core faculty activity is to shape. Parker Palmer points out "in the very act of educating we are in the process of forming or deforming the human soul."[11] Thus, all education is formation of one kind or another. There is no doubt that education forms students in deep ways; the question is whether it is intentional—and to what ends? At faith-based institutions, it is the wisdom community, those shared dreams, values, commitments, practices, and identity that give depth and direction to formation in students. Faith-based institutions have something in mind, usually far beyond what is described in the catalog. Of course, formation is happening to all of us all the time, and students' college experiences remain integrally connected to their lives. Still, the beliefs, values, and practices of the community are powerful shaping influences, and professors must take seriously their roles as mentors and guides.

James Smith wonders what would happen if faith-based institutions decided that education was primarily about what we love rather than what we know, and suggested that the essential nature of education is formational. In Smith's words:

I have been claiming that an education—whether acknowledged or not—is a formation of the desires and imagination that creates a certain kind of person who is part of a certain kind of people. The facts and information learned as part of the process are always situated and embedded in something deeper that is being learned all along: a particular vision of the good life.[12]

We agree with Smith, and we suggest that the "something deeper" in which the learning process is "situated and embedded" is a local and particular wisdom community. The shared values, practices, and commitments of the wisdom community give direction and distinction to much of the forming. There has been a robust discussion from ancient times to the present day about the practices that form persons. It is beyond the scope of this book to enter into that discussion (as tempting as that is), but we will identify and briefly describe three strategies that faculty members can utilize when representing the wisdom community: *proclamation, demonstration,* and *application.*

**Proclamation.** Simply put, professors need to profess, to proclaim what is important and why they do what they do, and to live honestly and openly before their students. Students need to hear what an institution has in mind, what is important "in this place," why faculty members choose to do their work here, and why local practices have such deep implications. Arthur Holmes claimed that "Faith and moral formation are acquired usually and best, not by force of argument or weight of objective evidence, but by entering into the life of a community and making its heritage one's own."[13] After quoting this same passage from Holmes, Clifford Williams adds, "When we embrace a Christian community of learning, our own Christian learning develops and matures."[14] Students need to know that.

In a Quaker institution, for example, we should explain why there are no head tables at banquets, why everyone goes by first names, and why peace and discernment processes are so important. Theological and communal commitments drive and shape these practices, and in turn participants are shaped by the practices. And people do not engage in these practices by accident; they have deep meaning and the people who practice them intend to fulfill specific aims. In other wisdom communities, students may need an explanation why social action is so critical, why forgiveness as Jesus described it in the Sermon on the Mount is so crucial, why the Great Commission is so compelling, why God's sovereignty is so central, or why we must read the Bible carefully and prayerfully but not literally, or, in some cases, why we should read it literally. As students and faculty join a faith-based wisdom community, we must take care to proclaim and explain to students the distinctive values, commitments, practices, and liturgies that will shape their lives, particularly so if we expect students to take this life together seriously and work with us and others to sustain it.

**Demonstration.** Proclamation is a necessary but insufficient action. True, we must be clear about what we believe and about what practices shape our common life, but we must demonstrate these practices in our daily life together. Faculty can go by first names and have no head tables as a practice demonstrating that every person is of equal importance, but if they act like the staff are second-class citizens and go about competitively promoting themselves over other colleagues, they will lose the value of the practice. If an institution proclaims that it is committed to women in leadership but all the senior leaders are male, students will see through the chatter in a New York minute. Words and deeds: we must demonstrate by our actions—personally and corporately—those things which we claim to be important. In every case, "the place teaches by example."[15]

**Application.** Finally, students need to be guided and nurtured as they engage in wisdom community practices, as they are being formed. This becomes a messy process at times, to be sure. But if we accompany consistent proclamation and demonstration with authentic opportunities to enter in, the proclamation and demonstration will bear fruit. Institutions must think carefully about the activities and programs they plan and provide. These activities and programs will form students, for good or ill. Activities can communicate that the classroom experience is central, or that classrooms take a backseat to social and sports activities. As representatives of the wisdom community, faculty must teach and intentionally shape, aiming at something concrete. What would happen if formational activities (proclamation, demonstration, and application) were evaluated along with course design and information acquisition? An interesting proposition!

## To Send

A Dutch proverb, long painted on blue and white Delft tiles, reads: "*Van het concert des levens krijgt niemand een program.*" ("In the concert of life, no one gets a program.") How true! Understandably, students desperately want a program, and many come to faith-based campuses convinced and convicted that with enough earnest prayer and self-denial, they will get the answer. Of course, life rarely unfolds that way. And without a program, students look to faculty to help them find a way forward. We thus get both a sacred trust and a daunting obligation. As representatives of the wisdom community, faculty teach, shape, *and* send.

Chris Anderson observes that all teachers want their students to accept complexity, to understand that "things are more complicated than they first appeared."[16] We agree. Most undergraduates, and many graduate students, have an insufficiently developed theology, faith, or view of the world to carry them through what life will bring their way. Christian faith isn't an insurance policy against difficulties, disappointments, sickness, meanness, or pain. Life is messy, and the mess will come our way. Students need to face the reality that life as they conceive it is terribly simplistic, and faculty need to remember that fear often accompanies such deconstruction and uncertainty—and fear is debilitating and destructive to formation. The ultimate assurance that faculty can give their students is this: life is messy, but God is faithful.

Former Calvin College President William Spoelhof was fond of saying that, although we do not get a program for the concert of life, "there is a conductor."[17] While facing the deconstruction of their perhaps simplistic notions of calling, students need to hear that they are not alone, that someone *is* calling them. Just as Samuel needed Eli's wisdom to understand that the voice in the middle of night was God's voice, so students need assistance and mentoring to hear and respond to God's calling—especially in a culture with such banal, persistent voices and blaring, empty sounds. Students need to find their vocation. In the words of Walter Brueggemann, they need "a purpose for being in the world that is related to the purposes of God."[18] To find that purpose, they need to be able to hear the Voice, and for that task, they may sometimes need our guidance.

Students need to realize that life is complex, that they are not alone, and that God is not silent. In addition, they need assistance in understanding the wisdom of patience in preparation. Few of us have a complete life map given to us. For most of us it is a matter of next steps and clues, an honest scavenger hunt. As professors, we would do well to be transparent about that fact in our conversations with students. They need to know that faculty struggle with vocation too, that we wonder what our work means. And students need to hear that the best thing they can do, especially when they do not sense any clear direction, is to lean in and prepare. Even with no particular end in sight, they will not waste their time if they take full advantage of the opportunities they have in that moment to learn and grow.

Finally, sending students is often a matter of helping them let go of dreams and desires that simply will not work and helping them to see how to lean into the possible. For example, a student comes to the university with the dream of being a surgeon, but the reality is that she will not make it into medical school. She needs other options—and there are many good ones. Or a student has a deep passion for literature and writing, but he is being pushed by parents to major in computer science ("You need a job to pay bills, son"). Maybe he needs to drop a major and take another one, or maybe he needs to plan to do both. Maybe he needs to think carefully about what he is called to do in view of the gifts he has, while remembering that bills have to be paid, too. In short, students need wise friends.

Ultimately, God's call is most likely to be found at the intersection of abilities and opportunities. At the very least, that is an excellent place to start looking. We need to remind students that the God of the university is not a trickster. God does not give one dreams, abilities, and opportunities only to snatch them away on a whim. Given the abilities they have and the opportunities lying before them, God calls students to prepare and choose wisely; that is their vocation during their years of studying. Ultimately, the God of the universe does have something in mind. We are all of us called to be holy persons. Within that context, we have the freedom to make our way as wisely and prayerfully as possible. Students need to hear that, too.

Would it not be interesting if faith-based institutions evaluated and rewarded faculty members for guiding students in their understanding of vocation and finding their calling? What would happen if our colleges aligned their faculty promotion and tenure systems to recognize and reward teaching, shaping, and sending, giving those core activities a higher priority than individual research and scholarship? What would happen if Christian colleges rewarded B with the hope of getting B, not A? The results could be staggering.

## Embracing the Institution's Call:
## To Tend the Wisdom Community

Thus far in this chapter, we have examined the core activities of teaching, shaping, and sending that we envision in the reconceived faith-based institution we are describing here. These core activities flow from and are themselves shaped by a particular wisdom community. We have also suggested a realignment of institutional priorities in the evaluation of faculty performance to support those core activities. In addition to what we have already discussed, we note three critical institutional practices as well—core practices that shape the content and vitality of a wisdom community: *the practice of hospitality, the pursuit of truth,* and *the embrace of covenant.*[19] Our understanding and practice of these three activities shape the essence of a particular wisdom community. The result is that not all wisdom communities are alike, and neither are all wisdom communities healthy. Thus, these activities are fundamentally important, and we must practice them with faithful love and thoughtful care.

### The Practice of Hospitality

Aurelie Hagstrom writes, "Christian higher education must recover and appropriate hospitality as a theologically significant moral category, one that benefits both the cultivation of community with colleges and universities as well as the pursuit of scholarly inquiry in the classroom."[20] We agree. The practice of hospitality benefits the cultivation of community—the wisdom community—and not all wisdom communities understand or practice hospitality in the same way. Where do our communities draw the line between "them" and "us?" In fact, how is "the us" determined? When and how is the stranger welcomed? What are the mechanisms by which the gatekeepers of the dominant tradition practice boundary maintenance?

Hagstrom suggests, "the more one is rooted on one's own identity and traditions, the more open one can be to others."[21] While that may certainly be true, we can think of many instances where those rooted in the tradition remain dug in, closed, and fearful, building more walls than bridges. As the eminent theologian and church historian Martin Marty observes, when Christian educators attempt to ward off "all expressions of the very culture in which their graduates must live and move and have their being,"[22] we do them a grave disservice. We agree with Marty and, in view of Hagstrom's suggestion, we desire to see our students gain sufficient confidence in their own story and identity that they can welcome their neighbor with no need to fear what so many call *the other*.

And hospitality extends not only to openness to other people and cultures, but also to other ideas and expressions of faith. It is our experience that trustees are usually the least hospitable constituency when it comes to welcoming and discussing differing ideas and beliefs. Faculty members are much more open and willing to do so. It is interesting to note that the body that spends the least amount of time in community (and on campus) has the greatest power to define what is acceptable and what is not acceptable to discuss when it comes to fundamental beliefs and institutional positions on major issues. We recognize that trustees serve as stewards of the university; inevitably, they must act as gatekeepers. We are not attempting to criticize the role of trustees in faith-based institutions as much as to point out that care and conversation are needed to be sure that they too understand and practice the formative nature of hospitality. Problems arise when conversations stop or discussions must go underground. When this happens, the wisdom community suffers and becomes malformed.

At the heart of hospitality is a deep humility, one which acknowledges that we know—but only in part—and that we see—but through the glass darkly. There are things scholars and teachers honestly do not know or have completely figured out. This we need to confess. Any wisdom community must see that its core tasks include determining how to navigate the territory between what is known and what is not known. There must be a place for mystery and a way to learn from those outside our own traditions and communities. Yet far too often, community members end up talking to those they already know, treating those outside their circle with fear and suspicion. Or worse yet, they simply go about their business as if others do not exist. They are invisible.

At conferences, for instance, we see administrators and faculty from denominational, friendship, and interest groups walking around like schools of fish. And we also see established and accomplished faculty who, having paid both kinds of dues, know their place (near the center of the circle, somewhere just to Jesus's right) and by a thousand gestures large and small let those outside the circle know their place. They rarely invite others to join their conversations or dinner parties. Such exclusion may root itself in a lack of social skill, but we fear this type of behavior is a bit more insidious. There is a subtle arrogance about the superiority of one's own tradition or theology or one's accomplishments, the very antithesis of humility. If such behaviors emerge in public meetings—especially expressly Christian ones—we fear they will show up on home campuses, too. When they do, community shrivels, and students lose out.

Finally, our understanding of grace and to whom it is extended shapes the practice of hospitality. Grace can be a great leveler. For example, Quakers see "that of God" in everyone. If God is at work in everyone, then hospitality is more likely to be extended to other persons and ideas than if we view others as *the other*, as not like us, dangerous, fallen, or foreign territory to be conquered. In those instances, we are likely to hear the advice Eli Lapp gave to John Book (played by Harrison Ford) in the movie "The Witness" as he prepared to go to town: "You be careful out among the English."[23] Such an admonition guides our behavior in the town, reminding us to keep to ourselves and to treat others with suspicion. As we emphasize at several points in this chapter, our theological commitments shape our practices, which in turn shape the wisdom community—and us.

## *The Pursuit of Truth*

How a faith tradition understands the pursuit of truth is fundamentally important for the development of a particular faith-based wisdom community. Has the truth already been revealed in the Sermon on the Mount or in the Great Commission? Are Scriptures are to be read literally? Is the essence of truth the proper understanding of revelation proclaimed by church authorities? Has it all been figured out, or is there room for the continuing, vigorous pursuit of truth?

Faith traditions come at these questions very differently, and the answers to such questions matter greatly because they shape the nature of discourse in each particular wisdom community. For example, some faith traditions look at the Bible as all-sufficient—*solo scriptura*. There is little room for discussion. Others emphasize both Scripture and tradition, although Scripture usually takes the pre-eminent position. Wesleyans hold that we need Scripture, tradition, reason, and experience (Quadrilateral) to find and discern truth. Quakers practice a "three-legged stool" of discernment: Scripture, the inner voice of Christ, and the community of believers. However, various Quaker communities differ regarding which is of primary importance. Precisely what is discussable and negotiable on campus is an important question in any faith-based community.

In addition, some traditions place high importance on the authority of the church; others do not. Some traditions read Scripture literally; others do not. Quakers and Wesleyans, for example, while having a high view of Scripture, would be inclined to read it carefully and prayerfully, but not literally. They would also be more open to listening to the Holy Spirit or the inner voice of Christ. Many Baptists see the Great Commission as central, while most Mennonites place greater emphasis on a peace witness and on social justice issues. These differences in faith and practice shape a particular wisdom community. And certainly not all faith communities within the same tradition are exactly alike. Some are more faithful to the guiding tradition; others have difficulty even identifying it. Still others are in the midst of deep directional changes or financial challenges. This is another reason why it is so important for a faith-based wisdom community to be clear about its guiding theology and core identity. Without a deep and abiding sense of true north, any road will do.

We believe that the rare air of faith-based higher education is discourse, and healthy wisdom communities practice it and work diligently to maintain and protect it. They know students who are invited into conversations that matter are shaped deeply by those experiences. When faculty have the freedom and encouragement to discuss life as it is and face difficult questions with care and courage, good things happen. However, when discourse is discouraged or relegated to conversations in parking lots and hallways after the public meeting, the wisdom community suffers, and students and faculty end up malformed.

### The Embrace of Covenant

In addition to the practice of hospitality (shaped by grace and humility) and the pursuit of truth (embodied in discourse), members of faith-based wisdom communities make promises to each other (they are asked to embrace a covenant). What is promised and the extent to which these vows are taken seriously have a profound influence on faculty and students.

Most of us smile when watching young people exchange marriage vows. Although weddings are a very serious sacrament, many of us wonder if the bride and groom have any idea at all as to what they are promising, or getting into. Usually they do not, and perhaps it is better to plunge in and let life unfold a step or two at a time. And we smile the same way while watching freshmen as they are inducted as members of the academic community during fall orientation or at an early academic convocation, thinking that they have no idea what they are getting into either. Perhaps it is better that way, too, that we let them plunge in and let life unfold a step or two at a time. We do wonder, however, if it would be better to be more transparent and precise about the promises we ask students to make and the implications of their making them.

Unfortunately, some seasoned faculty members and deans also smile this way when they meet new faculty colleagues at fall faculty sessions. They may look at the newly minted PhDs and think, "They don't have a clue." Here's the rub: they need to have a clue. They are joining a wisdom community with real expectations, values, practices, and concerns. Promises need to be made and kept. Faculty members are charged to teach, shape, and send with something clearly in mind. Faith-based institutions intend to accomplish something particular, and we cannot afford to let new faculty just get it as they go along.

If faith-based institutions take seriously the reality that new faculty are hired to be representatives of the wisdom community and we expect them to make and keep a covenant with the institution, then at least three processes will rise in importance. The first is *hiring*. We often hear that hiring a new faculty member is more important than building a building, potentially a multimillion dollar decision. We agree. We point out, however, that most institutions spend far more time, effort, and resources when planning a building or even a parking lot—because we can't afford to make a mistake, the CFO will say. Institutions cannot afford to make a mistake in hiring either, because a faculty member will articulate and embody the values of the wisdom community in ways that a building never will.

To be clear, we are not saying that institutions do not take hiring seriously. Most do, but we are saying that it is often done poorly. Far too often, hiring is seen primarily as a departmental task, but we argue that the academy should view the hiring of new faculty members as a campus-wide endeavor. Individual departments are often too small or isolated to think more globally about the community that the new faculty member will join. The focus goes quickly to teaching schedules, the vita, and scholarly interests. Considerations about institutional fit are often deemed secondary or ignored altogether, particularly so if the candidate has an otherwise strong vita. Time and again we have heard search committees argue, "This is a strong scholar! Yes, we know that they may not be such a great fit for us, but we can work on that." Such logic leads to million-dollar mistakes.

And most departments do not hire very often; thus, they remain amateurs at the task. An institution would do well to have a clear interview and hiring process that involves persons with extensive experience at the task. If not, the search may stumble and bumble along. When this happens, many solid candidates simply walk away and look somewhere else, but the stories of rude and failed search committees take on lives of their own. In the end, the wisdom community is diminished.

It is important to remember that a faith-based institution asks each faculty member to covenant with the community. Indeed, faculty members need to teach and do scholarship, but the essential question is whether or not they can effectively represent and embody the wisdom community, whether or not they will take the covenant seriously and keep their promises. Faith-based institutions ask for everything, and they should. However, such expectations of faculty members require a search process that is careful, thoughtful, professional, and particular.

If hiring the right person is important, then *orientation* is critical. Most faith-based institutions have some type of new faculty workshop or ongoing faculty class, and some are exemplary. We believe that the formal orientation period for a new faculty member should be three years at minimum and perhaps six years to be effective. In addition to instructional strategies and expectations for scholarship, it is critical to unpack carefully the theological commitments of the wisdom community and place them in a local and historical context. Colleges often overlook the reality that much of the orientation of a new faculty member occurs informally and organically at the department level. Provosts and deans who run new faculty orientation programs regularly express frustration that their work has been undermined by the bad habits and attitudes of departmental colleagues. One effective strategy is for each new faculty member to be assigned a mentor, akin to a spiritual director, and preferably one outside the department.

Finally, if promises are to be kept, then *maintenance* is important, too. Over time, we argue, the wisdom community becomes who is hired, what is allowed, and what is practiced. The operative question is how seriously faculty and administrators take the covenant and who provides corrective action when needed. Often, corrective action falls to the administrative structure—chairs, academic deans, and provosts—to step in when issues of civility, impropriety, or commitment arise. We find, however, that wisdom communities are at their best when faculty colleagues step in and say, "Hey, that behavior won't go here. We expect more from you. That won't cut it." When promises are made and colleagues take them seriously enough to hold each other accountable, the covenant remains strong. Surely, institutions receive direction from presidents and deans, but wisdom communities draw their strength from those who take seriously the task of teaching, shaping, and sending. Given this truth, we see that trustees are not alone in being entrusted with the welfare of the community; faculty also serve in this trust capacity, stewarding the health of the wisdom community.

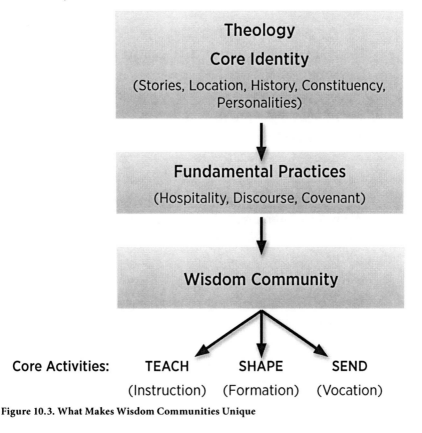

Figure 10.3. What Makes Wisdom Communities Unique

One final comment about tending the wisdom community—in addition to the *dominant theological orientation*, the other primary shaper of the local wisdom community is the *core identity* of that institution. How the institution understands itself, views its location, remembers its history through the stories about events and personalities, and how it interprets the spirit and influence of different constituency groups will all work to provide a certain local character, producing and shaping a particular community unlike any other wisdom community. That is why all Nazarene, Quaker, Church of Christ, Christian Reformed, Wesleyan, or Baptist institutions are not all alike, even if they are closely affiliated and embracing the same theology. Tip O'Neill, as we quoted much earlier in the book, loved to say that, "Ultimately, all politics is local."[24] We suggest that all wisdom communities are ultimately local, too.

## Conclusion: Embracing the Future of Faith-Learning Integration

Let us be honest. The discussion about the integration of faith and learning has been a long, and sometimes tired, conversation. Rather than renaming the conversation, perhaps it is time for faith-based institutions to reconsider their approach. What if they looked less to intellectual integration of the faith with our disciplines (what, in Chapter Two, we called epistemological and curricular models) and more to the embodiment of a particular tradition? What if they paid less attention to identifying the philosophical assumptions underpinning the disciplines and more to the practices, values, and expectations of their own wisdom community?

What if faith-based institutions aspired less to be recognized in the R1 world and more to be seen as world-class T1 (transformational) institutions? What if they looked at the fundamental faculty activities less as instruction, research, and service and more as teaching, shaping, and sending? What if deans and chairs saw their work less as managers and more as tenders of the wisdom community? What if faculty members saw their primary work less as research and more as authentic representation and stewardship of the local wisdom community?

And what if faith-based institutions proudly claimed our own unique mission, professing and demonstrating that we are in the transformation business? What if we aligned our reward structures to support our claims to that mission? What if we took seriously the advice Stanley Hauerwas gave to Bethany Theological Seminary?

The first advantage you have is lack of numbers. The Brethren
Church has never been a part of the American Protestant establishment. You have nothing to lose, so you might as well be faithful
to your heritage to the extent that heritage has been faithful to the
Gospel. That means that you do not have to imitate.[25]

What if institutions worked as though we had nothing to lose but our false
sense of importance and nothing to gain but the Kingdom? This, it seems to
us, is the future of faith-learning integration in the faith-based university:
to represent, embody, and care for the local wisdom community that, in
turn, shapes our students and sustains our work?

# Afterword

We started writing this book with the intent of weaving together two threads of an ongoing conversation about the integration of faith and learning, particularly in faith-based institutions. In some important ways, these conversations have gone past each other. One conversation—mainly among scholars—has focused on integration from, shall we say, the 30,000 foot level: integration definitions, clarification of terminology, questions concerning the plausibility and paucity of Christian scholarship, and implications for the future, to name only a few of the threads in the scholarly discussion. At its best, it is a yeasty and important conversation, helping those institutions and faculty who claim Christ to approach their callings faithfully and thoughtfully. When it is not at its best, this can become a one-size-fits-all conversation with little recognition of or room for theological distinctives and local identities. And as interesting as these discussions are to scholars, practitioners who have to open shop on Monday morning often find them a bit impractical and unrealizable. Much like Will Rogers' solution to the problem of finding and fighting German U-boats during WWI—drain the ocean—these discussions arc so high above the day-to-day reality of Christian colleges that they become superfluous. As one administrative colleague puts it, "You people can build condos in the air but someone has to pay the rent."

The other conversation—mainly among practitioners—has focused primarily on how faculty bring and share faith in their work, the implications of doing so (or not), and the prospects of secularization, a subject that dominates the worries of many trustees. At its best, this conversation can give life and direction to faculty who have heard a deep call to the scholarly vocation. Unfortunately, these conversations often get so caught up in local politics and theological fusses that it is hard to distinguish the forest from the trees.

Too often, we see the failure to connect these two important conversations at promotion and tenure time, when faculty are asked to provide concrete evidence that they are integrating faith and learning. Many faculty feel unprepared to do so. We deeply believe institutions that name Christ have a right to expect faculty to make their faith evident in their work. Certainly all institutions have the responsibility to live up to their own recruiting brochures. When Christian higher education operates at its best, practitioners and scholars get together and talk about how to hire, orient, and support faculty in their work; how institutions can avoid the slippery slope to nowhere; and how administrators and faculty together can preserve the unique heritage and traditions that shape their institutions' identities. When Christian higher education is not at its best, conversations turn into gripe sessions, administrators and trustees find fault with the faculty who (they think) lack spirit and commitment, sharing strategies about herding cats and asking (above all else) how to avoid litigation. And scholars look at practitioners with fear and suspicion, sensing a loss of power, academic identity, and theological focus. In essence, the conversation is so close to the ground that it loses perspective and a sense of true north.

This reminds us of a metaphor from a delightful book by Gordon MacKenzie, *Orbiting the Giant Hairball.*[1] For our purposes, think of the hairball as the day-to-day institutional reality all of us face. If you get too close to the hairball, you know what happens. Caught up in the daily drama, you lose your perspective, creativity, and bearings. But if you fly too high and lose touch, you become disconnected, uncaring, and irrelevant. The key, according to MacKenzie, is to establish an orbit close enough to the hairball to be relevant and high enough to stay out of the gunk. In this book, we tried to bring together the scholarly conversations (which are sometimes too far out) and the practitioner conversations (which are sometimes too close in) and thereby to establish a successful orbit for the two. You will have to judge if we were successful in that venture.

We realize that more work remains to be done. We suggest that scholars and practitioners need to be working and thinking together deliberately rather than engaging in parallel conversations about faith and learning. While no one needs another meeting, would it be helpful to have a conference dedicated specifically to this task? We believe that it could be a valuable conversation—together. And why not end the meeting with a session on "where do we go from here?" All of this assumes, of course, that we want to go somewhere together rather than stay in our own small groups, giving papers and presentations to each other, then publishing the proceedings. We need to do better than that if we are going to orbit the giant hairball together.

We believe that the witness of Ernest Boyer holds promise as a model for faith and learning integration in the public sector. Much like Parker Palmer, Boyer had national standing and influence, and faithfully lived out his spiritual commitments without making them primary or expecting others to adopt his ways. He worked as a faithful presence, neither ashamed to name Christ nor compelled to exclude other voices from the conversation. We agree with James Davison Hunter that living as a faithful presence where planted is a better way of thinking about the Christian call than devoting our waking hours to changing our entire world—a bit too high of an orbit, we fear.[2] Junior faculty desperately need mentors and role models, and Boyer's life provides a great model to emulate.

We believe that Boyer's "other" dimensions of scholarship—teaching, integration, and engagement (or application)—have much to offer faculty at faith-based institutions. In fact, faculty at faith-based institutions may have a decided edge in this type of scholarship, particularly since they lend themselves so nicely to smaller, flexible institutions with limited resources, to collaboration and sharing with colleagues, and to the language of faith integration and service. In other words, these scholarly dimensions fit the mission of faith-based institutions to a tee, and they take nothing away from the scholarship of discovery. They can all get along.

Of course, it is important for senior and junior faculty to be in the same orbit. Senior faculty will need to step up and let go of the notion that only the scholarship of discovery counts, that it is the only legitimate scholarship. And they will have to work harder to counter the prevailing reward structure that preferences research and discounts other forms of scholarship. This can be done through work on promotion and tenure committees, clearly the province of the faculty at most institutions. Senior faculty need to lead. And junior faculty will have to step up, too. Rather than trying to fill resumés with a list of disjointed scholarly presentations and publications, they will need to carefully plan and pursue a thoughtful, well-documented scholarly agenda. This is honest but hard work. If the faculty can get in the same orbit concerning scholarship, they can avoid the hairball at tenure decision time without drifting off into the atmosphere of irrelevance.

We believe that faculty members and administrators need to find a common orbit, too. Over the past two decades, faculties in all types of institutions have lost much of their previous influence over institutional matters. This is disconcerting on several levels. First, a faculty in large part carries the institutional ethos, the institutional glue, if you will. Their voice and perspective are critical for any institution earnestly seeking to navigate faithfully the competitive terrain of the post-modern, post-denominational (and in many respects, post-Christian) twenty-first century. Our experience is that many voices are needed for an institution to make its way successfully and faithfully. Depending totally on administrative instinct and purview lands an institution squarely in the hairball more times than not. On the other hand, it is only fair to say that faculties can spend months and months editing a document or fussing over rather insignificant details and distinctions while the building is on fire. They can orbit so high above the daily realities that presidents and provosts often find their discussions irrelevant to the daily demand for decisions to be made in light of market realities. To administrators, faculty honestly look sometimes like they not only build castles in the air, they live in them too! If faculty and administrators orbit together, however, they can avoid both administrative shortsightedness and faculty nearsightedness. We really do need each other.

Finally, we believe that Christian college faculty, presidents, provosts, and trustees must have the courage to remain true to their institution's mission rather than chasing the call of the academy, despite pressures from many sides to do so. If the orbit around the mission gets too high, the college can lose its distinctiveness and it can begin to look and act like every other institution. This, it seems to us, is a kiss of death. And if the orbit is too low, it loses direction and gets caught up in the local terrain and crashes. That is a kiss of death of another kind, but death nonetheless. The key is to fly high enough to be credible and low enough to be in touch with all that makes each institution dynamic and distinctive. In this regard, we trust that this book has provided some help to faculty and administrators who work in institutions that name Christ, and who are called to love God with everything they have, which of course includes their faith and their learning. Fly!

# Notes

## Chapter 1

[1] R. G. Green, "Tenure and Promotion Decisions: The Relative Importance of Teaching, Scholarship and Service," *Journal of Social Work Education* 44, no. 2 (2008): 126.

[2] For more depth on the concept of social knowledge about tenure and promotion, see Mackenzi Anne Huyser, "Faculty Perceptions of Institutional Commitment to the Scholarship of Engagement," *Journal of Research on Christian Education* 13, no. 2 (2005): 251–85.

[3] E. A. Lynton calls this *outreach* in *Making the Case for Professional Service* (Washington, DC: American Association for Higher Education, 1995). We use *service* and *engagement* interchangeably here.

[4] S. Weibe and L. Fells, "Thinking Around Tenure: Ducking Under the Finish Line," *Journal of Educational Thought* 44, no. 1 (2010): 17.

[5] Lewis Carroll, *Alice's Adventures in Wonderland and Through the Looking Glass: In One Volume*, introduction by Arthur Prager; illustrated by John Tenniel (New York: Dell, 1992), 124.

## Chapter 2

[1] Frank Gaebelein, *The Pattern of God's Truth: The Integration of Faith and Learning* (New York: Oxford, 1954).

[2] Joel A. Carpenter and Kenneth W. Shipps, *Making Higher Education Christian: The History and Mission of Evangelical Colleges in America* (St. Paul, MN: Christian University Press, 1987); William C. Ringenberg, *The Christian College: A History of Protestant Higher Education in America* (Grand Rapids, MI: Christian University Press, 1984).

[3] Those wanting to explore Reformed understandings of higher education would do well to look at these volumes: Calvin College Curriculum Study Committee, *Christian Liberal Arts Education* (Grand Rapids, MI: Calvin College / Eerdmans, 1970), a work widely recognized as reflective of the thinking of Nicholas Wolterstorff; Richard

Mouw, *He Shines in All That's Fair: Culture and Common Grace* (Grand Rapids, MI: Eerdmans, 2001); Cornelius Plantinga, *Engaging God's World: A Christian Vision of Faith, Leaning, and Living* (Grand Rapids, MI: Eerdmans, 2002); and Al Wolters, *Creation Regained* (Grand Rapids, MI: Eerdmans, 1985). We also recommend the works of Nicholas Wolterstorff, such as "The Mission of the Christian College at the End of the 20th Century," *Faculty Dialogue* 10 (1988): 37–46; "Can Scholarship and Christian Conviction Mix? A New Look at the Integration of Knowledge," *Journal of Christian Education* 47, no. 2 (2004): 99–118; also two volumes of collected essays, both edited by Gloria Goris Stronks and Clarence Joldersma, *Educating for Life: Reflections on Christian Teaching and Learning* (Grand Rapids, MI: Baker, 2002), and *Educating for Shalom: Essays on Christian Higher Education* (Grand Rapids, MI: Eerdmans, 2004).

[4] Richard L. Pratt, *Every Thought Captive: A Study Manual for the Defense of Christian Truth* (Abilene, TX: Abilene Christian University Press, 2011); David W. Gill, *The Opening of the Christian Mind: Taking Every Thought Captive to Christ* (Downers Grove, IL: InterVarsity, 1989); Kenneth W. Hermann, *Every Thought Captive to Christ: A Guide to Resources for Developing a Christian Perspective in the Major Academic Disciplines* (Kent, OH: Radix Christian Studies Program, 1985); and Donald W. King, *Taking Every Thought Captive: Forty Years of Christian Scholar's Review* (Abilene, TX: Abilene Christian University Press, 2011).

[5] H. Richard Niebuhr, *Christ and Culture* (New York: Harper and Row, 1951).

[6] In fact, the concept of *worldview* has generated debates quite similar to those spawned by *faith-learning integration*. See, for example, Douglas Jacobsen and Rhonda H. Jacobsen, *Scholarship and Christian Faith* (New York: Oxford University Press, 2004); and James Smith, *Desiring the Kingdom: Worship, Worldview, and Cultural Formation* (Grand Rapids, MI: Baker Academic, 2009).

[7] Others have examined the conceptual properties of this language. See, for example, Brian David Millis's dissertation, "Faith, Learning and Christian Higher Education" (Griffith University, 2004); and Theo Vandeweg, "Integration of Faith and Learning: A Reflection upon its Meaning in the NRC Context," in *Teaching from a Christian Perspective: An Anthology Sponsored by the Netherlands Reformed Congregations (NRC) Educator's Association*, ed. James W. Beeke, Martien Vanerd Spek, and Theo Vandeweg (Grand Rapids, MI: Netherlands Reformed Congregations Educator's Association, 1997), 56–73. See also Lesli DeAnn Welch's dissertation, "An Analysis of the Integration of Faith and Learning in Evangelical Secondary Schools" (Southern Baptist Theological Seminary, 2008). See Larry Burton and Constance Nwosu's research on student definitions and perceptions of faith-learning integration, "Student Perceptions of the Integration of Faith, Learning, and Practice in a Selected Education Course," at http://www.andrews.edu/~burton/2004PortfolioMaterials/Scholarship/Presentations/Nonjuried/College%20Faith.2.18.03.pdf/.

[8] Ken Badley, "The Faith/Learning Integration Movement in Christian Higher Education: Slogan or Substance?" *Journal of Research on Christian Education* 3, no. 1 (1994): 13–33. This comparison of evangelical and Reformed understandings of faith and learning may be of interest as well: "Two Cop-Outs in Faith/Learning Integration: Incarnational Integration and Worldviewish Integration," *Spectrum* 28, no. 2 (1996):

105–18. Finally, this excellent article continues to figure centrally in the discussions of faith-learning integration: William Hasker, "Faith Learning Integration: An Overview," *Christian Scholar's Review* 21, no. 3 (1992): 234–48.

[9] Historical examples include Paul Komisar and James McClellan, "The Logic of Slogans," in *Language and Concepts in Education*, ed. B. Othaniel Smith and Robert H. Ennis (Chicago: Rand-McNally, 1961), 195–214; and Israel Scheffler, "Educational Slogans," in *Philosophical Essays on Teaching*, ed. Bertram Bandman and Robert S. Guttchen (Philadelphia: Lippincott, 1969), 107–16.

[10] Clarence Joldersma, "Faith-Learning Integration: A Substantive Example that Transcends Sloganeering," *Journal of Research on Christian Education* 5, no.1 (1996): 67–88; and David L. Wolfe and Harold Heie, *Slogans or Distinctives: Reforming Christian Higher Education* (Lanham, MD: University Press of America, 1993).

[11] One contemporary who wants to get rid of the phrase, Perry Glanzer, has argued persuasively that faith and learning language fails to catch all the work that Christian colleges ask their faculty to do. He believes that the phrase *Christian scholarship* more adequately catches our work in research and writing. See "Why We Should Discard 'the Integration of Faith and Learning': Rearticulating the Mission of the Christian Scholar," in the *Journal of Education and Christian Belief* 12, no. 1 (2008): 41–51.

[12] At the time of writing, no dictionary has yet provided an entry for this popular phrase, although we know that one such article should appear the same year as our volume. See Louis Gallien, "Integration of Faith and Learning," in *Encyclopedia of Christian Education*, ed. George Thomas Kurian and Mark A. Lamport (New York: Scarecrow, 2014).

[13] This section is summarized from an article, "Clarifying Faith-Learning Integration: Essentially Contested Concepts and the Concept-Conception Distinction," *Journal of Education and Christian Belief* 13, no. 1 (2009): 7–17.

[14] Ludwig Wittgenstein's concept of family resemblances may be helpful here. Were he to address this question, he would likely tell us to look not for a single common thread but rather for overlapping similarities. See *Philosophical Investigations*, translated by G. E. M. Anscombe (New York: Macmillan, 1953), 67–68.

[15] Walter Bryce Gallie first introduced the idea of essentially contested concepts in "Art as an Essentially Contested Concept," *The Philosophical Quarterly* 6 (1956): 97–114; and "Essentially Contested Concepts," in *The Importance of Language*, ed. Max Black (Englewood Cliffs, NJ: Prentice-Hall, 1962), 121–46. Other examples of work built on Gallie's work include Mark Edward Criley's dissertation, "Contested Concepts and Competing Conceptions" (University of Pittsburgh, 2007); and Josep Macia, "On Concepts and Conceptions," *Philosophical Issues: Concepts* 9 (1998): 175–85.

[16] Historically, Christian believers have carried on such conversations regarding philosophy. Since integration language came into use, psychology was the first discipline in which significant numbers of Christian believers attempted to create such dialogue.

[17] Perspectival integration may imply a combination of saturation-degree dialogical integration and saturation-degree incorporation.

[18] We recognize that speaking of "where" faith-learning integration happens might strike some readers' ears as a bit too metaphorical. In an article that has become essential reading among seminary educators, Dan Aleshire has written that, despite our objections to assessing matters of faith, when we claim learning happens, we have to admit that it happens somewhere and so should be measurable. We believe his comment applies to faith-learning integration; it must happen somewhere. See "The Character and Assessment of Learning for Religious Vocation: M. Div. Education and Numbering the Levites," *Theological Education* 39, no. 1 (2003): 1–15.

[19] See Lois Lamdin, "Curricular Coherence and the Individual Student," in *Opposition to the Core Curriculum*, ed. James W. Hall and Barbara L. Kevles (Westport, CT: Greenwood, 1982), 69–83.

[20] Barbara St. Clair and David L. Hough, *Interdisciplinary Teaching: A Review of the Literature* (Springfield, MO: Department of Curriculum and Instruction, Southwest Missouri State University, 1992). Also, see Jeffrey C. Davis, "A Profession of Blended Beliefs," *Pedagogy* 10, no. 2 (2010): 317–44.

[21] For example, see Francis Bridger, "The Problem of Integration in Theological Education," *British Journal of Theological Education* 4, no. 3 (1992): 23–34. Also see Bridger's "Desperately Seeking What? Engaging with the New Spiritual Quest," *Journal of Christian Education* 44, no. 1 (2001): 7–14.

[22] Elizabeth C. Sites, Fernando L. Garzon, Frederick A. Milacci, and Barbara Booth, "A Phenomenology of the Integration of Faith and Learning," *Journal of Psychology and Theology* 37, no. 1 (2009): 28–38.

[23] See, for example, Derek Curtis Bok, *Beyond the Ivory Tower: Social Responsibility of the Modern University* (Cambridge: Harvard University Press, 1982); and Peter Werner, "The Future of the Integrated Curriculum in Physical Education: Guarded Optimism," *Teaching Elementary Physical Education* 10, no. 6 (1999): 11–13.

[24] An example that illustrates the longevity of this view is that of J. Billington, "Universities Have Fallen Down on the Job of Teaching Values," *Faculty Dialogue* 1, no. 2 (1984): 27–32. More recent work is also at hand, such as that of Jennifer S. Ripley, Fernando L. Garzon, M. Elizabeth Lewis Hall, Michael W. Mangis, and Christopher J. Murphy, "Pilgrims' Progress: Faculty and University Factors in Graduate Student Integration of Faith and Profession, *Journal of Psychology & Theology* 37, no. 1 (2009): 5–14. Laurie Mathias researched students' perceptions of Wheaton College faculty. Her dissertation, "Dual Citizenship in Athens and Jerusalem: A Portrait of Professors who Exemplify the Integration of Faith and Learning at Wheaton College," leaves professors with some distinct responsibilities for faith-learning integration (Regent University, 2007). See her article, "Professors who Walk Humbly with Their God: Exemplars in the Integration of Faith and Learning at Wheaton College," *Journal of Education and Christian Belief* 12, no. 2 (2008): 145–57.

[25] Tiana Tucker, personal correspondence, August 15, 2013.

[26] See *The Idea of a Christian College*, 2nd ed. (Grand Rapids, MI: Eerdmans, 1987); *Shaping Character: Moral Education in the Christian College* (Grand Rapids, MI: Eerdmans, 1991); and *Building the Christian Academy* (Grand Rapids, MI: Eerdmans, 2001).

[27] See Ken Badley, "The Community of Faith as the Locus of Faith-Learning Integration," in *Alive to God: Studies in Spirituality Presented to Jim Houston*, ed. James I. Packer and Loren Wilkinson (Downers Grove, IL: InterVarsity, 1992), 286–95.

[28] This section is summarized from a chapter-length treatment of the locus question that appears as "Where Does Faith-Learning Integration Happen?" in *Faith Integration for Schools of Education*, ed. Maria Pacino and Marsha Fowler (Indianapolis: Precedent, 2012), 56–73.

## Chapter 3

[1] Thomas O'Neill with Gary Hymel, *All Politics is Local and Other Rules of the Game* (Massachusetts: Bob Adams, 1994), 208.

[2] Steven Kerr, "On the Folly of Rewarding A, While Hoping for B," *Academy of Management Executive*, 9, no. 1 (1995): 7–14.

[3] William H. Bergquist and Kenneth Pawlak, *Engaging the Six Cultures of the Academy* (San Francisco: Jossey-Bass, 2008), 1–2.

[4] John Millett, *Management, Governance and Leadership* (New York: AMACOM, 1980), 17–21.

[5] While recognizing that institutions do not expect faculty to adopt different models of faith and learning integration as they progress up the ranks, they usually do expect faculty to become more sophisticated in their articulation of the relations between faith and learning.

[6] CCCU is the Council of Christian Colleges and Universities, a higher education association of 174 intentionally Christ-centered institutions around the world. The 119 member campuses in North America are all fully accredited, comprehensive colleges and universities with curricula rooted in the arts and sciences.

[7] For example, we know of an instance where a political science professor was dismissed for bringing in, of all things, a Democrat to speak to his class. We also know of a president who was in earnest planning to move the campus to a new location without any input from senior staff, faculty, or trustees.

[8] George Fox University, *Faculty Handbook* (2012), 29.

[9] For example see Arthur Holmes, *The Idea of a Christian College*, 2nd ed. (Grand Rapids, MI: Eerdmans, 1987); George Marsden, *The Soul of the American University: From Protestant Establishment to Established Non-Belief* (New York: Oxford University Press, 1994); James T. Burtchaell, *The Dying of the Light: The Disengagement of Colleges and Universities from Their Christian Churches* (Grand Rapids, MI: Eerdmans, 1998). Robert Benne's response to Burtchaell's lament appeared as *Quality with Soul: How Six Premier Colleges and Universities Keep Faith with Their Religious Traditions* (Grand Rapids, MI: Eerdmans, 2001).

[10] Many echo Arthur Holmes (*The Idea of a Christian College*) here and ask to see Christian faith brought to bear on every aspect of campus life.

[11] Randy Basinger, provost, Messiah College, personal correspondence, September 13, 2013.

[12] David Alexander, president, Northwest Nazarene University, personal correspondence, September 18, 2013.

[13] Dennis Lindsay, provost, Northwest Christian University, personal correspondence, September 16, 2013.

[14] James Edwards, president, Anderson University, personal correspondence, September 13, 2013.

[15] Calvin College, *Faculty Handbook*, (July 2013), 40.

[16] Lee University, *Faculty Handbook & Constitution*, sections 4–7.

[17] Mark Noll, *The Scandal of the Evangelical Mind* (Grand Rapids, MI: Eerdmans, 1994), 1.

[18] See Douglas Jacobsen and Rhonda H. Jacobsen, *Scholarship and Christian Faith* (New York: Oxford University Press, 2004); and James Smith, *Desiring the Kingdom: Worship, Worldview, and Cultural Formation* (Grand Rapids, MI: Baker Academic, 2009).

[19] Steve Bedi, provost emeritus, Taylor University, personal correspondence, September 13, 2013.

[20] Kerry Fulcher, provost, Point Loma Nazarene University, personal correspondence, September 13, 2013.

[21] We highlight and commend Azusa Pacific University's approach to documenting faith-integration in Chapter Eight.

[22] David Alexander, president, Northwest Nazarene University, personal correspondence, September 18, 2013.

## Chapter 4

[1] Douglas Jacobsen and Rhonda H. Jacobsen, *Scholarship and Christian Faith* (New York: Oxford University Press, 2004), 120. Also see their "A Response to the *Pneuma* Essays on Faith and Scholarship," *Pneuma: The Journal of the Society of Pentecostal Studies* 27, no. 1 (Spring, 2005): 157–60.

[2] Jacobsen and Jacobsen, *Scholarship and Christian Faith*, 50.

[3] Mark F. Goldberg, "A Portrait of Ernest Boyer," *Educational Leadership* 52, no. 5 (1995): 46.

[4] James Baldwin, "Sonny's Blues," in *American Short Stories Since 1945,* ed. John G. Parks (New York: Oxford University Press, 2002), 245.

[5] Douglas Jacobsen, "Theology as Public Performance: Reflections on the Christian Convictions of Ernest L. Boyer," (Presidential Scholar's Lecture, Messiah College, Grantham, Pennyslvania, 2000), 1.

[6] Ibid., 3–4.

[7] Ernest Boyer, *Selected Speeches: 1979–1995* (Princeton, NJ: Carnegie Foundation for the Advancement of Teaching, 1997), 110.

[8] Charles Glassick, Mary Huber, and Gene Maeroff, *Scholarship Assessed* (Princeton, NJ: Carnegie Foundation for the Advancement of Teaching, 1997), vii.

[9] Goldberg, "Portrait of Ernest Boyer," 46–48.

[10] Boyer, *Selected Speeches,* 60.

[11] Ibid., 80, 126.

[12] Ibid., 61.

[13] Ibid., 125.

[14] Ibid., 109–13.

[15] Ibid., 65.

[16] Ibid., 121.

[17] Ernest Boyer, "Reflections on a Church-Related Higher Education," *The Cresset* 57, no. 5 (1994): 7.

[18] Vachel Lindsay, "The Leaden Eye," in *Collected Poems by Vachel Lindsay* (New York: Macmillan, 1926), 69–70.

[19] Boyer, *Selected Speeches,* 116.

[20] Ernest Boyer, *Scholarship Reconsidered: Priorities for the Professoriate* (Princeton, NJ: Carnegie Foundation for the Advancement of Teaching, 1990), 16.

[21] KerryAnn O'Meara and Eugene Rice, *Faculty Priorities Reconsidered* (San Francisco: Jossey-Bass, 2005), 28.

[22] Boyer, *Scholarship Reconsidered,* 15.

[23] Ibid., 13.

[24] S. F. Aldersley, "Upward Drift Is Alive and Well: Research/Doctoral Model Still Attractive to Institutions," *Change* 27, no. 5 (1995): 50–56.

[25] Glassick, Huber, and Maeroff, *Scholarship Assessed,* 22.

[26] Ibid., 36.

[27] Ibid., 50.

[28] J. M. Braxton, W. Luckey, and T. Helland, *Institutionalizing a Broader View of Scholarship through Boyer's Four Domains* (San Francisco: Jossey-Bass, 2002).

[29] Robert Diamond, ed., *Field Guide to Academic Leadership* (San Francisco: Jossey-Bass, 2002), 280.

[30] O'Meara and Rice, *Faculty Priorities Reconsidered,* 293–300.

[31] Ibid., xi.

[32] Ibid., 305–6.

[33] Todd C. Ream, guest ed., *Christian Higher Education* 13, no. 1 (2014).

[34] Kathryn Boyer, *Many Mansions: Lessons of Faith, Family, and Public Service* (Abilene, TX: Abilene Christian University Press, 2014).

[35] Ernest Boyer, "Creating the New American College," *Chronicle of Higher Education* (March 9, 1994): A48.

## Chapter 5

[1] Carolin Kreber notes this failure to come to a consensus in her chapter, "Conceptualizing the Scholarship of Teaching and Learning and Identifying Unresolved Issues," in her own edited volume, *Scholarship Revisited: Perspectives on the Scholarship of Teaching* (San Francisco: Jossey-Bass, 2001), 1–18.

[2] Ernest Boyer, *Scholarship Reconsidered: Priorities for the Professoriate* (Princeton, NJ: Carnegie Foundation for the Advancement of Teaching, 1990), 24–25.

[3] Maryellen Weimer, "Learning More from the Wisdom of Practice," in Kreber, *Scholarship Revisited*, 47–52.

[4] Ronald Smith, "Expertise and the Scholarship of Teaching," in Kreber, *Scholarship Revisited*, 74.

[5] Ibid., 76.

[6] Ernest Boyer, *Selected Speeches: 1979–1995* (Princeton, NJ: Carnegie Foundation for the Advancement of Teaching, 1997), 126.

[7] Ibid., 65.

[8] Ibid., 77.

[9] Ibid., 88.

[10] Smith, *Scholarship Revisited*, 76.

[11] This definition of scholarship was proposed by Shulman and Hutchings in Lee Shulman and Pat Hutchins, "About the Scholarship of Teaching and Learning," The Pew Scholars National Fellowship Program, (Menlo Park, CA: The Carnegie Foundation for the Advancement of Teaching, 1998), 9.

[12] J. M. Braxton and M. Del Favero, "Evaluating Scholarship Performance: Traditional and Emergent Assessment Techniques," *New Directions for Institutional Research* 114 (2002): 19–31.

[13] J. M. Braxton, W. Luckey, and T. Helland, "The Inventory of Scholarship," in *Institutionalizing a Broader View of Scholarship Through Boyer's Four Domains* (San Francisco: Jossey-Bass, 2002), 141–46.

[14] Smith, *Scholarship Revisited*, 76.

[15] Pat Hutchings and Lee Shulman, "The Scholarship of Teaching: New Elaborations, New Developments," *Change* 31, no. 5 (1999): 11–15.

[16] Laurie Richland, "Scholarly Teaching and the Scholarship of Teaching," in Kreber, *Scholarship Revisited*, 61.

[17] Hutchings and Shulman, "Scholarship of Teaching," 11–15.

[18] Mary Taylor Huber, Pat Hutchings, and Lee Shulman, "The Scholarship of Teaching and Learning Today," in *Faculty Priorities Reconsidered*, ed. KerryAnn O'Meara and Eugene Rice (San Francisco: Jossey-Bass, 2005), 36.

[19] Richland, *Scholarship Revisited*, 61.

[20] Huber, Hutchings, and Shulman, *Faculty Priorities Reconsidered*, 38.

[21] We borrow this image from the advertisement for EDS systems, available at http://www.youtube.com/watch?v=Y7XW-mewUm8 (or available by typing "building planes in the sky" into a search engine or YouTube).

[22] In Chapter Nine, we return to this idea that each period or piece of scholarship can be viewed as part of a lifelong arc or trajectory when academic work is viewed as vocation.

[23] One (unnamed) observer has labeled some of these pressures as "the beginning of the unbundling of the American university." See Ann Hulbert, "How to Escape the Community-College Trap," *The Atlantic* 313, no. 1 (January–February, 2014), 68–72.

[24] Pat Hutchings, Mary Taylor Huber, and Anthony Ciccone, *The Scholarship of Teaching and Learning Reconsidered* (San Francisco: Jossey-Bass, 2011), 87.

[25] Ibid., 88–89.

[26] The authors know the correct spelling of *light*.

[27] Charles Glassick, Mary Taylor Huber, and Gene Maeroff, *Scholarship Assessed: Evaluation of the Professoriate* (San Francisco: Jossey-Bass, 1997), 36.

[28] Madeleine L'Engle, *Walking on Water: Reflections on Faith and Art* (Wheaton, IL: Harold Shaw, 1980), 121–22.

[29] Richard Hughes, *How Christian Faith Can Sustain the Life of the Mind* (Grand Rapids, MI: Eerdmans, 2001), 135–36.

[30] One of the authors (PA) served as vice president of academic affairs at Anderson University with then President Robert Nicholson. He heard Nicholson use this phrase many times.

[31] Sam Keen's *Apology for Wonder* remains one of the best books to address wonder (New York: Harper and Row, 1969). Anne Lamott ties wonder to prayer in *Help, Thanks, Wow: The Three Essential Prayers* (New York: Penguin/Riverhead, 2012). Paul Griffiths sets wonder in a theological framework and distinguishes it from curiosity in *The Vice of Curiosity: An Essay on Intellectual Appetite* (Ithaca, NY: CMU Press, 2006).

[32] Nathan Hatch, "Evangelical Colleges and the Challenge of Christian Thinking," in *Making Higher Education Christian: The History and Mission of Evangelical Colleges in America,* ed. Joel Carpenter and Kenneth Shipps (St. Paul, MN: Christian University Press, 1987), 167.

[33] Douglas Jacobsen and Rhonda Hustedt Jacobsen, *Scholarship and Christian Faith* (Oxford: Oxford Press, 2004), 52.

[34] We know of the academy's love of the phrase *the other*. We offer *the neighbor* as an alternative capable of invoking biblical responses to the person different from ourselves.

[35] Arlin Migliazzo, ed., *Teaching As an Act of Faith* (New York: Fordham Press, 2002). Among the many titles in this genre of books that examine faith and the academic disciplines, we also recommend these two edited volumes: Deane Downey and Stanley E. Porter, *Christian Worldview and the Academic Disciplines: Crossing the Academy (*Eugene, OR: Wipf and Stock, 2009); and Roger Lundin, *Christ Across the Disciplines: Past, Present, Future* (Grand Rapids, MI: Eerdmans, 2013).

[36] Of course, there are many other sources that provide leads for faith–learning scholarship in the disciplines. We note two here: a website developed by Jane Scott, Public Services Librarian at George Fox University: http://www.georgefox.edu/offices/murdock/Services/Faculty/FaithLearningBib/index.html and the CCCU Resource Library, particularly the series entitled "Through the Eyes of Faith:" http://www.cccu.org/Search?q=Through%20the%20Eyes%20of%20Faith.

[37] David I. Smith and James K. A. Smith, *Teaching and Spiritual Practices* (Grand Rapids, MI: Eerdmans, 2012), 20.

[38] K. Jo-Ann Badley and Ken Badley, "Slow Reading: Reading along *Lectio* Lines," *Journal of Education and Christian Belief* 15, 1 (2011): 29–42. Given the earlier discussion of humility, one author of the present work (KB) wishes to point out both that his co-author (PA) contributed this example to the text and that K. Jo-Ann Badley, dean of seminary at Ambrose University, actually inspired and led the article on *lectio divina*.

[39] See Todd C. Ream, Jerry Pattengale, and David L. Riggs, eds., *Beyond Integration* (Abilene, TX: Abilene Christian University Press, 2012).

[40] Jacques Maritain, *Education at the Crossroads* (New Haven: Yale University Press, 1943), 39.

[41] Glassick, Huber, and Maeroff, *Scholarship Assessed*, 61–65.

[42] Hebrews 11:8.

## Chapter 6

[1] Ernest Boyer, *College: The Undergraduate Experience in America* (New York: Harper & Row, 1987).

[2] Ibid., 131.

[3] Ibid., 132.

[4] John Hattie and H. W. Marsh "The Relationship Between Research and Teaching: A Meta-Analysis," *Review of Educational Research* 66, no. 4 (1996): 507-542.

[5] For example, see John H. Braxton, William Luckey, and Patricia Helland, *Institutionalizing a Broader View of Scholarship Through Boyer's Four Domains* (San Francisco: Jossey-Bass, 2002); Charles E. Glassick, Mary Taylor Huber, and Gene I. Maeroff, *Scholarship Assessed* (San Francisco: Jossey-Bass, 1997).

[6] Ernest L. Boyer, *Scholarship Reconsidered* (San Francisco: Jossey-Bass, 1990), 15, emphasis in original.

[7] Braxton, Luckey, and Helland, *Institutionalizing a Broader View*, 39.

[8] Boyer did not carry this concern alone. Many have addressed the pressures on academic research and some of the wrong responses academics are prone to make to those pressures. One good example comes from P. Arne Vesilind, "The Responsible Conduct of Academic Research," in *The Academic's Handbook*, ed. A. L. Deneef, C. D. Goodwin and E. S. McCrate (Raleigh, NC: Duke University Press, 1988), 104–111; see also Mark Bauerlein's essay, "The Research Bust," in *The Chronicle of Higher Education* (December 9, 2011): B4–5.

[9] Boyer, *Scholarship Reconsidered*, 21.

[10] Ibid., 18. Also see Pat Hutchings, Mary Taylor Huber, and Anthony Ciccone, "Getting There: An Integrative Vision of the Scholarship of Teaching and Learning," *International Journal for the Scholarship of Teaching and Learning* 5, no. 1 (2011): 1–14.

[11] Ibid., 19.

[12] Ibid., 20.

[13] C. P. Snow, *The Two Cultures and the Scientific Revolution* (New York: Cambridge University Press, 1961).

[14] Among many others, Sherry Turkle has traced this line of argument in her many books, but especially in *Alone Together: Why We Expect More from Technology and Less from Each Other* (New York: Basic Books, 2011).

[15] Ken A. Dill, "Strengthening Biomedicine's Roots," *Nature* 400 (1999): 309–10.

[16] Dale Dauphinee and Joseph B. Martin, "Breaking Down the Walls: Thoughts on the Scholarship of Integration," *Academic Medicine* 75, no. 9 (2000): 88.

[17] With many others, we recognize the continuing problems of definition with such terms as *integrative* and *interdisciplinary*. See Giovanni Gozzer, "Interdisciplinarity: A Concept Still Unclear, *Prospects* 12, no. 3 (1982): 281–92; Brian Hudson, "Reclaiming Scholarship as an Integrating Dimension of Academic Work for the Impact of Research on Teaching and Learning in Higher Education," *Scottish Educational Review* 43, no. 1 (2011): 24–20; L. le Grange, "The Scholarship of Integration (Re) Considered," *South African Journal of Higher Education* 21, no. 5 (2006): 506–14; Victoria N. Salmon, "Practicing Boyer's Scholarship of Integration: A Program for Community College Faculty—Revised," *English in the Two-Year College* 32, no. 1 (2004): 64–70; and Veronica Boix-Mansilla, "Learning to Synthesize: Toward an Epistemological Foundation for Interdisciplinary Learning," *The Oxford Handbook of Interdisciplinarity*, ed. R. Frodeman, J. T. Klein, and C. Mitcham (New York: Oxford University Press, 2010), 288–306.

[18] Snow, *Two Cultures*, 53.

[19] Alan M. Rubin, "Is Boyer Misguided or Misused? The Scholarship of Confusion," *Journal of the Association for Communication Administration* 29 (2000): 260–64.

[20] Ibid., 261.

[21] Ibid., 263.

[22] Ibid., 263.

[23] Ibid., 263, emphasis added.

[24] Ibid., 263.

[25] Mark Hirschkorn reviews some of the literature on how stories and rumors influence candidates for tenure and promotion. See "How Vulnerable Am I? An Experiential Discussion of Tenure Rhetoric for New Faculty," *Journal of Educational Thought* 44, no. 1 (2010): 41–54.

[26] Cole Dawson, vice president for academic affairs and dean of the faculty, Warner Pacific University, personal correspondence, December 20, 2013.

[27] Braxton, Luckey, and Helland, *Institutionalizing a Broader View*, 143–45.

[28] Carole A. Barbato, "Scholarship of Integration: Pushing, Blurring, and Connecting Theoretical Perspectives," *Journal of the Association for Communication Administration* 29 (2000): 242.

[29] Ibid., 243.

[30] Mordechai Gordon, "What Makes Interdisciplinary Research Original? Integrative Scholarship Reconsidered," *Oxford Review of Education* 33, no. 2 (2007): 195–209; doi: 10.1080/03054980701259642.

[31] Anne Hofmeyer, Mandi Newton, and Cathie Scott, "Valuing the Scholarship of Integration and the Scholarship of Application in the Academy for Health Sciences Scholars: Recommended Methods," *Health Research Policy and Systems* 29, no. 5 (2007): 5; doi:10.1186/1478–4505–5–5.

[32] Marcia Bundy Seabury, "Interdisciplinarity: Some Possibilities & Guidelines," *Issues in Integrative Studies* 22 (2004): 52–84.

[33] The idea of creation having aspects, and the disciplines reflecting on those aspects is adapted from Herman A. Dooyeweerd, *A New Critique of Theoretical Thought, Volume 1: The Necessary Presuppositions of Philosophy*, tran. David H. Freeman and William S. Young, (Paris: Uitgeverij H. J., 1953). Also see Al Wolters, *Creation Regained* (Grand Rapids, MI: Eerdmans, 1985).

[34] One of us has explored this at greater length, albeit for a secular audience, in "Resistance to Curriculum Integration: Do Good Fences Make Good Neighbors?" *Issues in Integrative Studies* 27 (2009): 113–37.

[35] Central examples include these three: Mark A. Noll, *The Scandal of the Evangelical Mind* (Grand Rapids, MI: Eerdmans, 1994); George M. Marsden, *The Outrageous Idea of Christian Scholarship* (New York: Oxford University Press, 1997); and Douglas Jacobsen and Rhonda Hustedt Jacobsen, *Scholarship and Christian Faith* (New York: Oxford University Press, 2004). Also see Harold Heie's *Learning to Listen, Ready to Talk: A Pilgrimage Toward Peacemaking*, (Lincoln, NE: iUniverse, 2007), especially chapter 22 on Christian scholarship; and Andrew Sloane's examination of Nicholas Wolterstorff's work in *On Being a Christian in the Academy: Nicholas Wolterstorff and the Practice of Christian Scholarship* (Edinborough: Paternoster, 2003); and Elmer J. Thiessen, "Refining the Conversation: Some Concerns about Contemporary Trends in Thinking about Worldviews, Christian Scholarship and Higher Education," *Evangelical Quarterly* 79, no. 2 (2007): 133–52. The largest professional organization focused on interdisciplinarity and integrative studies, the Association for Integrative Studies, ran Matthew S. Haar Farris's article, "Toward Interdisciplinary Studies as a Spiritual Exercise" in their May 2011 newsletter, *Integrative Pathways*, 33, no. 2, 3–10. Significantly, the article did not appear in their journal, but to publish it at all is to recognize perspectives on interdisciplinarity that are not strictly secular. See the article at http://www.units.muohio.edu/aisorg/pubs/news/11MAY.pdf.

[36] In this regard, we recommend Ellen T. Cherry's essay, "To Know, Love and Enjoy God," *Theology Today* 59 (2002): 173–77.

[37] "Oliver Wendell Holmes quote," at http://www.gotknowhow.com/quotes/oliver-wendell-holmes-i-would-not-give-a-fig-for-the-simplicity-this-side-o/.

## Chapter 7

[1] Many scholars note the ongoing character of what Boyer began; for example, see Robert M. Diamond and Bronwyn E. Adam, *The Disciplines Speak II: More Statements on Rewarding the Scholarly, Professional, and Creative Work of Faculty* (Washington, DC: American Association for Higher Education, Forum on Faculty Roles & Rewards, 2000).

[2] Ninetta Santoro and Suzanne L. Snead, "I'm Not a Real Academic: A Career from Industry to Academe," *Journal of Further and Higher Education* 37, no. 3 (2012): 384–96.

[3] Ernest Boyer, *Selected Speeches: 1979–1995* (Princeton: Carnegie Foundation for the Advancement of Teaching, 1997), 92.

[4] Ibid.

[5] Ibid., 89.

[6] Ernest Boyer, *Scholarship Reconsidered: Priorities for the Profession* (Princeton: Carnegie Foundation for the Advancement of Teaching, 1990), 57.

[7] Robert Bringle, Richard Games, and Edward Malloy, *Colleges and Universities as Citizens* (Boston: Allyn & Bacon, 1999), 3. Also see Kristin Ahlberg, Edward Countryman, Debbie Ann Doyle, Bill Bryans, Kathleen Franz, John R. Dichtl, Constance B. Schulz, Gregory E. Smoak, and Susan Ferentinos, "Tenure, Promotion and the Publicly Engaged Academic Historian," (2010), accessed from Organization of American Historians, http://www.Oah.Org/About/Papers/Press_Releases/Wgephs_Report.Pdf."; Brenda L. Bass, Howard L. Barnes, Kyle L. Kostelecky, and William Michael Fleming, "Service Learning and Portfolios: Enhancing the Scholarship of Integration and Application," *Journal of Teaching in Marriage & Family* 4, no. 1 (2004): 79–99.

[8] Ibid., 22.

[9] Charles Glassick, Mary Huber, and Gene Maeroff, *Scholarship Assessed* (Princeton: Carnegie Foundation for the Advancement of Teaching, 1997), ix.

[10] Ibid., 25.

[11] J. W. Braxton, W. Luckey, and T. Helland, "The Inventory of Scholarship," in *Institutionalizing a Broader View of Scholarship Through Boyer's Four Domains* (San Francisco: Jossey-Bass, 2002), 141–46.

[12] This definition of scholarship was proposed in Lee Shulman and Pat Hutchins, "About the Scholarship of Teaching and Learning," The Pew Scholars National Fellowship Program, (Menlo Park, CA: The Carnegie Foundation for the Advancement of Teaching, 1998), 9.

[13] Amy Driscoll, "Tracing the Scholarship of Engagement Through my Professional Memoirs," in *Faculty Priorities Reconsidered: Rewarding Multiple Forms of Scholarship*, ed. KerryAnn O'Meara and R. Eugene Rice (San Francisco: Jossey-Bass, 2005), 42.

[14] Linda Samek, provost, George Fox University, personal correspondence, December 15, 2013.

[15] Linda Mills Woolsey, dean of the college and vice president for academic affairs, Houghton College, personal correspondence, December 16, 2013.

[16] Doyle Lucas, director of DBA program, Falls School of Business, Anderson University, personal correspondence, December 16, 2013.

[17] David Clark, vice president and dean, Bethel Seminary, Bethel University, personal correspondence, December 16, 2013.

[18] Jonathan Parker, provost, California Baptist University, personal correspondence, December 16, 2013.

[19] All biblical references and citations are taken from the New Revised Standard Version unless specifically indicated otherwise.

[20] We join Tertullian (*Prescription Against Heretics*), who famously glossed this same verse long before we did.

[21] Carl R. Rogers, *Freedom to Learn* (Columbus, OH: Merrill, 1969). Others expressing sentiments similar to these include E. Bain-Selbo, "From Pride to Cowardice: Obstacles to the Dialogical Classroom," *Teaching Theology & Religion* 6, no. 1 (2003): 3–8; William P. Brown, "Thirsting for God in the Classroom: A Meditation on Psalm 42:1–8, *Teaching Theology and Religion* 6, no. 4, (2003): 187–89; chapter 15 on intellectual snobbery in Joseph Epstein, *Snobbery: The American Version* (Boston: Houghton Mifflin, 2002); and Sheila Delany, *Chaucer's House of Fame: The Poetics of Skeptical Fideism* (Chicago: University of Chicago Press, 1973).

[22] Deirdre McClosky, "Humility and Truth," *Anglican Theological Review*, 88, no. 2, (2006), 181–95.

[23] In Chapter Nine, we discuss the concept of conversation and our duty as academics to participate responsibly in the academic conversation that has gone on in our field before we arrived there to do our work. We believe that responsible participation implies respectful listening which, in turn, implies reading diligently.

[24] Boyer, *Scholarship Reconsidered*, 21.

## Chapter 8

[1] The pairing appears in as many words in such places as Romans 15:18, 2 Corinthians 10:11, Colossians 3:7, and 1 John 3:18. Without the specific language of words and deeds, walking the talk is arguably a theme in Scripture. We note Gay Lynn Voth's article, "The 'Word' in Deed: Mennonite Brethren Attitudes toward Faith and Learning," *Direction* 37, no. 1 (2008): 7–18.

[2] Peter Weir and Tom Schulman, "Dead Poets' Society," (United States: Touchstone Pictures 1988).

[3] Arthur W. Chickering and Marcia Mentkowski, "Assessing Ineffable Outcomes," in *Encouraging Authenticity and Spirituality in Higher Education*, ed. A. W. Chickering, J. C. Dalton, and L. S. Auerbach (San Francisco: Jossey-Bass, 2006), 221.

[4] We should note the possibility that some might react to the idea of assessing faith and learning integration because the academy has found itself in an environment increasingly obsessed with and driven by assessment. See Simon Head's book review

essay, for example, "The Grim Threat to British Universities," *New York Review of Books* (January 13, 2011): 58–64.

[5] Recognizably, some elements of faith will always remain invisible to assessment. Nevertheless, current institutional realities demand that institutions and individuals give an account of their work, so we will use the framework, albeit with caution. We do so aware of the plentiful literature on character, morality, spirituality, and their assessment (compared to the relative shortage of research on the assessment of faith and learning integration). We list here just a sample of the literature that might inform our current question, albeit from other conversations: H. Astin and A. Antonio, *The Impact of College on Character Development* (Los Angeles: Higher Education Research Institute, Graduate School of Education and Information Studies, University of California, 1999); D. Basinger, "The Measurement of Religiousness: Some Philosophical Concerns," *Journal of Psychology and Christianity* 9, no. 2 (1990): 5–13; E. A. Daniel, "Exploring the Process of Assessment: Report on the ATS Workshop on Assessing Theological Learning," *Theological Education* 39, no. 1 (2003): 93–100; D. O. Moberg, "Assessing and Measuring Spirituality: Confronting Dilemmas of Universal and Particular Evaluative Criteria," *The Journal of Adult Development* 9, no. 1 (2002): 47–60; H. F. Reisz, "Assessing Spiritual Formation in Christian Seminary Communities," *Theological Education*, 39, no. 2 (2003): 29–40.

[6] Distinguishing institutions and individuals leaves us with this question: At what levels should we expect institutions to deliver clarity . . . to department, to college or school, to all faculty individually? If we take the last answer as correct, how should the institution proceed with this task? If we remain at the level of the whole institution, then faith-learning integration remains unembodied and unlocated; institutional articulation is only part of the question. Regarding faith-learning integration, institutions cannot "do it."

[7] Daniel Aleshire, "The Character and Assessment of Learning for Religious Vocation: M. Div. Education and Numbering the Levites," *Theological Education* 39, no. 1 (2003): 1–15.

[8] Some might want to add another dimension to this matrix. Recognizably some faculty will be more explicit about faith than others, and some will be more adept at faith-fully framing courses and assignments. But another criterion or continuum invites inspection: the repulsive / winsome (inviting) criterion. That is, a person could be very explicit and open about faith and repel other people by his or her manner (or lack of manners). Should we assess, or how do we assess if faculty actually take steps to become more winsome in their manner and approach to the faith-full framing of their research, service, and classroom work? We answer *yes*, we must assess this question, but we leave that work for a future time. Other criteria we have not built into this framework may also apply. For example, some faculty attend to the faith foundation of their work in a more organizational and formal way, while others can do so more spontaneously and informally. We will not suggest an answer to the question of whether anyone should assess faculty on this continuum (as if we preferred one form of faith expression over another), but we recognize it as an important matter to explore. In Chapter Two, we noted the possible contribution of Wittgenstein's concept of family resemblances. The recognition of such resemblances would honor the reality that different professors have different conceptions of faith-learning integration and

thus that no single assessment instrument can possibly do justice to all our work, in different disciplines, different courses, and different venues with our different inclinations, our widely varying interests, and the range of our passions. See Ludwig Wittgenstein's *Philosophical Investigations*, trans. G. E. M. Anscombe (New York: Macmillan, 1953), 67.

[9] Our book on (other people's) hypocrisy awaits the removal of a couple of logs from our own eyes.

[10] The dean was pushing for the hire of a faculty member who obviously had little Christian faith to articulate or practice.

[11] At the time of writing, with employment increasingly tight for academic workers, Christian colleges can choose from dozens and sometimes hundreds of applicants for most positions that come open. In our experience, not many of these applicants can articulate a coherent vision for Christian higher education. So, is the ox in the ditch or not? In one sense, yes. In another sense, no.

[12] Admittedly, some have argued that a Christian college needs to have some non-Christian colleagues on the faculty, if only to keep the Christians honest and to be sure that they walk their talk. Elton Trueblood made such an argument. See, for example, Elton Trueblood, *The Idea of a College* (New York: Harper, 1959).

[13] Sadly, one can easily imagine a situation where a committee prefers and promotes the hypocrite of the upper left quadrant because of his or her skill at talking the talk. That would be a sad indictment indeed if the same committee denied our Teresa a promotion on the grounds of a thin essay.

[14] Those interested in this distinction should see these passages: Romans 5:18, 2 Corinthians 10:11, Colossians 3:7, 1 John 3:18.

[15] We recognize that words and intentions differ from each other and that some observers might say intentions should be extrapolated from deeds rather than from words. Here, we have elected to include intentions with words. For a careful philosophical treatment of some of the distinctions between words, actions and achievements, see Gilbert Ryle, *The Concept of Mind* (New York: Barnes and Noble, 1949). Following Ryle's task-achievement distinction would yield a more sophisticated and precise framework for anyone assessing faith-learning integration, but doing so would also produce a less-accessible framework.

[16] Wisely, we think, we will leave this questions to biblical scholars and theologians.

[17] Some may want to require that the institution make explicit its recognition of the conceptual problems and differences in theological commitments that attach to this ideal. Such recognition likely implies that it recognizes in its policies and documents the varied ways people speak about the same ideal, using such language as faith-learning integration, teaching from a Christian worldview, bringing Christian faith to bear, realizing Christian faith, and teaching out of a Christian perspective.

[18] We provide here only the criteria themselves without indicating to what degrees which institution should meet them. Obviously, any institution wanting to implement what we describe here would need to go through the process of identifying what constitutes having met a given criterion at each specified level. That process would entail agreeing on which adjectives and adverbs to use to describe each

level. For example, note this brief list of terms: astute(ly), careful(ly), complete(ly), comprehensive(ly), conscientious(ly), deft(ly), diligent(ly), exhaustive(ly), extensive(ly), full(y), methodical(ly), meticulous(ly), rigorous(ly). We believe such work must be done but will not suggest anyone should volunteer for such work unless their institution has already adopted Boyer's view of the scholarship of engagement. Interestingly, Azusa Pacific University has already done much of this exact work; see the next endnote.

[19] http://www.apu.edu/faithintegration/resources/guidebook/

[20] They did not produce the book to fit Boyer's framework, but we have adjusted their language here to accord with Boyer's language. They introduce teaching and inquiry/discovery on page 7 but then treat both at length later in the document (pages 31–42).

## Chapter 9

[1] Michael Billig summarizes some of the effects of disciplinary specialization as well as fracturing within disciplines and their effects on scholarly writing and publication. See *Learn to Write Badly: How to Succeed in the Social Sciences* (New York: Cambridge University Press, 2013). He refers several times to the difference between producing writing with big words for small circles (disciplinary specialists) or smaller words for big circles (accessible writing for intelligent general readers; pp. 15, 17).

[2] In this regard, we note the work of Paul Griffiths, *Intellectual Appetite: A Theological Grammar* (Washington, DC: Catholic University of America, 2009); and *The Vice of Curiosity: An Essay on Intellectual Appetite* (Ithaca, NY: CMU Press, 2006).

[3] We borrow the idea that every culture has a taken-for-granted stock of knowledge from Alfred Schütz, *The Phenomenology of the Social World*, trans. George Walsh and Frederick Lehnert (Evanston, IL: Northwestern University Press, 1967).

[4] Tiana Tucker, personal correspondence, August 15, 2013.

[5] In *How to Write Badly*, Billig deals at length with several results of the crank-it-out attitude, with clunky writing prominent among them.

[6] Anne Lamott, *Bird by Bird: Some Instructions on Writing and Life* (New York: Anchor/Random, 1995).

[7] Again, this is one of Billig's complaints throughout *How to Write Badly*.

[8] Lots of books on writing deal with scheduling writing, some as an antidote to the other kind of writer's block. We recommend the treatment in Paul Silvia's *How to Write a Lot* (Washington, DC: American Psychological Association, 2007), 11–28. A Web search for the string "outer writer" will also produce some helpful insights from people aiming at writing productivity rather than writing inspiration, a concept often connected to discovering one's "inner writer."

[9] Mortimer J. Adler, *The Great Conversation: A Reader's Guide to Great Books of the Western World* (Chicago: Encyclopedia Britannica, 1990). We are aware of the criticisms of the Great Books. Euro-centrism notwithstanding, our point in quoting

this title is simply to underline that academics who would write do enter a pre-existent conversation.

[10] This is not a book on writing, but we do want to point to one common weakness of academic writing that diminishes the author's voice. We call it a disappearing act because the writer disappears: forgoing the first-person pronoun. Writing without "I" or "we" leads many academic writers to use the passive voice ("it will be shown that") or personification ("the next chapter will make clear that"), both moves that weaken writing.

[11] Gloria Stronks and Doug Blomberg, eds., *A Vision with a Task: Christian Schooling for Responsive Discipleship* (Grand Rapids, MI: Baker, 1993).

[12] Andrew Anderson, "A Field of Questions: W. P. Kinsella Comes to Ithaca," in *Baseball, Literature, Culture: Essays, 2002–2003*, ed. Peter Carino (Jefferson, NC: McFarland, 2004).

[13] We will not deal at length with the deeper psychological and sociological aspects of e-mail, but we recommend two titles: John Freeman, *The Tyranny of E-mail: The Four-Thousand-Year Journey to Your Inbox* (New York: Scribner, 2009); William Powers, *Hamlet's Blackberry: A Practical Philosophy for Building a Good Life in the Digital Age* (New York: Harper, 2010). Do not read these books if they will distract you from writing.

[14] Nostalgia alert: we are not techies, but one of us did develop bibliographic database software for WordPerfect 5 for DOS. The other first learned to program on a self-built Heathkit computer using Benton Harbor BASIC.

[15] Some readers may find interesting reading in the meta-element article in *Wikipedia*. Do not be distracted by the meta-joke article nearby.

[16] Mihaly Csikszentmihalyi, *Flow: The Psychology of Optimal Experience* (New York: Harper and Row, 1990).

[17] Some word processors continuously show the word count in a corner of the screen. Others require the writer to go through a couple of steps. We encourage writers with the continual word counts to make the information on the screen part of a purposeful attempt to increase awareness of their writing processes. We encourage those who have to click on Tools in order to get a word count to form the habit.

[18] Speaking of e-mail, we recommend that our readers periodically dump all their sent e-mail from one day into a word processor file and then do a word count. Our daily output of e-mail should serve as proof both that we apparently do have the time to write and that we can write hundreds or even thousands of words in one day if we keep our buns on the chair and our hands on the keyboard.

[19] We refer here to Stephen King's claim that there are four kinds of writing: bad, competent, good, and great. He believes that "While it is impossible to make a competent writer out of a bad writer, and while it is equally impossible to make a great writer out of a good one, it is possible, with lots of hard work, dedication, and timely help, to make a good writer out of a merely competent one." *On Writing: A Memoir of the Craft* (New York: Scribner, 2000), 142.

[20] We know that in parts of the academy, jaw-droppingly impenetrable writing seems to have won the day. Those who want or need to write such prose to see their work published are welcome to ignore this section.

[21] We say this cautiously. Faculty at Christian colleges should conduct and publish interdisciplinary work not because it will be published or because Boyer said they should. They should do it because God's world has many aspects, all of them connected, and all of them sustained and held together by Christ's creative power (Col. 1).

[22] Reading aloud will not necessarily help the writer identify weaknesses in the argumentation or conceptual framework of the piece, another reason to form or join a writing professional learning community and to use an editor.

[23] Like our readers, we believe that is likely for the good, inasmuch as we do not need more journals with more articles than we have now. But we assume that the quality of our readers' work would be above average and that more of it should appear in print. Purely as a matter of interest, we note R. Campbell and A. Meadows's estimate that roughly 1.5 million scholarly articles appeared in 2009. See "Scholarly Journal Publishing: Where Do We Go from Here?" *Learned Publishing* 24, (2011): 171–81. A. E. Jinha estimated a year earlier that 50 million scholarly articles had been published by that time. See "Article 50 Million: An Estimate of the Number of Scholarly Articles in Existence," *Learned Publishing* 23, (2010): 258–63. Without a milligram of cynicism, we want to suggest that not all these articles warranted publication.

[24] See, for example, Freeman, *The Tyranny of E-mail.*

[25] At the time we were writing this book, Amazon's "Advanced Search" feature appears only after the user has searched one title under the "Books" menu. The "Advanced Search" menu includes an option to select the dates of publication, and you can type a recent or future date into that dialog box. Searching both Amazon and Books in Print will yield overlapping but somewhat different lists of forthcoming titles, not all of which will ever actually appear in print. Readers should know of one additional resource, WorldCat, a meta- (and mega!) library catalogue maintained by the state of Ohio and sustained by user fees from all participating libraries. WorldCat contains the records of thousands of libraries around the world. Every catalogued title in every participating library will appear in WorldCat, implying that forthcoming titles do not appear there but that all member libraries' extant titles—over 100 million books at the time of writing—do appear.

[26] Silvia, *How to Write a Lot.*

## Chapter 10

[1] In Chapter Eight, we named as a criterion for assessing the individual faculty member that he or she be able to articulate a vision of faith-learning integration with some theological and biblical sophistication. We listed that criterion recognizing that some will find it objectionable and that we expect too much of some faculty.

[2] Of course, the idea of a university being transformational is not new, but the nomenclature "Transformational Institution (TI)" is our own.

[3] Steven Kerr, "On the Folly of Rewarding A, While Hoping for B," *Academy of Management Executive* 9, no. 1 (1995): 7–14.

[4] Jose Ortega y Gassett, *Mission of the University* (New York: Norton, 1944), chap. 6. We have appropriated the idea of thinking about what institutions are to be primarily and to be in addition from chapter titles in Ortega's *Mission of the University*. We recognize that he was not speaking specifically about the mission of faith-based institutions.

[5] David Hassel, *City of Wisdom: A Christian Vision of the American University* (Chicago: Loyola University Press, 1983), 60–82. Hassel's writing has influenced our thinking about wisdom communities. We commend and recommend this title to those interested in this topic.

[6] For example, see J. H. Pryor, K. Eagan, Blake L. Palucki, S. Hurtado, J. Berdan, and M. Case, *The American Freshman: National Norms Fall 2012* (Los Angeles: Higher Education Research Institute, UCLA, 2012), 4.

[7] We are not sure if professors need a repertoire or an arsenal of methods. Some seem to teach well with just two or three learning strategies, compensating for the apparent lack of variety with other qualities. We will not sort out the question of instructional quality in this book.

[8] Vic Heasley taught chemistry at Point Loma Nazarene University for over forty years and was recognized by students and faculty colleagues as a great professor, connecting his classes to the wisdom community on a daily basis.

[9] Parker Palmer deals with this idea of the big subject in both *The Courage to Teach* (San Francisco: Jossey-Bass, 1998), and *To Know as We Are Known: A Spirituality of Education* (San Francisco: Harper, 1983).

[10] Dwight Kimberly, a biologist at George Fox University, was known for his excellent teaching, his humility, and his genuine care for students. He was a wisdom keeper who practiced the Five E's throughout his career.

[11] Parker Palmer, "Toward a Spirituality of Higher Education," in *Faithful Learning and the Christian Scholarly Vocation*, ed. David Henry and Bob Agee (Grand Rapids, MI: Eerdmans, 2003), 75.

[12] James Smith, *Desiring the Kingdom: Worship, Worldview, and Cultural Formation* (Grand Rapids, MI: Baker Academic, 2009), 29.

[13] Arthur Holmes, *The Soul of the Christian University* (Grand Rapids, MI: Calvin College, 1997), 34.

[14] Clifford Williams, *The Life of the Mind* (Grand Rapids, MI: Baker Academic, 2002), 82.

[15] A. Bartlett Giamatti, *A Free and Ordered Space* (New York: Norton, 1988), 59.

[16] Chris Anderson, *Teaching as Believing: Faith in the University* (Waco, TX: Baylor University Press, 2004), 200.

[17] Gaylen Byker, "The Embarrassment of Riches," in *Keeping Faith: Embracing the Tensions in Christian Higher Education*, ed. Ronald Wells (Grand Rapids, MI: Eerdmans, 1996), 19.

[18] Walter Brueggemann, "Covenanting as Human Vocation," *Interpretation* 33, no. 2 (April 1979): 126.

[19] John Bennett, *Academic Life: Hospitality, Ethics, and Spirituality* (Boston: Anker, 2003). We wish to acknowledge the thoughtful work and profound influence that John Bennett has had on our understanding and identification of core institutional practices. In this book, he concludes with the following: "Only when educational leaders and all who participate in higher education allow themselves to be truly formed as well as informed by conversation and hospitable teaching, scholarship, and service, can the academy be true to itself. . . . I have suggested that this challenge is best met when we commit to hospitality, conversation, and covenant. . . . They are best demonstrated, however, rather than simply talked about" (187–88).

[20] Aurelie Hagstrom, "Christian Hospitality in the Intellectual Community," in *Christianity And the Soul of the University*, ed. Douglas Henry and Michel Beaty (Grand Rapids, MI: Baker Academic, 2006), 120. Other good treatments of hospitality include these: D. W. Anderson, "Hospitable Classrooms: Biblical Hospitality and Inclusive Education," *Journal of Education & Christian Belief* 15, no. 1 (2011): 13–27; Bennett, *Academic Life*; and Jane McAvoy, "Hospitality: A Feminist Theology of Education," *Teaching Theology and Religion* 1, no. 1 (1998): 20–26.

[21] Hagstrom, "Christian Hospitality," 129.

[22] Martin Marty, "The Church and Christian Higher Education in the New Millennium," in *Faithful Learning and the Christian Scholarly Vocation,* ed. Bob Agee and Douglas Henry (Grand Rapids, MI: Eerdmans, 2003), 59.

[23] "The Witness," directed by Peter Weir, Paramount Pictures, 1985.

[24] Thomas O'Neill with Gary Hymel, *All Politics is Local and Other Rules of the Game* (Boston: Bob Adams Publishers, 1994), xv.

[25] Stanley Hauerwas, *The State of the University: Academic Knowledges and the Knowledge of God* (Oxford: Blackwell, 2002), 208.

## Afterword

[1] Gordon MacKenzie, *Orbiting the Giant Hairball: A Corporate Fool's Guide to Surviving with Grace* (New York: Penguin, 1998).

[2] James Davison Hunter, *To Change the World: The Irony, Tragedy, and Possibility of Christianity in the Late Modern World* (New York: Oxford Press, 2010).

# Acknowledgments

We tell our students that learning is a communal act. So, too, is writing a book about faith and learning. With hearts full of thanks, we wish to acknowledge several persons for their assistance and encouragement. From George Fox University, we both wish to thank Jane Scott, Public Services Librarian. She fielded a number of urgent requests from us, and always delivered the needed information quickly and agreeably. And we want to recognize and thank our colleague in the College of Education, Marc Shelton, for his thoughtful work with Ken on the College of Education white paper focused on Boyer's expanded understanding of scholarship. Hundreds of colleagues, students, and workshop participants have rounded the corners of our vision of faith and learning and of the understandings of promotion and tenure we present herein. We thank them all, literally too many to name. Finally, a thank you to George Fox University for Ken's sabbatical during which we wrote this volume.

CPSIA information can be obtained
at www.ICGtesting.com
Printed in the USA
FSOW02n2314060217
30505FS